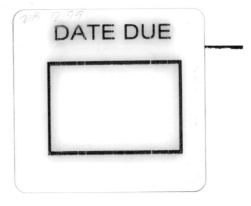

# Images, Miracles, and Authority in Asian Religious Traditions

# Images, Miracles, and Authority in Asian Religious Traditions

EDITED BY

## Richard H. Davis

WestviewPress

*A Division of* HarperCollins*Publishers*

Copyright © 1998 by Westview Press, A Division of HarperCollins Publishers, Inc.

Published in 1998 in the United States of America by Westview Press, 5500 Central Avenue, Boulder, Colorado 80301-2877, and in the United Kingdom by Westview Press, 12 Hid's Copse Road, Cumnor Hill, Oxford OX2 9JJ

A CIP catalog record for this book is available from the Library of Congress.
ISBN 0-8133-3463-2

The paper used in this publication meets the requirements of the American National Standard for Permanence of Paper for Printed Library Materials Z39.48-1984.

10    9    8    7    6    5    4    3    2

# Contents

# Illustrations

# Editor's Note

The essays in this volume discuss materials in Chinese, Japanese, Pali, Sanskrit, Tamil, Thai, and several other languages of Asia. The editor spent considerable time and effort hoping for a miraculous intervention that would enable his computer to produce acceptable diacritic marks in the proper font for transliterating the various languages according to scholarly conventions. However, no such miracles were forthcoming, and it became necessary finally to remove the diacritics from names, texts, and terms in Asian languages altogether. (The same problem did not occur with diacritics for French and German.) I trust that most readers will not miss the lost markings, and those who do will have to imagine their presence.

# Acknowledgments

The contributors to this volume are grateful first of all to the Association for Asian Studies. We held panels at the Annual Meetings of the A.A.S. on topics relating to images, miracles, and authority for three years, from 1991 through 1993, and the papers presented at those conferences served as the bases for the essays in this collection.

We all acknowledge the outstanding editorial assistance of John Jones, of the Department of Religious Studies, Yale University. His organization and careful attention to both the content and form of our contributions helped greatly in bringing our essays together into a coherent volume. The editor also thanks Amy Russell, a student at Bard College, for removing unsightly diacritics at a time when I could not bear going through the essays yet again.

A grant from the A. Whitney Griswold Faculty Research Fund at Yale University facilitated editorial work on the volume. Finally, the editor expresses his gratitude to Yale University and Bard College, for providing the settings and facilities within which this collection has come into being.

# About the Contributors

**Robert L. Brown** teaches the history of Indian and Southeast Asian art at University of California, Los Angeles. He is particularly interested in issues of artistic and cultural interchange, and has worked on these issues in his 1996 book, *The Dvaravati Wheels of the Law: The Indianization of South East Asia.*

**Richard H. Davis** is Associate Professor of Religion at Bard College. His most recent book is *Lives of Indian Images* (1997).

**Phyllis Granoff** teaches Sanskrit and Indian religions at McMaster University. Together with Koichi Shinohara, she has written *Speaking of Monks: Religious Biography in India and China* (1992). She edits the *Journal of Indian Philosophy.* Her current research is on sacred place in medieval India.

**K. I. Koppedrayer** received her M.A. and Ph.D. from the Department of Religious Studies, McMaster University. She is currently Chair of the Department of Religion and Culture, Wilfred Laurier University. Her publications include articles on south Indian philosophy, caste in India, and Native American religions.

**Donald F. McCallum** is Professor of East Asian Art at University of California, Los Angeles. He has written most recently on *Zenkoji and Its Icon: A Study in Medieval Japanese Religious Art* (1994).

**Koichi Shinohara** teaches East Asian religions at McMaster University. Together with Phyllis Granoff he has edited several collections of essays on religious biography, and has written a book, *Speaking of Monks* (1992), on biography in India and China. His current research is on sacred place in China.

# 1

# Introduction:
# Miracles as Social Acts

*Richard H. Davis*

Early on the morning of Thursday, September 21, 1995, Ganesha began drinking milk. Word quickly got around, and soon crowds gathered to watch in amazement as Ganesha imbibed spoon after spoon of the fresh white liquid.[1]

What made this remarkable was that Ganesha is a divinity, the elephant-headed son of Hindu gods Siva and Parvati, and stone statues of Ganesha were consuming the offerings of milk. Worshipers would hold spoons up to the Ganesha statues and the milk would disappear, just as if Ganesha had sucked it up through his trunk. Hindus regularly "feed" their religious icons during the rites of worship known as *puja* and believe that these divinely animated images consume the "subtle portion" of the food, but they do not expect the icons to eat or drink the visible, material portions of the offerings. So Ganesha's more perceptible drinking on the twelfth day of the lunar fortnight, a day particularly sacred to Siva and his family, evoked great wonder and commotion among his human devotees.

No one was quite sure just where or how the miracles started, but several sought to take credit for being first to apprehend them. One temple priest in Delhi claimed that a worshiper had dreamed that Ganesha needed milk, while another priest at the more famous Birla Mandir explained that at 12:30 a.m. the temple bells had started ringing and he had heard a voice saying that Shiva and Parvati were thirsty. Wherever it all began, those who observed the miracle vigorously spread the word, and by 4 a.m. people were lining up at local temples. Traffic stood still for hours in front of Delhi's largest temples. By noon supplies of milk had disappeared from the shops of Delhi.

News of Ganesha's milk drinking spread almost instantaneously not only by word of mouth, but also by all the electronic media modern technology has made available to Indians--telephone, radio, television, faxes, and soon enough the Internet. So rapid and effective was the communication of divine activity that countless Hindus in the cities of India and farther abroad in Kathmandu, Dubai, Hong Kong, London, Toronto, and New York left work or home that same day and flocked to their local temples to see if Ganesha was doing it there too. In Calcutta vendors jacked up the price of milk ten times over normal. In Bombay the stock market closed down when hundreds of traders made a milk-toting pilgrimage to the nearest temple--where Ganesha refused their offerings. Ganesha was making his presence known throughout the Hindu global village.

Hindus who observed Ganesha statues drinking milk spoke of the event's strangeness and their feelings of awe. "It was so shocking that I did it a few times just to make sure," one reported, "and each time the marble statue took the milk." The sheer unexpectedness of the phenomenon seemed to demand explanation. Many Hindus understood Ganesha's action as a sign, a revelation of His Being. Said Jaiprakash Pandey, a priest at the Mahalakshmi temple in Bombay, "God has a message for us. He is saying, 'This is not just stone. It is *me*.'" The miracle, they said, was God's way of reasserting his own existence by intervening supernaturally and strikingly in the normal routine of things. Others saw in it a portent of some impending cosmic transformation--the arrival of a new incarnation of Vishnu, the end of the present age of degeneracy, or perhaps the beginning of a millennium.

The widespread event inspired immediate coverage and commentary in the Indian and Western press. While they reported the long lines at the temples and the statements of the faithful, these reports also sought to explain the phenomenon in a variety of ways. Some sociological commentators pointed out that the milk miracle vindicated Hindu values at a time when many Hindu believers feel threatened by the competing ideologies of Islam, Christianity, and modern secularism. Here, it would seem, Ganesha was rebuking all those competitors who dismiss Hindu liturgical practices as "idolatry" by demonstrating just what an idol can accomplish. Others suspected a deeper conspiracy at work. The miracle was concocted, some charged, by Hindu nationalist groups such as the Bharatiya Janata Party and the Vishva Hindu Parishad (VHP) to "produce a surge of religious fervor." Leaders of these groups certainly did step into the act. Vishnu Hari Dalmiya, president of the VHP, offered his view to the press: "It was a divine act which the human mind cannot fathom or explain." Another prominent VHP spokesman, Ashok Singhal, asserted that the event heralded the coming golden age of Hinduism. However, not many imagined that these groups could have originated and engineered such an impromptu and dispersed happening.

The Indian Rationalist Society meanwhile claimed that Chandraswami, an influential and controversial Hindu guru who had been arrested a few days earlier for his alleged connections with bombings in Bombay in 1993, had orchestrated the entire tumult in order to insinuate his own miraculous powers. Chandraswami, it appears, was not distressed by the accusation. "I had invoked Lord Ganesha yesterday," he responded to the charge. "This is only the beginning of godly miracles." Presumably the miracles would continue until he was freed from detention.

Loyal to the secular premises of their profession, reporters in the major Indian and American newspapers and magazines felt obliged to convey skepticism about the veracity of the miraculous. *India Today* commissioned a professor of physics at the prestigious Indian Institute of Technology, Delhi, to explain Ganesha's milk consumption experimentally, in terms of the physical principles of surface tension, upward bulge, and siphon action, aided by an unconscious tilting of spoons on the part of the credulous and devoted. The magazine ran a series of photographs to prove the point. The *New York Times* devoted a long article to the "Guru Busters" of the Indian Science and Rationalists' Association, who have made it their uphill task to expose all religious trickery in India. The *Times* reporter described the head Guru Buster, Prabhir Ghosh, brandishing a Ganesha statue and a spoonful of milk for passersby in the Calcutta railway station, exclaiming, "See what a fraud it is! See what it is that the gurus and swamis are up to!"

Miracle, fraud, or both, Ganesha's milk drinking was nothing new in India, or for that matter elsewhere in Asia. (The speed with which the miracle was communicated and replicated around the globe, however, was entirely unprecedented in the history of world religions.) Throughout the religious literatures and popular traditions of the religions of Asia, we hear of icons that do remarkable things. They move their limbs and walk. They sweat and bleed like humans. They communicate with their devotees, and exhibit oracular powers. When lost or buried, they may appear in the dreams of holy men to reveal their hidden locations. While being transported, they may choose their new homes by suddenly becoming so heavy they break their vehicles. They emanate brilliant light. They produce visions of the past lives of their worshipers. They cure the sick. Such actions depart so dramatically from our commonsense expectations of what an inert piece of sculpted wood, metal, or stone can do that we label them "miracles."

The essays in this volume explore these tales and anecdotes of miracle-performing icons in Asian religious traditions. For three years, the contributors here and several others participated in a series of panels at the Association for Asian Studies annual conference addressing the topic of religious images and their miraculous deeds. The first year (1991) we discussed "Miraculous Images: The Power of the Sacred in Asian Religious Traditions." The following year the panel considered issues of political authority, "God and King: Miraculous Images and the State in Cross-Cultural Perspective," and in 1993 we focused more specifically on monastic traditions, "Monks and Images: A Cross-cultural Examination of Miraculous Images and the Monastic Community."

As we discussed and compared examples from south, southeast, and east Asia, involving Buddhist, Jain, and Hindu traditions, we found this theme leading us in several directions. First, it led us to look more closely at how these Asian religious traditions understood images as animate beings or embodied divinities. Second, we found a common concern in examining the nature of expectation and response towards icons and the miraculous. Finally, we shared an interest in investigating the roles of religious images in their religious and political settings, and the ways miracles and narratives of miracles function in situations of social change and conflict. This interest provided our main impetus. As Koichi Shinohara put it, all the papers dealt with the ways images work in Asian societies, and we focused on miracles in order to study this. Before I discuss some of these points as they appear in the essays, though, it will be helpful to say something about notions of the "miraculous," East and West.

## Miracles in the West

In speaking of unexpected actions by religious images as "miracles," we are choosing an English term with a Western semantic history grounded mainly in Christian theology and Enlightenment philosophical critique. There are parallel terms in Asian languages, as we will see below, but as a starting point we may unpack some of the meanings embedded within our Western category.

Miracles are actions or events that so differ from the expected course of things that they evoke astonishment and wonder. The word "miracle" itself derives from terms of response: Greek *meidian*, "to smile," and Latin *miraculum*, "to wonder." Etymologically, these are related to the Sanskrit root *smi*, also meaning "to smile," from which derives one of the most common Indic terms for an astonishing, wondrous event, *vismaya*.

As this definition suggests, miracles are social acts in several senses. They require an audience, a community of witnesses, who respond to the event with appropriate reactions of wonder, surprise, astonishment, and delight. Miracles also presume a set of socially shared expectations concerning what ought to happen, a common sense view of the normal way of things, from which the miraculous by definition deviates. It is precisely through their departure from the ordinary that miracles elicit pleasure and admiration. Hindus do not expect stone statues to drink milk physically, and find it remarkable when they do. In the West, the everyday order of things is most often subsumed within the term "nature." Nature represents the orderly, causal, and empirically intelligible way of things. In this tradition, nature is naturalized, assumed to be universal in application and potentially accessible to the comprehension of all humans. In contrast to the orderly and expectable operations of nature, the unanticipated eruption of the miraculous points in Western discourse to the "supernatural," to forces that are believed to act outside the usual parameters of nature.

Thomas Aquinas develops his definition of the miracle from the Latin etymology, and recognizes its supernatural causality. "The term miracle," he observes, "is derived from admiration, which arises when an effect is manifest, whereas its cause is hidden; as when a man sees an eclipse without knowing its cause. . . . A miracle is so called as being full of wonder, in other words, as having a cause absolutely hidden from all. This cause is God. Therefore those things which God does outside the causes which we know are called miracles" (Aquinas 1945: 980). Aquinas's definition brings in a third social aspect of the miracle: the attribution of agency. Those who witness or narrate the marvelous event ascribe the action to some agent that operates unseen beyond the limits of the ordinary. To do this, they call upon socially-held theological or meta-physical interpretive schemes that involve forces transcending the normal order. For Christians such as Aquinas, that agency must be God. The Christian God is the original creator of the natural order, and though this God does not normally intervene visibly within the creation, God may occasionally act to accomplish something so unusual that it must evoke wonder among human observers, and so lead them to look beyond the visible for explanation.

This suggests yet another way in which miracles are social acts. Within Christian discourse, miracles are understood as signs or communications, the signifying practice of God. Augustine, for instance, characterizes miracles in terms of God's direct concern to lead souls towards worship: "Therefore God, who made the visible heaven and earth, does not disdain to work visible miracles in heaven and earth, that He may thereby awaken the soul which is immersed in things visible to worship Himself, the Invisible "(Augustine 1950: 318). Humans ought to comprehend miracles as intentional and rhetorical acts on the part of God, intended to persuade and compel faith as well as to evoke astonishment. As God's communication, miracles should also be re-communicated among humans. In *The City of God*, Augustine expresses his annoyance with Innocentia of Carthage, who has been miraculously cured of breast cancer but fails to publicize the miracle (823-24). It is much better to do as the Hindus of Delhi did when they saw Ganesha statues drinking milk, and use all available means to tell others of the wondrous event.

Miracles often occur in situations of conflict, where differing systems of belief compete and questions of faith and power are directly at issue. This is when supernatural communications are most needed. Augustine cites the miracle contest between Moses and the Pharaoh's magi recounted in the Book of Exodus. The magi, he avers, achieved their results "by the magical arts and incantations to which the evil spirits or demons are addicted," but Moses, by contrast, "having as much greater power as he had right on his side, and having the aid of angels, easily conquered them in the name of the Lord Who made heaven and earth" (311). In this competition of "magical arts" versus "true miracles," the magi are accused of "criminal tampering with the unseen world," while Moses' miracles are produced "for the purpose of commending the worship of the one true God, and prohibiting the worship of a multitude of false gods" (312).

Miracles and narratives of miracles, then, constitute claims to religious authority. They do this not only through the affirmation of one's own miracles, as evidence of the potency of the particular unseen power accepted by one's community of belief, but also through the castigation or simple denial of the miracle claims of other groups. As in Augustine's description of the Egyptian magi, the positive term "miracle" is itself generally denied to rival claimants. There are other terms more suitable to characterize those purported miracles, such as demonic, criminal, impotent, and the like. As social acts, therefore, the narrating of miracles and likewise the subversion of competing claims to the miraculous both serve important polemical purposes.

We must recognize one more social aspect of the semantic history of miracles: the categorical denial of the miraculous. In the West this occurred within the setting of the Enlightenment and the growing confidence among intellectuals of the eighteenth century that empirical and scientific means of knowledge were sufficient to comprehend all phenomena. Western philosophers proposed to repudiate not only the supposed miracles of other traditions, as Augustine had done, but all claims involving miraculous occurrence and supernatural agency. Spinoza was the first to make the argument, but the most influential statement was put forth by David Hume in his controversial essay, "On Miracles," first published in 1748 as part of his *Philosophical Essays Concerning Human Understanding*.

"Nothing is esteemed a miracle, if it ever happen in the common course of nature," writes Hume. "There must, therefore, be a uniform experience against every miraculous event, otherwise the event would not merit that appellation" (Hume 1980: 115). Recognizing that we define miracles in terms of their transgression of the laws of nature, which are themselves established through our uniform human experience, Hume argues that so-called miraculous events may be rendered credible only through some superior proof. Hume then considers various kinds of testimonies concerning miracles, and rejects them all as flawed. There is no compelling proof, he concludes, "and therefore we may establish it as a maxim, that no human testimony can have such force as to prove a miracle, and make it a just foundation for any such system of religion" (127). Within the essay Hume acknowledges the role of reported miracles in establishing the authority of religious systems, and he points to human sentiment as the basis for our propensity to believe in unnatural events. "The passion of surprise and wonder, arising from miracles," he observes, "being an agreeable emotion, gives a sensible tendency towards the belief of those events" (117). Hume takes particular aim at the miracles of his own Christian tradition, such as those narrated in the Pentateuch. He also points to the greater abundance of supposed miracles among "ignorant and barbarous nations," thereby rhetorically suggesting a correlation between civilization and the dismissal of the miraculous. Those who accepted Hume's vision of a cosmos devoid of miracles could at least retain the satisfaction that they are no longer among the ignorant and barbarous orders.

Hume's rejection of all miraculous possibility inaugurated the establishment of a skeptical attitude towards the claims and narratives of miracles in all traditions, Western and non-Western alike. The veracity and historicity of miracles both ancient and modern continued to be debated, of course, but during the nineteenth century many Christians found themselves abandoning the miraculous (Mullin 1996). Academic approaches to the study of Christianity likewise sought to naturalize or demythologize the Biblical accounts of miracles. However, it is important to keep in mind that Enlightenment skepticism is by no means not universal among those who live in West. *Time* magazine recently reported the results of a poll in a cover article on "The Message of Miracles": 69% of Americans polled said they believed in miracles (Gibbs 1995: 65).

Humean skepticism, along with a confidence in post-Enlightenment ontological and epistemological premises as universal in scope and application, underlie most common Western scholarly approaches to Asian religions. When they consider Asian accounts of miracles, which are indeed abundant, Western scholars have often adopted interpretive strategies that emphasize pre-scientific bewilderment and priestly deception. Without the explanatory apparatus of Western science, they argue, Asians clumsily seek to explain natural events by invoking supernatural causes. So, in the case of Ganesha's milk consumption, naive Hindus observe the disappearing milk and infer divine intervention, where modern principles of physics offer a natural account. Second, they say, dishonest religious elites fabricate marvels for a gullible populace to enhance their own standing. Here the physics professor's alternative explanation and the Guru Busters' charge of fraud against the holy man Chandraswami for masterminding the miracle of milk find their intellectual lineages. Both critical strategies are united in ascribing all accounts of divine or supernatural activity to natural and human agency.

## Indian Miracles and Special Powers

People in Asia observe miraculous events, too, though there are no precise equivalents in Indic languages for the semantic field occupied by the term "miracle" in the West. One wishing to translate the word into an Indian language like Sanskrit--a missionary, say, translating Christian texts--would have a number of terms from which to choose. Some Sanskrit approximations stress the unusual character (*alaukika*) of an event, some emphasize the response of wonder and astonishment (*adbhuta, ascarya, vismaya*) it evokes, and still others might be chosen to point to divine or non-human agencies (*daiva, apauruseya, amanusya*) believed to cause the marvel (Apte 1987: 290).

Ancient Indians who wrote in Sanskrit, like most people at most times, maintained a sense of what could normally be expected to occur in everyday life. Most often they used the term *laukika*, derived from the word for "world" (*loka*), to denote the common, usual, ordinary, customary course of things in the world of human society. What is "normal" is to a significant degree culturally defined, of course, so Indians of the Buddha's time might well take for granted things that we would consider extraordinary, just as we would regard as ordinary many things that would astonish them. Nevertheless, for ancient Indians as for modern Westerners, things that departed from the normal way of things (*alaukika*) as they defined it would create surprise and wonder.

In his classical treatise on dramaturgy, Bharata discusses the psychology of wonder and its representation on the stage. For Bharata, the "marvelous" (*adbhuta*) is one of eight primary aesthetic sentiments (*rasa*) that drama ought to evoke in its audience. To create the sentiment of the marvelous within a play, he advises, an actor or actress must convey dramatically the emotional state of "wonder" (*vismaya*). This emotion arises in situations that transcend or "lie beyond" (*atisaya*) the normal. When something extraordinary occurs, feelings such as stupefaction, agitation, confusion, and fainting are natural human responses. Bharata calls these feelings subsidiary emotional components to the prevailing sentiment of wonder. To portray a character's emotional reaction to the extraordinary, Bharata recommends that the actor simulate some of its physical reactions: "gaping eyes, staring fixedly, hair standing on end, crying, sweating, joy, exclaiming, giving gifts, making involuntary sounds, and uncontrollably moving one's feet and hands (*Natyasastra* 6.74; Sivadatta 1894)." The Indian gestural vocabulary for expressing astonishment is one Westerners can readily recognize.

Bharata observes that there are two types of wonder: one he calls the "joyful" and the other "divine" (*daiva*). Something that brings great happiness, such as obtaining something one greatly desires, engenders a kind of joyful wonder, even though nothing altogether out of the ordinary may occur. The other type, the divine, involves a greater departure from everydayness. Seeing gods, for instance, causes wonder of a different sort, as does observing illusions and feats of magic. Here we are closer to the sphere of the miraculous.

For Western observers, deviations from the ordinary course of nature lead to the domain of the supernatural, and for monotheistic Christians, supernatural agency belongs preeminently or solely to the one God. By contrast, ancient Indians inhabited a cosmos made up of multiple worlds (*loka*s), often enumerated as seven or fourteen, each occupied by different types of beings and each adhering to different standards of normalcy. Within this universe, the world known directly to humans was only one of many. The expanded conception of the cosmos led to an implicit recognition of the relativity of miracles. What might seem wondrous to humans in their world could be perfectly expectable in the divine worlds of Indra or Brahman. Traffic between worlds, too, was relatively common, if we judge by classical Indian texts. Beings from divine realms regularly manifested themselves within the human world, and likewise human sages, yogis, and adepts of various types could visit divine worlds. With the eschatological premise of transmigration, Indians of ordinary attainments considered that their own souls too had inhabited and would inhabit other worlds in past and future lifetimes.

For the most part, Indians did not seek a single agency to account for all miracles, but rather recognized a multiplicity of possible agents: gods, various categories of semi-divinities, and unusually accomplished humans. (Some philosophers of monist or strong theistic orientation did try to unify all worldly movement within a single explanatory principle or power, but even they recognized the diversity of miraculous causes on a phenomenal level.) Gods were divine due to their superior capacities of knowledge and action, and they could use those powers in the human world to achieve effects that would seem miraculous to humans. But those same powers were also available to humans who practiced rigorous regimes of sacrifice, austerities, meditation, knowledge, devotion, or ritual.

Patanjali's classic treatise on the practice of yoga, for instance, catalogs a long list of special powers or "attainments" (*siddhis*) acquired by advanced practitioners: knowledge of past and future, understanding the language of all creatures, ability to read minds, capacity to disappear, ability to enter another's body, capacity to glow brilliantly, levitation, and many more (*Yogasutra* 3.16-44). These powers are not solely the preserve of yogis, however. As the commentator Vyasa observes, the various categories of gods in the divine regions enjoy many of the same powers that yogis work so hard to acquire. Moreover, there are still other ways of gaining such powers. "The attainments," admits Patanjali, "may be produced by birth, herbs, mantras, austerities, or meditation" (4.1). His commentator Bhoja explains this further. Birds are born with the ability to fly and great prodigies like Kapila (founder of the Samkhya school of philosophy) are born with perfect knowledge. Alchemists can build an invulnerable body by ingesting mercury. Some adept in the art of mantra are able to fly by repeating verbal formulae, and rigorous ascetics may acquire a host of special powers (Mitra 1883).

Indians considered powers such as those Patanjali and his commentators describe to be inhering human capacities theoretically available to all, rather than special gifts from God or other divinities. In the yogic psychology accepted by many soteriological schools of Indian thought, such powers were beyond the reach of most humans, since we are generally bound by a variety of fetters, constrained by our ignorance and lethargy, and too fully immersed in worldly activities that prevent us from undertaking the actions necessary to work our own liberation. It takes effort to overcome the forces of obstruction, and in Indian religious discourse many schools vied with one another to advocate the most effective method for doing so. Thus, while Bhoja accepted the powers of alchemists and mantra-adepts as valid, he argued that yogic meditation was the most reliable and essential means of attainment.

While non-theist orientations such as Patanjali's school of yoga saw no need for divine intervention in the process, theists usually accepted the role of grace--the "fall of Shakti" (*saktipata*) from Shiva onto a suitable candidate, for example, in the Saiva siddhanta school (Davis 1991: 90-92). Even theists, though, located this transforming moment of divine favor within a lengthy program of learning, ritual activity, and devotional exercise necessary to ready the novice for grace, and an even more rigorous program after God's power had fallen.

In a world of so many miraculous possibilities, one could not view miracles unambiguously as a unique God's acts of communication. Nevertheless, Indians certainly did consider miracles to have a rhetorical force. If the ability to accomplish supernormal feats served as an index of one's level of attainment, then the demonstration of this for an audience could well serve to compel recognition and acceptance of one's teachings.

Early Buddhist texts, for example, narrate various miracles produced by the Buddha Sakyamuni and his closest followers, especially Maudgalyayana, who was known as the "foremost of those with miraculous powers." One brief episode relates that a god in the Brahmaloka once entertained the erroneous idea that no humans were able to enter his divine world.[2] Using his power to read minds, the Buddha became aware of this and decided to disabuse the arrogant deity of his foolish notion. Traveling to the Brahmaloka "as easily as a strong man might stretch out his bent arm or bend his straight arm," the Buddha floated cross-legged above the god and transformed his body into fire. Wondering where his master had disappeared to, Maudgalyayana perceived with his "divine eye" the Buddha sitting in the Brahmaloka and immediately went to join him there. Three more of the Buddha's disciples followed him to the Brahmaloka, and soon all five of them hovered there, cross-legged and blazing, before the astonished god. Maudgalyayana asked if the deity still held to his wrongheaded view, and the god was forced to admit that he had been mistaken. More than this, he now accepted the core Buddhist tenet: "No longer can I say that I am eternal, I am permanent." The display of miraculous powers could have a powerful pedagogical force, even upon a divine audience.

For the most part, though, the Buddha worked his miracles for human audiences. Indeed, according to some Buddhist texts, this accounts for the birth of the Buddha among humans rather than among the gods with whom he shared so many attainments. As the *Sarasamgaha* puts it, since the Buddha's miraculous powers are common to other gods, they would have excited little wonder if he had been born in the Brahmaloka. Born as a human among other humans, however, the Buddha's powers compel attention and awe and thereby attract listeners for his teachings (Sasaki 1992: 9-10).

In India as elsewhere, miracles seem to occur most frequently at moments of challenge and conflict. As the early Buddhist texts of the Pali canon repeatedly recount, the Buddha and his followers engaged in many contests of supernatural feats, as well as more discursive debates of doctrine, with rival ascetics and religious wanderers. In one *Vinayapitaka* account, a wealthy merchant of Rajagriha attaches a bowl made of costly sandalwood to a high bamboo pole and issues a challenge: "I will give this bowl to any worthy mendicant or brahmin who has the power (*iddhi*, Sanskrit *siddhi*) to get it down" (Oldenberg 1880: 110-12). Teachers of various persuasions line up to claim the prize. (In fact, they are the same group of six heterodox teachers that the Buddha debates in another discourse.) Each declares that he is worthy and possesses powers, but none is able to fetch the raised bowl. Just then, the Buddhist monks Maudgalyayana and Pindola Bharadvaja came into town on their begging rounds, and they dare each other to get the bowl. Bharadvaja rises into the air, takes the bowl, and then circles three times around the city before alighting. Awed by the display of miraculous power, the merchant fills the bowl with sumptuous foods to honor the Buddhist adept. Bharadvaja, it would seem, has displayed his supernatural attainment in order to demonstrate the superiority of Buddhist teachings and practice over those of their opponents.

This scene has a satiric force, mocking the futile efforts of other rival teachers to accomplish even the simple superhuman feat of levitation. Generally, though, Indian miracle narratives do not deny miraculous powers to their opponents, nor do they castigate them as demonic in nature, as Augustine does in his recounting of Moses and the magi. Where miracles are taken as part of a singular God's supernatural intervention, it is difficult to accept the miracle claims of other religious communities who may ascribe them to forces or deities outside God's hegemony. Conversely, in a cosmos filled with many beings possessing the ability to accomplish out-of-the-ordinary feats, as in India, it was much easier to accept provisionally the claims of others.

Nevertheless, it was also important to assert the superiority of one's own. Indian religious literature is filled with stories of miracle contests, where an opponent's feats are matched and surpassed by the miraculous actions of the god or person proclaimed in that particular text. Typical of the genre is the battle between the South Indian Virasaiva saint Allamaprabhu and the leader of the Siddhas, an adept named Goraksa, reported in the *Sunyasampadane* and retold by A. K. Ramanujan (1973: 146). It seems that Goraksa had acquired an invulnerable magical body through his yogic practice, and that Allama mocked his power. Goraksa gave his opponent a sword and invited him to try cutting his body in two.

> Allama swung the sword at him, but the sword clanged on the solid diamond-body of Goraksa; not a hair was severed. Goraksa laughed in pride. Allamaprabhu laughed at this show-off and returned the sword, saying 'Try it on me now.' Goraksa came at Allama with his sword with all

his strength. The sword swished through Allama's body as if it were mere space. Such were Allama's powers of self-emptying, his 'achievement of Nothingness.' Goraksa was stunned--he felt acutely the contrast between his own powers and Allama's true realization, between his own-diamond-body in which the carnal body had become confirmed and Allama's body which has no body but all spirit. This revelation was the beginning of his enlightenment.

The polemical strategy is hierarchy, where the powers of one claimant are shown to surpass those of others. And here, as is often the case, the demonstration of superiority in miracles also carries a persuasive message.

When so many beings possessed supernatural powers, there was always the problem of deciding just who or what had caused some miracle. An audience observing some wondrous event might entertain several plausible hypotheses. In one discourse the Buddha himself raises this as a concern (Rhys Davids and Carpenter 1890: 211-223). The Buddhist lay-follower Kevaddha, a householder of Nalanda, asks the Buddha to have one of his mendicants use his superhuman capacities to perform a miracle (*iddhi-patihariya*) for the people of Nalanda. By such a demonstration, Kevaddha believes, the Buddhists can persuade the locals to have greater faith in the Buddha. The Buddha replies that he does not usually instruct his followers to perform marvels. When Kevaddha presses him, the Buddha explains that performing a miracle as a means of persuasion can backfire. A skeptic might well say, "Well, there is a magical charm known as Gandhari. The monk is just using that charm to perform this kind of marvel." Any public demonstration of superhuman powers acquired by monks, says the Buddha, makes him anxious since it could always be misinterpreted as the cynical use of magical techniques. The discourse closes with the Buddha persuading Kevaddha that the only reliable and effective "miracle" is the miracle of education (*anusasani-patihariya*), namely elucidating the main tenets of Buddhist doctrine. Likewise in the episode of the sandalwood bowl, the Buddha reprimands Pindola Bharadvaja for displaying his powers on such a slender pretext: "How could you demonstrate your superhuman miraculous powers to lay people for the sake of a pathetic wooden bowl, Bharadvaja? It's like a woman showing her panties for a miserable copper coin. . . . It will not help convert the unconverted." From this incident the Buddha lays down a rule for the monastic community, that "mendicants shall not demonstrate their superhuman miraculous attainments for lay persons."

In these instances the Buddha renounces the public performance of miracles by his disciples for strategic reasons: they may lead to confusion over cause and they are not always effective in the primary aim, which is to spread the Buddhist teachings. However, he was certainly willing to employ miraculous powers when a clear pedagogical purpose could be achieved, as in his visit to Brahmaloka. Some texts, however, give another reason to renounce such powers. Enjoyment of supernatural powers might become a seductive end in itself, and so deter the adept from still greater accomplishments.

In his commentary on the *Yogasutras*, Vyasa describes one such scenario in dialogue form. When a yogi reaches a stage where he possesses the attainments, says Vyasa, the gods come to him with offers almost too good to resist. "Stay here," they entreat the yogi.

> Enjoy yourself here. Here's a delicious meal. Here's a beautiful woman. Here is a potion that prevents old age and death. Here is a ship that flies through the sky. Here's the tree of life. The heavenly Ganges, the adepts, the great sages, the finest most obliging celestial courtesans, divine powers of hearing and seeing, a diamond-like body--all these you have earned through your own virtues. Now accept them. This is the undecaying, ever youthful, never dying realm that the gods love. (Prasada 1924)

But pass them up the yogi must, if he is to attain the highest stages of yogic meditation. Vyasa directs the yogi experiencing temptations from divine realms to remember his primary aim.

> I was sizzling on the terrible coals of samsara, [the yogi should reflect]. I was spinning in the darkness of birth and death. And somehow or other, I got hold of the lamp of yoga, which disperses the gloom brought on by the five afflictions. These temptations born of thirst are winds that could extinguish that lamp. Now that I have obtained the light, how could I let myself be tricked by this mirage of temptations and turn myself back into fuel for the blazing fire of samsara. So farewell, temptations. You are like dreams, desirable only to the weak.

The yogi who remembers where he has come from and what his final aim is will not be tempted to use his attainments for personal pleasure, and only through this renunciation can he attain that aim.

The voluntary disavowal of displaying or enjoying superhuman powers is not the same as the Enlightenment denial of the miraculous as a category, of course. In ancient India, there were also those who were skeptical towards extraordinary powers and supernatural events. They were designated as representing the Carvaka or Lokayata ("this worldly") persuasion, which made an argumentative practice of denying all non-empirical notions, such as transmigration, Vedic eternality, divine intervention, as well as any claims of miraculous phenomena. However, the Lokayata school left few if any independent treatises documenting its own viewpoint, and consequently they appear in Indian philosophical literature most often in the role of disputants who always lose, propounding doctrines the texts wish to refute. It is difficult to tell just how widely Lokayata views might have been shared in India.

In the nineteenth century, under colonial conditions, Western Enlightenment-based ideologies made a profound impact on upper-class Indian attitudes, and many religious reformers sought to accommodate Indian philosophical and religious traditions with the new premises and values of their colonial rulers. In the literature of Hindu reform and renewal lay a new critique of supernatural powers and the miraculous.

For example, the founder of the Arya Samaj, Dayananda Sarasvati, explained the beginnings of his skepticism with an episode from his youth. Dayananda's father, he relates, was a devout worshiper of Shiva, who once insisted on taking Dayananda to the all-night fast and vigil at the local Shaiva temple on the night of Shivaratri. While his father, the other devotees, and even the brahmin priests failed to stay awake, the young Dayananda doused his eyes with cold water to prevent sleep. He watched in confusion as a mouse crawled over the image of Shiva before him and began to eat the food offerings. "Thoughts upon thoughts crowded upon me," remembers the adult Dayananda, "and one question arose after the other in my disturbed mind" (Dayananda Sarasvati 1879: 10). Finally he awakened his dozing father to ask how the "hideous emblem" of Shiva in the temple could be identical with the Great God of the Hindu scriptures. After what he had seen, Dayananda told his father, "I feel it impossible to reconcile the idea of an Omnipotent, living God, with this idol, which allows the mice to run over his body and thus suffers his image to be polluted without the slightest protest." Finally his father allowed the boy to return home, where Dayananda recovered from hunger and fatigue, but he was never able to recover his innocent belief in the value of worshiping images.

While credulous elders slumber, the alert youth sees for himself the materiality and powerlessness of the idol--the anecdotal moment of enlightenment appears as the starting point for Dayananda's later project of reform. In his magnum opus, the *Satyartha Prakasa* ("Light of truth"), Dayananda carries out a thorough going assault on what he terms Hindu "idolatry," in favor of the innovative reformulation of the Vedas that he advocates as the true and proper basis for modern Hinduism. Along the way he debunks all miraculous claims made on behalf of images. His fictive interlocutor cites miracle after miracle, and Dayananda disputes each one. When the Muslims of Aurangzeb's time came to break the temple idols of Benares, the disputant relates, a Shiva Bhairava image miraculously sent gigantic bees out of the temple to chase away the invaders. Nonsense, replies Dayananda. "It is not the miracle of the idols. There might have been bee-hives there. It is the nature of the bees that they run to sting those who disturb them" (Dayananda Sarasvati 1894: 454). Why then, asks the opponent, do so many believe in miracle-producing divine images? "Just as sheep follow one another blindly, fall into a pit and cannot save themselves," Dayananda answers, "similarly these men having blind faith follow one another, fall into the pit of idolatry and lead a miserable life." Dayananda employs all the familiar explanatory strategies--natural causes, priestly deception, popular gullibility--to subvert the miraculous. Much like Hume, Dayananda is comprehensive in his attack on miracles and devotes chapters to the tenets and erroneous claims of Buddhism, Jainism, Islam, and Christianity, but he strikes at the miracles of his own religious tradition with particular vigor.

Enlightenment ideologies, scientific empiricism, and Hindu reformers have all undoubtedly had their effects on many Indians in the colonial and post-colonial periods. Ganesha's milk drinking in the heart of modern urban India, however, reminds us that miracles still do happen. Or, if one prefers an Enlightenment perspective, it shows that the desire to perceive the extraordinary and wondrous in the midst of the mundane, which is the psychological basis of the miraculous, still remains strong among contemporary Hindus, just as it does among a majority of Americans.

## Images, Miracles, and Authority

The essays in this volume deal more specifically with one type of miracle, those enacted by religious icons or images. The worship of religious icons, both in public temples and monasteries and in more private domestic shrines, has long been a central mode of ritual and devotional practice among the Hindu, Buddhist, and Jain traditions of India. With the international expansion of Buddhism (and to a lesser extent, of Hinduism) into east and southeast Asia, icons traveled too.

With material objects like carved images, the threshold of the miraculous is more modest than it is with persons, since we do not generally expect such objects to do anything. Yet in Asian religious traditions images do, or are said to do, all sorts of things. When they do sweat, or bleed, or cry, or move about, people often pronounce it contrary to expectations, wondrous, a miracle. On Ganesha's day of thirst, something eminently normal for even a young infant was taken as miraculous when performed by an icon. And just as Ganesha's milk drinking was taken as an omen, the simple actions of an icon may often take on oracular significance. As Koichi Shinohara's essay on "Changing Roles for Dynastic

Images" in this volume relates, when an ancient Chinese Buddha image sweats it may well portend danger to the kingdom, and if its head falls off, the end of the dynasty may follow soon. It is wise to pay attention when images act.

The first essay in the volume, Robert Brown's "Expected Miracles," addresses the question of definition. In a religious setting where actions that we might consider miraculous are taken as normal and expectable, where then is the miracle? To illustrate his point, Brown offers the example of the famous seventh-century Chinese Buddhist traveler Xuanzang, who retells the stories he heard during his tour of India of miracle-producing Buddha images (and also of Hindu icons) with a prosaic nonchalance, as if these wondrous actions are, if not exactly normal, then at least unexceptional. So too with inscriptions from Thailand of the Sukhothai period, the laconic mode of narration of marvels suggests that "miracles are the expected active aspect of the image." This does not mean that such acts are reduced to the routine insignificance of everydayness. While not unique or shocking in a Buddhist setting, argues Brown, these expected miracles are still full of meaning, "characterized by shared forms and meanings that are readily recognized, understood, and acted upon." They help confirm a particular view of the world, rather than upset it.

In Brown's essay, the expected nature of image miracles leads him to a critique of (citing the work of Gregory Schopen) the "protestant pre-suppositions" typical of much Buddhist scholarship, and in particular of the long-standing postulation of a hierarchical split between a "rational" monastic elite and a "superstitious" laity (Schopen 1991). According to this scholarly bifurcation, narratives of miraculous feats performed by the Buddha, by eminent monks, or by Buddha images may have been of great moment to the unsophisticated populace, but the more rationalistic monks would have disavowed these unlikely stories. The evidence for this division, though, is not persuasive, Brown reminds us. After all, Xuanzang was one of the most learned monks of his time.

The proliferation of expectable miracles in Buddhist sources also leads Brown to ask how Buddhist images are able to act as they do. What is the relation of a Buddha image to the Buddha? Where does the icon gain its powers? Do these powers originate with the image itself, with the superhuman spirits that may come to inhabit or animate it, or with the worshipers who make it and surround it with ritual, devotion, and hopeful expectation? Several essays in this volume discuss the theological premises that enable images to perform miracles, and this is the central concern of Robert Brown's second essay. In "Miraculous Buddha Images," Brown begins by describing the idiosyncratic predilection of the famous Emerald Buddha of Thailand for ducks' eggs, and its tendency to wring the necks of those foolish enough to tell lies in its presence. Just how are we to understand the odd and distinctive characteristics of this eminent image?

Brown reminds us that the Buddha Sakyamuni was a great miracle worker. He cites the evidence of early Buddhist narrative art, where "gods and men, the supernatural and the phenomenal, the miraculous and the quotidian exist together," linked indivisibly within the same pictorial frame. Within the Indian premises of the time, as I have argued above, the Buddha Sakyamuni enjoyed his miraculous abilities as a result of powers or "attainments" theoretically available to all, but possessed by the Buddha in the highest degree. Physical relics like the Buddha-tooth of Sri Lanka and the ashes of the Buddha placed inside stupas retain some miraculous power, most often, because they are remnants of the Buddha's bodily being. One might expect that Buddha images, also sharing in the Buddha's nature, derive their capacities from this participation. However, Buddha images do not perform the same miracles that the Buddha Sakyamuni does, as the Emerald Buddha's violent execution of liars most strikingly illustrates. Brown argues that it is the image's material being, not its Buddha-nature, that serves as source for these more idiosyncratic acts, and that we might well look elsewhere than Buddhist doctrine in order to understand the cults of miraculous Buddha images found throughout the Buddhist world.

Phyllis Granoff also takes up the theology of images in her essay on "Divine Delicacies." Examining medieval Jain narrative literature, Granoff argues that Jains of that period did not distinguish clearly between representations of the Jina and the Jina himself. In Jain devotional hymns, likewise, seeing the image of the Jina is identical with seeing the Jina. Granoff considers a series of medieval Indian stories involving the act of making likenesses to show that the identification of signifier and signified, image and reality, that we see in Jain literature is not in fact restricted to religious or ritual contexts. Rather, she argues, all art objects may partake of the subtle essence of that which they represent, and in that sharing of essence lies the power of images in India.

Granoff's essay also introduces a new theme: the role of miracles and miracle stories in competition between different religious persuasions. Feeding and food transactions are central activities in all major Indian ritual traditions, whether it be feeding sacrificial food to the Vedic gods, giving food to Jain and Buddhist mendicants, or making food offerings to divinities embodied in images. The Buddhists had often elaborate tales of miraculous feeding. Granoff shows how the Jains, in competition with the Buddhists for food offerings and much else, developed counter narratives of food miracles that satirize the Buddhist stories. While accepting the veracity of the event, for instance, the Jain retelling might alter the agent, or use the story to contrast the gluttony of Buddhist monks with the more rigorous Jains. We begin to see here how miracles and narratives of miracles could be employed in a contentious religious setting not only to buttress the claims and teachings of one school, but also to demote and subvert the claims of others.

K. I. Koppedrayer's essay also examines the role of images and miracle narratives in constituting religious authority, this time in a late medieval Hindu setting. Focusing on an important South Indian Saiva religious center, the Dharmapura Adhinam, Koppedrayer shows how the often-repeated story of its founder, Gurujnanasambandhar, revolves around a series of wondrous events by which he miraculously acquires an icon of Shiva Cokkanatha, locates a suitable teacher, and then receives spiritual consecration (*abhiseka*) from a thunderstorm. This final marvel, where the founder stands all night holding a torch that continues to burn through a heavy downpour, leads his teacher to confer onto Gurujnanasambandhar the authority to establish his own lineage, and thus serves as the central event in the founding of the non-brahmin monastic center. As Koppe-drayer argues, the miraculous consecration resolves a difficult problem. In the Saiva siddhanta school, traditionally, certain rights and powers had been reserved to five select lineages of Saiva brahmins. How could a non-brahmin lineage outside this circumscribed priestly group gain credibility or authority? Here the "miracle makes up for what ordinarily might be questioned" by ascribing the consecration to Shiva's own agency, through the medium of rain, confirmed the next morning by the (probably brahmin) teacher. Gurujnanasambandhar's religious descendants propa-gate the religious authority he originally gained by maintaining ongoing ritual interactions with the Cokkanatha image that he first acquired.

In "Jina Bleeds," Phyllis Granoff shows that in medieval India particular images were often closely linked not just to the continuing prestige of religious orders, but more broadly to the foundation and continuing prosperity of the political order as well. Such assumptions were widely shared. Hindu, Buddhist, and Jain texts all made similar assertions on behalf of their images, and the chronicle and panegyric literature of medieval Indian kingship also reflected a royal acceptance of the necessary association of king and deity, and the need to maintain a relationship with divinity through regular ritual interactions with the god in its iconic form. Not surprisingly, considering this set of premises, images might serve as indices of royal fortune. As early as the *Mahabharata*, "images in the temple cry and shake and vomit blood, foretelling of the terrible destruction of the impending battle."

Against this background, Granoff observes, the Indian invasions by Turkic military forces affiliated with Islam beginning in the early eleventh century presented a special challenge to both religious groups and secular leaders. The successful Muslim attacks on the temples of all image-worshiping sects seemed to contradict the confident Indian assertions of the power of miraculous images, and to demonstrate instead their apparent impotence. Granoff examines Jain stories dealing with unusual images under pressure from Muslim attack. While at least some Jain images retain miraculous abilities in post-invasion narratives, they seem most often to exercise their capacities within a more modest ambit. As Turkic military elites come to control much of northern India, Jain images work wonders on behalf of the Jain community rather than for the kingdom as a whole. This shift in the scope of the miraculous, Granoff argues, corresponds with a retreat by the Jain community as a whole, from acting as participants in a pan-Indian debate to a more exclusive and parochial concern with the health and integrity of the community of Jain faithful. The character of miracles that images work may well change in accord with a change in the circumstances where they work them.

Koichi Shinohara also observes historical shifts in the types of miracles Chinese Buddhist images are said to perform, in his essay on "Changing Roles for Miraculous Images." Examining a collection of miracle stories compiled by the seventh-century monk Daoxuan, Shinohara finds that many of the narratives reflect a close connection between images and the Buddhist community, and between images and secular political authorities. As Granoff shows for India, so too in these Chinese narratives, the body of an eminent image often bears a homologous relationship to the monastic body of the Buddhist Sangha or to the body politic, such that the actions of an image may be observed to predict the future of these social groups. During the anti-Buddhist period of the Northern Zhou, for instance, miracles of sudden disappearance and the miraculous preservation of images under duress became prominent, no doubt reflecting the persecuted Buddhist community's anxiety and desire to persevere. Ironically, religious and political instability seems to require more miraculous conduct on the part of images. Shinohara shows that with the restoration of order and a climate favorable to Buddhism under the Sui and Tang dynasties in the seventh century, miraculous images appear to lose their role as royal oracles, and stories no longer emphasize the previously cozy relationship between Buddhist images and the royal court.

In Koichi Shinohara's second essay, the agency shifts from the mira-culous image to the monk who serves as its guardian, but this essay also illustrates the political roles images might play in changing historical circumstances, and also the kinds of extraordinary loyalty miraculous images might inspire among Buddhist monastics. Using Daoxuan's bio-graphy, Shinohara traces the life of Zhuli, and particularly his relationship with two miraculous images. The first was "King Udayana's image," an image that came from India and had been closely associated with Emperor Wu, the famous pro-Buddhist ruler, and the second was an image of Lamp-Lighter Buddha that had won the respect of the Song dynasty's first ruler. Through his close political ties with the Sui rulers, and especially with prince Guang (later the second Sui emperor), Zhuli was able to move these two images to Changlesi and support them in a manner suitable to their prestige. No doubt the images had political value to the Sui ruler as well, since both had been closely associated with previous southern dynasties and at Changlesi they could lend their charisma to the new imperial line. With the beginning of the Tang dynasty Zhuli's situation became more precarious, and when Fu Gongyou led a rebellion in the area he threatened to move the images across the river as part of a general attack on the Buddhist institutions of the area. To protest the displacement of his two favored images, Zhuli finally performed self-immolation in front of the temple. His sacrifice did not prevent Fu Gongyou's expropriation of the images, but it did succeed in the long run, since the two Buddhas were restored to their home by the mid-seventh century.

The final essay in the volume takes us to Japan, and deals with "The Replication of Miraculous Icons." Donald McCallum focuses on two extraordinary cult images, the Amida Triad of Zenkoji and the Seiryoji Shaka. According to their traditional accounts, both images were supposed to have been created in India during the time of the Buddha Sakyamuni. Likewise, many of the Chinese Buddhist images Shinohara discusses, and also the Emerald Buddha of Thailand, are traced back to India and linked with the Buddha, Asoka, or other great figures in the early history of Indian Buddhism. With both the Amida Triad and the Seiryoji Shaka, subsequent travels brought them in contact with still other great figures and transformative moments in Buddhism, as if the biographies of such images served as a metonym for the history of the religion itself. The Seiryoji Shaka, it is said, arrived in the Chinese capital along with the famous Indian translator Kumarajiva, and the Amida Triad voyaged from Korea to Japan in the sixth century just when Buddhism was officially introduced there and immediately became a central icon in the disputes over the adoption of Buddhism in Japan. During the Kamakura period, both images became centers of lively cultic activity.

As remarkable as their travels and many miraculous deeds are, these two images are still more unique as progenitors of families of identical icons. McCallum observes that the Amida Triad spawned approximately two hundred replications, while the Seiryoji Shaka was the source for about one hundred copies. The practice of reproducing certain prestigious icons, evidently at its peak during the thirteenth and fourteenth centuries, raises in new form the questions about the character of religious images and the bases of their powers addressed previously in the essays of Brown and Granoff. To what extent do replicated icons share in that which they replicate? By copying an image, can one also reproduce its charisma and its powers? McCallum reports cases where dream oracles demanded the fabrication of new copies and where marvels like a "gushing forth" of relics accompanied the installation of a replicated icon, as if the new images required their own miracles to confirm their independent status as objects of power, even as they retained their explicit connection with the primary icon from which they had been copied. Yet the texts do not explain precisely the source of their powers. In the end, McCallum concludes, the relationship of original and replication remains somewhat mysterious.

Perhaps it is well to end with McCallum's note of ambiguity. Dealing with several religious formations and many distinct schools of thought over a considerable span of time and covering different cultural and civilizational zones of South, Southeast, and East Asia, the participants in the A.A.S. panels and the contributors to this volume could hardly expect to come up with all-embracing principles or explanations. We do hope, however, that by investigating a broad range of Asian religious icons, their many miracles, and their varied relations with religious and political authority, we will encourage others to pay attention when images act, or when Ganesha begins drinking milk again.

## Notes

1. This discussion of Ganesha's milk-miracle is based on the following accounts of the event in newspapers and news magazines: *India Today* (October 15, 1995), *Los Angeles Times* (September 23, 1995), *New York Times* (Sept. 22 and Oct. 10, 1995), *Ottawa Citizen* (Sept. 22, 1995), and *Vancouver Sun* (Sept. 22 and 23, 1995).

2. *Samyutta-nikaya*, Brahmasamyutta 6.1.5. Feer, ed., 1, pp. 144-46; Rhys Davids 1, pp. 182-84. I thank Phyllis Granoff for allowing me to read her then-unpublished paper on "The Ambiguity of Miracles: Buddhist Understandings of Supernatural Power" (now forthcoming from *East and West*), from which I have borrowed several key references.

# 2

## Expected Miracles: The Unsurprisingly Miraculous Nature of Buddhist Images and Relics

### Robert L. Brown

*It is the power of expectation rather than the power of conceptual knowledge that molds what we see in life no less than in art.*

E. H. Gombrich (1969: 225)

In recent years the Virgin Mary has appeared miraculously several times to the Catholic Latino community of Los Angeles. In one appearance the Virgin took form in the dust and dirt on the window pane of a woman's apartment. Crowds of hundreds of people formed to see the image, causing the landlord to order the window removed. The removal was shown on local television news, and as the workmen carried the pane away people desperately attempted to touch the image. Then a bizarre scene took place. The people were almost entirely Latino, but a white man suddenly appeared in the crowd shouting that he saw nothing but dirt on the window and that the people were deluded. In a moment a Latina woman shouted back at him, saying "Of course you can't see the Virgin. You aren't Catholic and you're white!" (See *Los Angeles Times*, March 25, 1993).

This woman understood well the power of expectations. She expected the miracle in the sense that she anticipated its possibility and the form it would take, the Virgin's shape in an unusual material and place. She knew that this white man had no such expectations. Like this doubting man, many people today do not expect miracles. Even the Catholic Church is highly suspicious of such miracles as the window-pane Virgin (*Los Angeles Times*, July 13, 1994). For Buddhists in ancient India and Southeast Asia this was not the case, as images and relics were considered miraculous by their nature. The notion we may hold today that a miracle is a unique, unanticipated, and unexplained event does not apply to the miracles of these images and relics. As with the Virgin's appearance for many in the Los Angeles crowd, Buddhists generally regard a miracle as an anticipated event, but its expected nature does not detract from its significance and power. Indeed, it contributes to them.

## Xuanzang's Expected Miracles

Modern art historians have a varying but fairly standard approach to the study of Buddhist images. They talk about the image in terms of sources in an attempt to say why it looks the way it does, and discuss how it in turn relates to later images. They talk about the image's gestures and symbolic content, about its style, and perhaps about its social or cultural context.

Xuanzang, a Chinese monk who was in India for some sixteen years in the seventh century, mentions images often in recording his experiences in the *Records of the Western Regions*.[1] However, Xuanzang never discusses the kinds of information most valued by modern art historians. He is either unaware of or does not care about style and iconography, the dual horns on which art historians pin their study. On one hand, this seems self-evident; we do not expect Xuanzang to be a modern scholar. On the other hand we might expect that the categories of information for modern scholar and ancient pilgrim would be somewhat similar, while their use or value might be different. Is the modern scholar's expectations of the image so different from Xuanzang's as to make the image difficult or impossible to recognize in the terms in which he saw it?

Xuanzang basically records only four characteristics about the images he mentions: their size, the material they are made of, their location, and their miraculous nature. The first two, size and material, can be further defined, as Xuanzang was interested mostly in large images and in images made of precious materials. There are some exceptions, but when he notes a small image, as in one instance an image of Maitreya, he justifies its mention by saying that "although of small dimensions, its spiritual presence is great...." (Beal 1884: ii, 61). The sizes of many of the images he records are huge: a 1000-foot long sleeping Buddha and a 100-foot tall metal Buddha at Bamiyan (Afghanistan), for example. The precious materials he mentions are usually gold, silver, and jewels, but in Bengal he saw an eight-foot tall Buddha image of green jade. How truthful, or better how "factual," are such observations?

Very few of the actual images Xuanzang mentions have, as far as I am aware, been identified in South Asia. There are colossal Buddha images, specifically at Bamiyan, but these are made in relief in rock and mud; no sleeping Buddha has been found; and a 100-foot metal Buddha appears unlikely, although Martha Carter has argued that we should take Xuanzang at face value and that one actually existed at Bamiyan (Carter 1985: 119ff.). I can at least envision the possibility of colossal images made of wood and covered with gilded copper sheets; indeed, Xuanzang says that the Bamiyan image was cast in parts. But the largest extant metal Buddha image of which I am aware is very much smaller, the over seven-foot tall Sultanganj image from Bihar (see Harle 1986: fig. 157). It dates to the seventh century and could have been made just when Xuanzang was in Bihar. He also mentions a 100-foot copper image of Siva in Banares. While I know of no tradition of colossal Hindu images, some stone images of Hindu images are big. The seventeen-foot relief image of Mahadeva at Elephanta is the largest I know (see Harle 1986: fig. 97), and there is the freestanding theriomorphic Varaha at Eran at over eleven feet (see Harle 1986: fig. 74), but nothing compares in size to the extant Bamiyan Buddhist images.

What about Xuanzang's references to precious materials? Although we have very few extant Buddha images made of gold and silver, presumedly because most have been melted down and lost, they certainly existed. It is also possible that images Xuanzang said were gold were bronze covered with gold leaf. It is not clear, however, what he meant by images made of jewels. Some bronzes had inlaid gem stones, but such inlay was always used sparingly for Indian Buddhist images, particularly for images as early as the seventh century. There was a practice of putting jewels on Buddha images, of crowning and bejewelling them, which Xuanzang himself mentions, and thus it appears that he differentiates this practice from images made with jewels. It is usually thought that it was in the seventh and eighth centuries, just when Xuanzang was in India, that the Buddha image began to be depicted with jewels--crown, necklace, armbands--worn over his monastic robe. Xuanzang saw such images, as he tells us that stone jewels are real jewels that have turned to stone over time.

Xuanzang is thus highly selective in the images he describes, using precious materials and large size as two criteria for selection. While it may seem obvious to us why size and material would have impressed Xuanzang, it is not really clear what he associated these with. It was not an historical framework he was using. He was not attempting, for example, to associate the images' large size and precious material with certain patrons or to place them into some historical chronology. Time, for Xuanzang, is more or less two simple categories, the present and a relatively un-differentiated past, usually defined only in terms of individuals' lifetimes, most usually the lifetime of the Buddha or of Asoka. Xuanzang is not looking at the images for clues to position them historically but rather to judge their spiritual power and place them within Buddhism. Because the images are rarely linked to any human agency, they appear as if self-immanent. With their wondrous size and priceless material, they appear not so much as artistic or archaeological facts, but rather as part of a miraculous epistemology, a way of knowing through the miraculous.

Xuanzang's *Records* is a record of Buddhism, not of historical events. Modern scholars may tend to see his book more as history than religious myth because Xuanzang, following literally in the footsteps of other Chinese monks, has added an actual geography to the Buddhist record. This movement through actual space is the structure in which the religion is retold. He is not "making up" the geography, just as he is not making up the Buddhist narrative. The importance of the geography tells us why the third of the points given above, location, was recorded by Xuanzang in reference to the images.

Xuanzang's accurate geography is actually a lucky bonus for modern scholars, more a product of the Chinese pilgrimage tradition than any interest Xuanzang may have had in reporting a "true" landscape. Xuanzang readily incorporated into his record what he had only heard about a place or monument. For Xuanzang the accuracy of his account did not rely on his testing of facts and information. Indeed, his landscape was one in which facts are explained by the miraculous or supernatural: for instance, a ditch is where someone went down into hell; the woods are the result of a discarded tooth stick of the Buddha; the city is destroyed by dragons; a pool is where crocodiles eat swimmers having bad character and spare those with good; boats sink due to *nagas* who lust after the relics they are carrying. These are not quaint stories connected to places but are how Xuanzang explained his world.[2]

The fourth of the images' characteristics that interested Xuanzang is specifically their miraculous nature. The miracles the images perform are fairly restricted in type. By far the most common form of miracle is the appearance of light. Light is an indication of spiritual power or authenticity. It can be emitted by any spiritual object, such as a footprint or a stupa, as well as an image. Stupas by far outnumber images of the Buddha in the *Records*, not, I think, because the relic outranks the image in Xuanzang's mind, but merely because it is above all the stupa that marks the geography. The standard structure for Xuanzang's narrative is to use the stupa to start each story, so that the stupa becomes both a geographical as well as a narrative measure of the text. A stupa can be built to indicate a wide variety of events and people, such as to note *jatakas*. One stupa even fell from heaven. The stupa is not strictly a relic mound for Xuanzang.

Besides producing light, surprisingly few other types of miracles are mentioned by Xuanzang for images. There are several instances when Buddha images move. One in Gandhara circumambulates the stupa and stops a robbery, for example. Some images produce cures when touched (see Brown 1997a).

Can we attempt, as I did with the size and material of the image, or as Alexander Cunningham and others have done with the geography (Cunningham 1871), to judge the accuracy of Xuanzang's miracles? The empirical testing of Xuanzang's geographical references is relatively easy and it tends to show a high level of empirical accuracy. The testing above of Xuanzang's references to Buddha images of colossal size and precious material, on the other hand, led to rather ambiguous conclusions. If pressed, we might be tempted to say that Xuanzang sometimes exaggerated or misunderstood what he saw. But any attempt to judge the accuracy of the miracles immediately appears difficult. As those who believe in miracles point out, empirical methods tend to fail when judging miracles.

The Buddhist images I have mentioned--of the Buddha, the stupa, the footprints--are not the only objects that reveal miracles in the *Records*. Hindu images also perform miracles. There are a number of instances when Xuanzang mentions the miraculous power of Hindu images. At times he attempts to indicate a Buddhist superiority, as when he explains that an image of Siva is in a bending pose because it has arisen to bow to the baby Buddha. But it is not the case that only some, and specifically Buddhist, images are miraculous. This is of some importance, as it argues that miracles are in the nature of images, not just Buddhist images.

Indeed, Xuanzang's epistemology of the miraculous locates miracles in the nature of reality, not just of religion. One commentator writing on Xuanzang calls him miracle-loving, and then goes on to use his *Records* like a modern factual history (Wriggins 1987). Xuanzang did not love miracles so much as believed they explained his world. Thus he is as matter-of-fact recording the miracles images perform as he is recording the images' sizes and materials. Miracles are not presented as surprising. Nor can I find instances of Xuanzang doubting the miracles he describes, although the text is often ambiguous at best as to what miracles he "actually" saw.

## Hierarchical Expectations

I have mentioned several times differing expectations regarding the nature and appearance of miracles, whether among the individuals in the Los Angeles crowd at the appearance of the Virgin or between Xuanzang and the modern scholar. These expectations break into two simple categories, a belief or not in miracles. The modern scholar probably would expect that the Buddha image could not perform miracles, and that miracles should either be proven empirically or be doubted. Xuanzang expected Buddha images to perform miracles, which he says they did, and which he never doubted. While it is easy and correct to point out that there is no reason Xuanzang should have modern expectations, this does not avoid the problem that with such varying and mutually exclusive expectations the Buddha image is a completely different object for the modern scholar than for Xuanzang. Indeed, the hermeneutical examination by modern scholars of elite Buddhist texts tends to leave out the image altogether.

This focus on text and doctrine also leaves little room for the examination of miracles. Recently Gregory Schopen has written on the Buddha image in the broader context of scholars' approach to Indian Buddhism. Finding an often skewed understanding of Buddhism today, he writes in "Archaeology and Protestant Presuppositions in the Study of Indian Buddhism" that "Buddhist scholars...and historians of religions are all working from the same assumption as to where religion is located" (Schopen 1991: 19), which is in the texts and not in the practice of the religion. Schopen attributes this assumption largely to Protestant Christianity, and what it means for us here is that aspects of a religion that center on images and relics, the locus of practice and of miracles, has been neglected by scholars as truly part of the religion. The goal of recovering a true or pure Buddhism located in the texts, one attributable to the original teachings of the Buddha and uncorrupted by superstition, is indeed at the foundation of Buddhist scholarship and continues to be of central importance today (see Clausen 1975).

This notion is not confined to Western scholars' understanding of ancient Buddhism. A. B. Griswold locates it as defining the difference between elite and popular Buddhism as practiced in contemporary Thailand:

> The two tendencies are divergent, not to say contradictory. In modern Siam there is, on the one hand, the official Doctrine, rational and humanistic, a "religion without a god," preached by learned monks and accepted by modern-minded Buddhists. On the other hand there is the popular religion, full of superstition and magic. These two exist side by side, with mutual tolerance (Griswold 1953: 7).

However, in the very next paragraph Griswold continues:

> For the last hundred years the highest ecclesiastical authorities have sought to strip Buddhism of its superstitious accretions, to restore the pure Doctrine of renunciation and gentleness taught in the fifth century B.C. by the greatest of human teachers - the Sage of the Sakyas, the Lord Buddha (Griswold 1953: 7).

Mutual tolerance, perhaps, but the hierarchy is clearly marked and those of the pure Doctrine are actively involved in ridding Buddhism of its "superstitious accretions." It would appear that Protestant Christianity and Western Buddhist scholarship have contributed to the views of the highest ecclesiastical authorities in Thailand during this last hundred years, although Griswold feels that the rationalist elite existed (in small numbers) among the Buddhists earlier, and he speculates that they were at Sukhothai in the thirteenth and fourteenth centuries.[3]

That there was a spectrum from the rationalist to the superstitious (to use Griswold's terms) that determined the expectations regarding miracles within Buddhism throughout its history seems clear, and that the hierarchy runs from rationalist texts to superstitious practice also seems, in its broadest outlines, correct, with images and relics having to do with practice. While textual scholars may find this statement a disconcerting generalization, I will remind them that Edward Conze could write his text-based book on *Buddhist Thought in India* (Conze 1973) without (as far as I can see) ever mentioning miracles, saying:

> This book deals exclusively with the monkish elite and their life of meditation. As a religion, Buddhism had also to make provision for the masses, whose bhaktic and magical beliefs are only lightly touched upon here. The Tantra, which is a literary elaboration of the Stupa-worship of the laymen, therefore also falls outside the purview of this book(Conze 1973: 32).

Where I would question Conze, and Griswold, is the extent to which these two understandings of Buddhism were ever kept separate, either between monk and layperson or between learned and ordinary monk. Xuanzang was among the most learned and renowned monks of his time, yet we see no rejection by him of "*bhaktic* and magical beliefs." And while the Bangkok ecclesiastical authorities may discourage non-rational views among Thai monks, many of the most famous twentieth-century Thai monks have had lives filled with the magical and the miraculous (see, for example, Keyes 1982).

Nor do I see why Conze's meditating monks should be placed in opposition to those with magical beliefs, as magical powers are often said to be produced by the monks and the Buddha through a power called, in Pali, *iddhi* (Sanskrit *siddhi*), a power that comes in levels and is created primarily through meditation. It is the power mastered most fully by Buddha's pupil Mogallana, called "the chief of those with magic powers," and it includes a variety of forms, such as flying through the air. The Buddha had frequently to restrain his monks, and particularly Mogallana, from too frequently using these powers to perform miracles. This power was not available only to the Buddhists, however, although in the Buddhist texts the stories are usually told in terms of the monks having real magical powers while the others (Jains or Ajivikas, for example) were merely charlatans who were faking them.

It seems that the power that explains the ability to produce miracles is rather clearly identified in this regard, with a not particularly mysterious nor mystical way of achieving it. In short, when we are talking about human beings (including the Buddha) performing miracles, the super-human power needed for their performance is more of an understandable human achievement than an incomprehensible characteristic of a divinity. It appears to me that within the context of the Buddha's life, the possession of *iddhi*, the ability to perform miracles, and the occurrence of the miracles themselves are not outside of natural laws for Buddhist believers and thus not unexpected.[4]

If the miracles performed by the Buddha and his monks are explained in terms of their source of power and expected in their occurrence, they also are limited in the forms they take. The Buddha performed the same miracles over and over and at different times, such as the fire and water miracle which he performed in a number of contexts when he would rise into the air, fire springing from his shoulders and water pouring from his feet. Likewise, the Buddha and his monks often fly through the air. Or, as Phyllis Granoff discusses in her article "Divine Delicacies" in this volume, the Buddha performs miracles having to do with food. If we take a moment to think about another Indian deity, Krsna,[5] we see that he does not perform these miracles, but spends his time killing demons, lifting mountains, making love in multiplications, and so forth, miraculous efforts not performed by the Buddha. The point is that miracles are specific to individuals, deities,[6] and religions and are limited in forms. There are, of course, many interesting explanations as to which miracles are performed and why, but in the most fundamental way it is a matter that individuals and deities perform miracles that are meaningful, practical, and useful rather than willful and arbitrary. Thus, for example, the Buddha and his monks flew through the air in large part because the Buddha and the *sangha* were teachers who were required to be in many places to spread the *dharma* and serve as a wide field for merit making.

## Expected Miracles at Sukhothai

I have already mentioned that Xuanzang notes in a matter-of-fact style in his *Records* the occurrence of miracles. T. H. Barrett in his article

"Exploratory Observations on Some Weeping Pilgrims" (Barrett 1990) has argued that the writings of the Chinese Buddhist pilgrims in India lacked emotion, and this may in part explain Xuanzang's prosaic references to miracles. A second possible explanation, that the miracles simply were not that important to Xuanzang, seems unlikely, however, due to the sheer number of the references. The most likely explanation for their often simple and brief notation is the expected nature of the miracles, not their lack of importance.

It is difficult to find sources for the practice of Buddhism in India that discuss miracles in as great detail as that of Xuanzang's *Records*. Nevertheless, turning now to the Thai and Pali Sukhothai-period (thirteenth-fifteenth century) inscriptions from Thailand, we find a similar laconic manner in which miracles are mentioned, and some striking similarities to Xuanzang's account both in the type and form of the miracles. This evidence appears to support the expected nature of image and relic miracles in the practice of Buddhism.

King Ramkamhaeng's famous first Sukhothai inscription, dated 1292, makes no mention of miracles. He records the erection and placement of several Buddha images, but true to the very simple and straightforward character of his Thai inscription, there is almost no elaboration. He does not tell us what his motivations were for making the images, and he describes them only as to size and, sometimes, material. Even the significant *cakravartin* act he performed in 1285, seven years before Inscription 1, the act of digging up relics in Si Satchanalai, is recorded simply in this way:

> In 1207 saka, a year of the boar, he [that is, Ramkamhaeng] caused the holy relics to be dug up so that everyone could see them. They were worshipped for a month and six days, then they were buried in the middle of Sri Sajjanalai, and a cetiya was built on top of them which was finished in six years (Griswold and Prasert 1971: 217).

There is no mention of the relics performing miracles; apparently the king and his people were satisfied with just looking at them. But this would change greatly within about fifty years when, in the middle of the fourteenth century, we get a near frenzy of relics being found or acquired, brought to Si Satchanalai and Sukhothai, and performing miracles. It is also at this point that there is a tremendous amount of building and image production at Sukhothai. These changes can quite confidently be linked to the increased influence of Sinhalese Theravada Buddhism.

The Sukhothai monk, Si Satha (Sriraddha), who is the subject of the mid-fourteenth century Inscription 2, brought back from Ceylon several relics of the Buddha, including a hair relic (Kesadhatu) and a neck-bone relic (Givadhatu) which he placed in Wat Mahathat (Mahadhatu) at the center of Sukhothai. The miracles these and other relics at Wat Mahathat performed are described in detail in the inscription, part of which follows:

> Then the great relics performed tremendous miracles, [sending forth rays] like ocean waves or great showers of rain. ....Some rays shone like the stars at night, or like liquid gold flowing brilliantly everywhere; some rays were like.....jewels, or like double and single gardenia flowers appearing all over the universe. ....The Kesadhatu performed a miracle....like flashes of lightning and streams of water, moving rapidly about in the sky in a marvelous manner (Griswold and Prasert 1972: 129-30).

Later the description continues: "...the relics came whirling down and made the circuit of the Golden Cetiya, shooting out rays which were marvelously beautiful to behold like crystal cart-wheels" (Griswold and Prasert 1972:131). Here now for comparison is Xuanzang, writing 700 year earlier, describing a relic miracle in India:

> At one time, from within the stupa there arose suddenly a smoke, which was quickly followed by a fierce flame of fire. On this occasion people said the stupa was consumed. They gazed for a long time till the fire was expended and the smoke disappeared, when they beheld a *sarira* [relic] like a white pearl gem, which moved with a circular motion round the surmounting pole of the stupa; it then separated itself and ascended up on high to the region of the clouds, and after scintillating there awhile, again descended with a circular motion (Beal 1884: i, 66).

In India and Thailand relics perform limited and specific miracles; they glow, send out rays of light, and fly in a circular motion. While there is concern for Xuanzang and for the Thais at Sukhothai whether a relic may be genuine, there is no question that genuine relics do exist, and that those that are real perform miracles. In other words, miracles are expected from a genuine relic and indeed identify a genuine relic.

Miracles also are expected during the life of the Sukhothai kings as they replicate the life of the Buddha. King Mahadharmaraja I, a contemporary of the monk Si Satha of Inscription 2, is likened in Pali Inscription no. 6 to Vessantara and Janaka and, when he renounced his kingship briefly for monkhood, "At that moment the earth quaked, unable to bear at all places the weight of his virtues. Then there were all sorts of other miracles: such is the usual course of things in the career of Bodhisattas" (Griswold and Prasert 1973: 164). Miracles are, simply, "the usual course of things."

Both King Mahadharmaraja and Bhikkhu Si Satha sponsored the making of many images of the Buddha. One that was probably made about this time (that is, mid-fourteenth century) is the Buddha at Wat Si Chum; there is some evidence that Bhikkhu Si Satha was involved in at least the building of the *mondop* that surrounds the image. An unusual feature of the *mondop* is a extremely narrow, pitch-dark tunnel in the walls that leads from near the entrance up steep stairs around the right side of the Buddha, then behind the image, to emerge on the roof. There is a small window cut behind the head of the enormous Buddha, and I have elsewhere suggested that the window was used as a means for a monk to speak, so that the voice appeared to come from the Buddha to the worshipers before the image (Brown 1997b). If so, this is not simply cynical trickery. The tunnel has implanted in its ceiling a series of engraved stone plaques illustrating the Jatakas, and there are Buddha Footprints (Buddhapada) in the ceiling along the way. The passage through the tunnel was not simply a means to get behind the Buddha to trick the worshipers but was a spiritual journey of its own. The monk speaking for the Buddha must have undertaken this journey by retracing the footsteps of the Buddha which would, I think, have given the Buddha image a truly miraculous voice.

Indeed, Buddhists in Thailand continue to ask Buddha images questions and to receive answers (see Textor 1966). Furthermore, each Buddha image can answer. Each Buddha image can, in this sense, produce miracles, with each Buddha image having the power to produce answers about future events or to produce desired future events. Returning to Xuanzang: he also expected Buddha images to work miracles. In fact, in terms of noting what the images *do*, Xuanzang restricts his comments pretty much to this, although the miracle could of course lead to other goals, such as indicating one's amount of merit. Xuanzang would not say that miracle producing is all that Buddha images do. He would certainly acknowledge, for example, that making and worshiping images creates merit. But my point here is that miracles are the expected active aspect of the image.

What is not clear, however, is the relationship of the image to the Buddha, and of both of these to producing miracles. If the Buddha produced miracles through his power of *iddhi*, for example, is this also what allows an image to produce a miracle? This issue is the focus of my second paper in this volume, "The Miraculous Buddha Image: Portrait, God, or Object?"

## Conclusion

The doubting man who turned up in the crowd to see the window-pane Virgin and the modern Buddhist scholar, however different their backgrounds, share a post-Enlightenment view of the empirical nature of reality that treats phenomenon as explained by scientific natural laws. When Samuel Beal published the English translation of Xuanzang's *Records* in the nineteenth century, he could not resist adding a footnote to the account of the relic miracle I quoted above (on p. 32), "This account probably refers to some electrical phenomenon. The surmounting pole of the stupa was provided with metal rings or discs, and was capped generally with a metal "pitcher" (so called). This would naturally act as a lightning conductor (Beal 1884: i, 66, f.n. 227)." With some relief, we now know what Xuanzang and the other people "really" saw, an event that can be explained according to natural scientific laws. I wonder if the relics at Sukhothai six centuries later that similarly twirled in circles, moved into the clouds, glowed, and then fell to earth would have been explained by Beal in the same manner.

The attempt to explain miracles as phenomena following natural scientific laws is one side of the rationalist coin, the other being the attempt to show that phenomena that defy such natural laws (that is, miracles) in fact cannot exist. David Hume, for example, has an influential section on miracles in his 1748 book *Philosophical Essays Concerning Human Understanding* in which he uses logic to argue that a miracle cannot occur (Hume 1748). The Western philosophical tradition follows Hume as a series of complicated and often technical discussions on the nature of miracles that focuses on the question of whether miracles actually occur or not (Swinburne 1970). On the other hand, the occurrence or not of miracles is not an issue for many in the Los Angeles crowd who came to see the Virgin, nor for Xuanzang and the Thai Buddhists discussed here. Miracles are expected to occur, although their occurrence can have important significance. They are not unique and shocking events that are un-explained and mysterious, but are characterized by shared forms and meanings that are readily recognized, understood, and acted upon.

### Notes

1. All my references for Xuanzang are to Beal's translation. I have not attempted to cite each reference by page, however, due to their frequency. Only those direct quotations are cited by page.

2. As explanations for phenomena, Xuanzang sometimes mentions merit or

desires (that is vows), but these are usually reserved to explain the form of future births.

3. Griswold has discussed the difference between the rationalist and the pious believers repeatedly, and is not unaware of the importance King Mongkut (r. 1851-1868) had on the rationalist form of modern Thai Buddhism, but he feels Mongkut only accentuated what was the true and original teachings of the Buddha (see Griswold 1974: 5-11 and Griswold 1960: 28-30).

4.. In this sense, the powers and what they produce are perhaps not even to be labeled as miracles. This dialectic between the natural and the supernatural seems to be highly fluid, however, when considering the life of the Buddha. While the Buddha may fly through the air under his own power generated through means accessible (at least theoretically) to everyone, and with no claims to being a deity, others who see him fly will call it a miracle and react to the Buddha as if he were superhuman. This is not only because people may simply be ignorant of the meditational process, but also because the two layers, the miraculous and the normal, appear side-by-side in the narrative even if they are contradictory or in opposition. For example, the Buddha Sakyamuni is said to be about nine meters tall, yet he is described frequently as going into ordinary people's homes without a problem. The texts (as well as their readers/listeners) feel no need to explain this apparent discrepancy. It is cited by Griswold, however, as one of the clashes of myth with reality that so bothered King Mongkut, leading to his attempts to rationalize Buddhism in nineteenth-century Thailand (Griswold 1961: 23; see also my discussion in "The Miraculous Buddha Image" in this volume).

5. The Hindu god Krsna works well for a comparison with the Buddha as he, like the Buddha, appears in human form. Indeed, frequently in the texts his divine character is obscured in that those around him, for example even his own mother, do not recognize him as divine.

6. Whether to call the Buddha a person or a deity depends, as discussed throughout this paper, on one's point of view.

# 3

# The Miraculous Buddha Image: Portrait, God, or Object?

*Robert L. Brown*

The Emerald Buddha, the most famous Buddha image in Thailand, is said to have a taste for certain foods, such as duck's eggs, and is known to wring the necks of those who tell a lie in its presence (see Figure 1). A second well-known image in Thailand, the Buddha Jinaraja in Phitsanulok, likes pig's heads and can predict health problems. Such characteristics of Buddha images are idiosyncratic and of a personal nature. They cannot be explained by references to Buddhist doctrine and texts but appear to have a "human" flavor to them--to be specific, illogical, emotional, and willful--to reflect a human nature. Yet, they are miraculous. Having a taste for certain foods is typically human, but for a statue to have such tastes is miraculous. Or, is it the Buddha who has such tastes? Already things are complicated, as we have the human and the divine, the phenomenal and the miraculous, the image and the Buddha becoming mixed and interrelated.

What is the agency for a miracle performed by a Buddha image? In attempting to answer this question I will deal with three strands of the Buddha's nature and history, that of the human, the divine, and the material. The miraculous is different in relation to each. For the human Buddha, that is, the historical figure Sakyamuni who lived in northern India sometime around the sixth century B.C.E.,[1] the assumption would be that, as with other humans, the ability to perform miracles is not a natural gift. Indeed, humans cannot normally perform miracles without aid from an exterior, usually supernatural, source. Indeed, humans cannot normally perform miracles without aid from an exterior, usually supernatural source. Or, as Richard Davis has outlined in the Introduction, humans can develop superhuman powers through yogic and Tantric practices, and the Buddha's yogic powers were supreme. Nevertheless, few modern scholars would accept yoga as a means to achieve miracles. As a god, the Buddha could presumably perform miracles, but the Western scholarship on Buddhism is replete with arguments that the Buddha cannot be considered a god, merely a revered human teacher.[2]

Despite modern doubting of the Buddha's ability to produce miracles as a human or deity, the Buddhist texts and art, from the earliest examples of each, describe and depict the Buddha performing miracles. In fact, for the art, the depiction of the Buddha's miracles, particularly in narrative imagery, dominates over other aspects from his life.[3] The scholars' argument is that, despite the prevalence and perseverance of the miracles in the Buddha's life, their presence is not part of original or true Buddhism, but a later addition from popular superstition. The centrality and importance of this view of Buddhism in the scholarly literature cannot be overstated, and I will discuss it below.

But this dialectic between Buddha as human teacher and divine miracle-maker rarely incorporates the issue of the place the miracle-producing images themselves take. The image is neither teacher nor god, but an object of some material, such as stone, metal, wood, or clay. Nevertheless, I will argue that the dialectic of a human or divine nature for Sakyamuni often informs our reading of the actual artistic objects. Further, I want to propose that the image's material nature and its role as an object in a ritual arena of practice may at times be the decisive indicators of its miracle-producing capacity.

## The Life of the "Human" Buddha in Texts

When David and Indrani Kalupahana wrote *The Way of Siddhartha: A Life of the Buddha*, published in 1982, they wanted "to eliminate the mythology that came to be associated with Siddhartha's early life as a result of his being elevated to the level of a transcendent being and to present him as a historical person (Kalupahanas 1982: vi)." The Kalupahanas are following a long-lived and influential scholarly tradition of attempting to uncover the historical, and thus "real," Buddha and by extension, his true and original teachings.[4] The basic assumption is that the miraculous descriptions have been added to the original historical facts, and thus the easiest way of historicizing the Buddha is simply to eliminate the miraculous and supernatural. The Kalupahanas attempt this most often by making the event, explained in the original text(s) as due to a metaphysical or miraculous agent or cause, explainable through a human psychological process of decision making or by giving the miraculous an allegorical or metaphorical interpretation.

For example, at Bodhgaya when Sakyamuni sits under the Bodhi Tree there are earthquakes indicating the importance of the events taking place. At one point, Sakyamuni touches the ground to call the earth, personified as a goddess, to witness his preparation for enlightenment, which causes the earth to shake. One text, the fifth-century *Lalitavistara Sutra*, says that "as the Bodhisattva [that is, Sakyamuni] touched the great earth, it trembled in six ways: it trembled, trembled strongly, trembled strongly on all sides; resounded, resounded strongly, resounded strongly on all sides" (Bays 1983:482). The Kalupahanas interpret the shaking as not due to a miraculous earthquake, but psychologically as a result of Sakyamuni's extreme intensity of purpose: "It was an enormous determination, a tremendous undertaking. His whole body trembled as he sat down, giving him the feeling that mother earth herself was trembling" (Kalupahanas 1982: 94).

A second scholar who has recently attempted a similar demystification of the Buddha's life is Hajime Nakamura. Unlike the Kalupahanas, however, whose retelling of the Buddha's life is written like a novel complete with dialogue, Nakamura has told the story using quotations from Buddhist texts interlinked with analysis and explanation. The passages he has chosen are, he believes, the earliest and thus those most reflective of the Buddha's own teachings and time, primarily selections from the Pali texts, particularly the *Sutta-nipata*, which he considers "first among the Early Buddhist canon" (Nakamura 1982:3). One way Nakamura determines which textual sections are early is by eliminating those passages which describe the Buddha as a deity or with supernatural powers, considering them as later corruptions of the historical facts. Nakamura's account is much more focused on the teachings of the Buddha than the Kalupahanas' book, which stresses his biography. This is because the life of the Buddha appears not to be emphasized in the earliest strata of texts and thus is not so strongly evident in Nakamura's quotations. The Kalupahanas have sorted through all of the available textual sources, which vary among themselves, in order to piece together a complete life story. In fact, the lack of a complete biography for the Buddha is cited as one of the reasons they wrote the book, for as they note "For some inexplicable reasons, no complete account of his life story was attempted until recent times" (Kalupahanas 1982:vi).[5]

It is worth pausing to ask to what extent this absence is because such complete accounts of an individual's life are in themselves modern constructs. The Buddha's biographies were always highly selective in the events recorded, and these events were cosmic in significance, intended not as traces of an individual's psychological inner dialogue and displays of independent volition, but as the recording of the universal *dhamma* which he taught and lived. In other words, no complete biography was required, as it was not the story of Sakyamuni as a unique individual whose life from birth to death was intrinsically interesting. What was worth knowing was the *dhamma* which he taught, concretized and exemplified in certain events from his own life. Thus, the Kalupahanas have attempted to humanize and modernize the Buddha by presenting a complete biography.

Whatever the differences in their books, the Kalupahanas and Nakamura share an archaeological approach to Buddhist texts, one that attempts to remove the accretions of later times to expose the original foundation. They assume there is a clear chronology of these accretions which can be determined, and they treat the story as made up of "facts" that need to be excavated from the confused matrix of the entire text. Also, they expect to and do reveal, in the end, a similar humanized Buddha, a person psychologically like you and me, whose doctrine and life can be told in a modern simple, clear, and rationalist vocabulary.

## The Life of the "Human" Buddha in Art

Given the notion of Buddhist texts as fields to be excavated for historical facts, it is appropriate to ask if a similar approach works actually using archaeology and art. In other words, can archeology and art be used in a similar fashion to reveal the true and original human Buddha? Indeed, Nakamura suggests just this in his introduction, saying, "As long as we have to rely upon written documents, the non-mythological Sakyamuni is almost impossible to discover. In order to bypass such limitations and reach the historical man, we have to rely upon solid proof--namely, archaeological materials (Nakamura 1977:3)." Rather surprisingly, considering this statement, Nakamura only very sparingly uses archaeological material in his book, mentioning, for example, remains identified by some scholars as King Bimbisara's bamboo grove monastery at Rajagrha where the Buddha sometimes stayed (p. 87), and most completely the archaeological remains from Piprahwa, sometimes identified as Kapila-vasthu, Sakyamuni's hometown, which includes an inscribed relic casket found in 1898 that appears to identify the contents as the relics of the Buddha (pp. 127-130). Unfortunately, these finds, as well as all others associated with the historical Buddha, remain controversial as to date and identification. Archaeology does not provide the sureness, the factual solidity, that Nakamura apparently hopes. In fact, many scholars believe that no art or monument datable to and associated with Sakyamuni's lifetime has been, or ever will be, found. Herbert Härtel, in an article that reviews the archaeological finds of the eight major sites associated with the Buddha's life recorded in texts, puts it this way: "To give it in a nut-shell: The hope to recover original structures and ruins of a town or habitation of the time of the Buddha, let us say Kapilavastu, is almost zero" (Härtel 1991:62).

While Härtel's article supports this position and seems convincing, for our purposes of looking for the "original" Buddha in the archaeological evidence, even if material is found that can be dated to his lifetime it would only be architectural, either now-vanished wooden architecture, such as the discovery of postholes, or possibly remains of mud stupas.[6] In other words, there is little or no hope of any decoration or art contemporaneous with the Buddha that would carry suggestions of doctrine or belief. Even the discovery of the Buddha's "true" relics would be of no help in themselves, but would depend on their context, and obviously could only be associated with material and events from a time after his death.[7] In any event, we must ask what any of this would tell us about what the Buddha taught or thought, the answer being, unfortunately, very little or nothing.

The earliest extant art that has a Buddhist iconography dates to about the first century B.C.E., thus at the least two hundred years after the Buddha's death, and it depicts Sakyamuni's life replete with miracles. This early Buddhist iconography is found usually associated with stupas, and includes material from such sites as Bharhut and Sanci.[8] The miraculous in these depictions includes a broad range of figures whose actions and appearance cannot be explained in direct phenomenological terms. Following the notion of the factual which is later embroidered by the miraculous or supernatural of the textual tradition, I want to consider whether the removal of the "legendary" in these earliest artistic scenes might produce a true, historical, and nonmiraculous Buddha figure.

I will say immediately that the exercise appears to produce very little helpful insight into the Buddha's human or historical life. There are several reasons for this. One is that the artistic reliefs are not so much narratives as icons, meant not to be read like word texts but to be used in acts of ritual piety that focus on the entire monument.[9] The life-scene reliefs are highly standardized in terms of inconography, which tends to increase recognition but to reduce comparative detail that might reveal historical information. Furthermore, the early reliefs depict life-scene events in a mixture of the earthly and the supernatural. Events that take place in heaven are shown in the same way, with the same kind of buildings and locations, as events on earth; the gods are usually depicted in the same way, with the same bodies and clothing, as human beings; and the gods usually act in the same way, for example give honor to the Buddha, as human beings. In fact, with respect to Bharhut, without the inscriptions on many scenes we would not know if they involved gods or men. Many scenes appear to show both men and gods participating together in the event. The "legendary" is not so much grafted onto the factual as both are part of one reality, one continuum of space and time in which gods and men, the supernatural and the phenomenal, the miraculous and the quotidian exist together. If this is true, it appears of little value to attempt to pry them apart, or to see one as being more real than the other.

Where, then, might the Buddha be placed in this continuum? It is one of the more interesting and intriguing facts that the earliest Buddhist reliefs do not show the Buddha in anthropomorphic form. Even the location and imagery of the Buddha in these reliefs is thus unclear, although it has usually been assumed that his presence was implied through the use of context. Susan Huntington has recently initiated an interesting discussion on this issue by her suggestion that most of the early Buddhist scenes usually understood to be life scenes are actually depictions of sacred places (Huntington 1991 and 1992). Here she is arguing against the notion of an aniconic period in early Buddhist art, a period during which the figural Buddha was not represented, but whose presence was suggested by the use of symbols.[10] As far as I understand her argument, she is saying that if we regard these supposed life-scenes as illustrations of actual places and practices (that is, of the time of the reliefs, for example, first century B.C.E. for Bharhut), we need not expect the Buddha figure to be depicted, since its absence is simply due to its absence at the contemporary scene, not to any religious, artistic, or philosophical concerns or prohibitions.[11]

I think the issue of how the Buddha was regarded, whether human or divine, and thus the nature of his life and the miracles he performed, is at play in Huntington's interpretation. She feels that the Buddha was never considered a god. In her article "Aniconism and the Multivalence of Emblems: Another Look" she gives a reference to Helmuth von Glasenapp's book *Buddhism--A Non-Theistic Religion*, which, she says, has "demonstrated [that] the Buddha was not a god"[12] (Huntington 1992:117). Huntington is responding here (as well as in her article as a whole) to Vidya Dehejia's article "Aniconism and the Multvalence of Emblems" (Dehejia 1991) where the latter had implied that Buddha was a god. While neither Huntington nor Dehejia focus on the divine or human nature of the Buddha, the question of whether the reliefs are depictions of a cosmic or purely earthly event must rely in part on whether the worshiper saw in them a divine and miraculous imagery.

As an example of how assumptions regarding the Buddha's nature are reflected in the interpretation of the reliefs, I will use the Prasenajit Pillar from Bharhut, which both Dehejia and Huntington discuss (see Figure 2). Dehejia says these are "three interrelated panels pertaining to the enlightenment" (Dehejia 1992:50), the upper one showing "the presence of the enlightened Buddha," the middle panel that of "four sets of gods...[who] arrive to praise the enlightened Buddha," (Dehejia 1992:51) and the bottom one "heavenly nymphs who...arrive to honor the enlightened Buddha" (Dehejia 1992:51).[13] Thus, there are three "simultaneous events," all from the life of the Buddha, and in the upper panel "the Buddha's presence...[is] indicated by aniconic emblems" (Dehejia 1992:51).

Huntington, on the other hand, suggests that the upper panel does not imply in any way the presence of the Buddha, but rather "shows devotees (at a time subsequent to the Buddha's enlightenment) indicating their reverence to the sacred place of the event and the sacred tree under which the Buddha attained enlightenment" (Huntington 1993:118). The middle panel

> ...does not require the presence of a Buddha image. Instead, I suggest that the scene is not the Buddha's enlightenment but rather just what it appears to be and just what its inscriptions suggest: it is the presentation of the role played by the celestial beings in this momentous event. If a camera had been present at the time of the Buddha's enlightenment, this scene might show what the camera would have found if it had turned to pan the audience. I suggest that these beings are immortalized in the artistic composition for their role as supporters and devotees of the Buddha (Huntington 1993:119).

Likewise for the bottom panel, these goddesses (they are called *apsara* in the inscriptions) are "devotees in their own right, like the *devas* in the scene above it" (Huntington 1993:120).

I find problematic Huntington's interpretation for at least two reasons. First, while the event of the Buddha's enlightenment does not require the presence of a Buddha image, it does require the presence of the Buddha. It is difficult not to find this presence in the upper panel, identified by its inscription as "Bhagavato sakamunino bodho," read as "enlightenment of the Holy One Sakyamuni" by Dehejia (Dehejia 1992:50) but as "the *bodhi* (tree) of holy Sakyamuni" by Huntington (Huntington 1990:403). In either case, the Buddha's participation in the event cannot be removed nor can it be removed from the mind of the worshiper. There is no reason to worship this tree unless the Buddha had reached enlightenment under it, and once that took place the Buddha's participation, whether he is indicated by an anthropomorphic image or not, is not forgotten when worshiping the tree. Aniconic here merely means that no anthropomorphic image is present to indicate this presence, the tree (and other objects) providing it.

The second problem I have with Huntington's interpretation is how the Buddha was regarded by the worshiper. When Huntington suggests that we imagine a camera present at the enlightenment and panning the audience, are we to assume that it would have captured an audience of deities? Indeed, the upper panel as well shows deities present. While the figures surrounding the tree and the two figures ambiguously located "above" the temple and whistling cannot be identified for certain as either gods or humans,[14] the two winged figures flying in the air around the tree are clearly not humans. How do their, and the other deities', presence fit with the notion that these are historical snapshots? Nor can one say that the deities in the middle panel are an actual human audience turned into a divine audience by the use of inscriptions, as there was no human audience present at the enlightenment. What audience does Huntington refer to here?[15]

I thus find Dehejia's interpretation much more convincing than Huntington's for these three scenes. In fact, my own interpretation would go somewhat farther than Dehejia's, as I would suggest that the three panels are not only linked in time but also in space, and that the artist intended to show the moment of enlightenment when the Buddha was surrounded by the gods as witnesses and celebrants, the two bottom panels being considered as literally sharing the space with the upper panel. That the Bharhut artist intended this can be seen by the way in which the elephant pillar rising from the middle panel extends into the artistic space of the upper panel, connecting the two. The scene, in short, is not an illustration showing contemporary worship of the tree at Bodhgaya but a scene of a cosmic and divine event, the most important moment in Buddhism, for which the artist has attempted to pull out all the stops. That the artist considered the Buddha at that moment, or the worshiper looked at these panels and thought of the Buddha as, a simple human teacher is, for me, extremely difficult to imagine.

## The Image of the Buddha as an Object

The reliefs on the fence at Bharhut surrounded a stupa which, we may suppose, contained relics, probably of the Buddha Sakyamuni.[16] Relics and aniconic reliefs re-present the Buddha at Bharhut. The appearance of the anthropomorphic Buddha image is the subject of enormous numbers of studies, and its date and place of creation continue to be hotly debated. The image could be seen, in terms of what already existed at Bharhut, as created to fill the empty spaces or replace the symbols in the reliefs, or to participate with the relic and stupa as an icon of worship. While other possible reasons for its invention may be suggested, they all assume that at least the image is a "portrait" that sets up a relationship between the icon and the Buddha, so that we are seeing the Buddha (however many times removed) when we see the image. Is it this relationship, then, that enables images to perform miracles?

The Emerald Buddha's ability to kill people, mentioned at the beginning of this essay, appears to be a surprising power for a Buddha image, if not even more so for the Buddha himself. The Emerald Buddha is today the best known Buddha image in Thailand, located at Wat Phra

Kheo within the compound of the Royal Palace in Bangkok. As H. R. H. Princess Maha Chakri Sirindhorn writes in the foreword to Prince Subhadradis Diskul's recently published *History of the Temple of the Emerald Buddha*: "The Temple of the Emerald Buddha is both a sacred structure and the repository of the spirit of the entire Thai people. ...It is a site where royal ceremonies are performed nearly the whole year round" (Diskul n.d.). Before 1932 and the present constitutional monarchy, one of these royal ceremonies involved the swearing of allegiance by the country's ministers to the king before the Emerald Buddha. The implications are clear: a false pledge of allegiance, a lie, would be detected by the Emerald Buddha and the punishment would be (a supernaturally-caused) death.

One might interpret this in straightforward terms of political legitimation; that religion is being used by those in power as a means to force, trick, and coerce others. This interpretation, one we are comfortable with today after the writings of Weber, Marx and others, assumes a great deal of cynicism and crafty manipulation on the part of the king and superstition and sheep-like acceptance on the part of most everyone else. That Buddha images had political resonance in Thailand, as elsewhere, is certainly true. But the power that such images as the Emerald Buddha possessed was shared by king and subject alike, and was, I want to argue, part of the image as object. That these objects are images of the Buddha is important, but their power to influence the people and the state stems most fundamentally from their ability to function as *objects* of power, rather than as portraits or symbols of the Buddha. The Buddha stands as a reference to the object, but is not the only reference. Indeed, I want to suggest that in these cases it is not the most important reference.

In 1934, Robert Lingat suggested that the Emerald Buddha was, before it was carved into a Buddha image, the sacred gem of the kings of Angkor (Lingat 1934). Just what the sacred gem meant for the Angkorian kings and their religion is still largely a mystery.[17] We know that it was present when Suryavarman I gathered together some 4,000 of his officials at the Royal Palace at Angkor in 1011 C.E. to receive their oaths of fealty. In part, their oath ran, "This is the oath which we...swear, all, without exception, cutting our hands, offering our lives and our devotion gratefully, without fault, to H. M. Sri Suryavarmadeva,... in the presence of the sacred fire, of the holy jewel, the brahmans and the *acaryas*. We will not revere another king, we shall never be hostile (to our king), and will not be accomplices of any enemy, we will not try to harm him in any way...(Briggs 1951:151)." If the oath is not kept, the result, requested within the oath itself, is to receive "royal punishments of all sorts." But the oath immediately adds that "If we hide ourselves in order not to keep this oath strictly, may we be reborn in the thirty-second hell as long as the sun and the moon shall last" (Briggs

1951:151). In other words, the power and results of the oath work, as with that made before the Emerald Buddha, without needing the king's presence.

The reason for associating the gem and the Buddha image is argued at length by Lingat, and the topic has been taken up by Frank Reynolds as well (Reynolds 1978). Here, I can only briefly outline these complex connections. The Emerald Buddha is made of a green stone, as yet geologically unidentified, but the material is clearly of importance. It is focused on in the various chronicles that trace the history of the image, where the Buddha is identified as being carved from a magical gem brought by the gods for that purpose from Mt. Vibul. The original request to the gods, by the sage Nagasena, was for the gem of the Universal King or *cakravartin* kept on Mt. Vibul, which, while turned down for this specific gem, was fulfilled by giving another gem (of equal value) kept in the same place. The *cakravartin's* gem (and thus the substitute one also) is associated with prosperity and fertility, specifically with the bringing of rains, as it was in India as is seen in a first century B.C.E. relief from Andhra showing the *cakravartin* rasing the gem to the sky which brings down the rain (see Figure 3) Reynolds discusses further associations of rain-making with both the green color of the stone and with "emeralds."

These chronicles place the sculpting of the image in India, followed by an eventful history of its moments, including a stay in, of all places, Angkor Thom, before ending up in Thailand. Thus, the connection the Emerald Buddha may have between Angkor and Thailand is reflected unequivocally in the chronicles. The royal nature of the gem itself is central because when carved into an image of the Buddha it is an imposingly powerful symbol of the close interrelationship of kingship and Buddhism, the two parts of the Thai (or any Theravada Buddhist) state. Indeed, for the king to possess the gem-Buddha is to possess control of both kingship and Buddhism. This symbolism is made concrete with the practice, traceable to the sixteenth century, of the king changing the clothes of the Buddha during each year: specifically, the Buddha wears the king's garb during the hot season, and changes to that of the monk during the rainy season. The Buddha, like the king (who traditionally has spent a period as a monk), is both a *cakravartin* and a monk. Frank Reynold's two wheels of the *dharma* are here revolving not only in unison but, in fact, as one.

The changing of the clothes of the Emerald Buddha that took place on November 3, 1933 that Lingat describes involved, as its central focus, the lustration of the Buddha. The water from the lustration was collected and used by the king first to sprinkle on his own head, and then, divided into several bowls of precious material, to be distributed among the waiting crowd, many or perhaps most of whom were royalty and elites. This ceremony, taking place after the 1932 coup, apparently did not involve oaths being sworn to the king.[18] Nevertheless, it is my speculation that the water in touch with the image was one underlying factor that gave power to the oath.

The notion of an oath being sworn by drinking water that has touched an object of power is well known in many areas of Southeast Asia. In Sumatra, the *Naga* stone from Sabokingking is inscribed with a text of an oath to a chief (Datuk) in which blessings and imprecations are enumerated (see Figure 4). The seventh-century Srivijayan chief's followers, apparently in the presence of the stone, spoke this oath and drank the water that was poured over the stone. The concept of drinking or swallowing an oath by drinking the water that has touched a powerful object is recorded into modern times in Sumatra (McKinnon 1985:2-5). It implies the ability of water to absorb and transfer the "power" of an object, so that the oath-taker literally ingests this supernatural power. The Sabokingking stone is particularly graphic in this imagery as the water would pass over the words of the oath, "absorbing" them, so that the oath-taker would be drinking the curse itself. Hiding oneself from the Datuk in order to avoid the oath's obligations, as with Suryavarman's followers or those who swore before the Emerald Buddha, would fail, as the Datuk's followers would literally have the curse, and its supernatural power to carry out its promises and threats, inside his body.

Drinking an oath was also a practice in Thailand. The *Jinakalamali*, a sixteenth-century Pali chronicle written in Chiengmai in northern Thailand, mentions the drinking of an oath several times. In 1517, for example, Emperor Tilakapanattu received the rulers of two Shan cities with their followers in Chiengmai. He "made them pay homage to the Order of monks of the Three Fraternites and the Three Pitakas together with the Sihala-image as the foremost (object of veneration), and making them solemnly pledge by troth in the presence of the Three Gems had them drink to their oath of allegiance (Jayawickrama 1968:164)." There are no details given of the actual ceremony, so I cannot say exactly how the drinking was associated with the image, but at least we can identify the Sihala image, as it is still in Chiengmai. Interestingly, the Emerald Buddha was also in Chiengmai in 1517. It had been brought to Chiengmai in 1481 by Emperor Tilakapanattu's great-grandfather, King Tiloka, and was installed in his then just-renovated Wat Chedi Luang.

What interests me particularly about the notion of using the Emerald Buddha image as the power (via the water) behind the oath, and then (as also discussed) as the *cakravartin's* gem, is that in both cases the focus is on the image as object. Certainly, in both cases we are dealing with supernatural and miraculous powers of the object. But neither relies on the specifically Buddhanature of the image. Finally, it may be argued that the lack of connection to the Buddha is not unique to the Emerald Buddha, but is true for most Buddha images (at least in Thailand); that indeed the image, when it is being addressed with a question or a vow and is miracle-producing, is seen as an object of power rather than as the Buddha. It is possible that the distinction is that the image, when it is producing merit, is seen as relating to the Buddha, while when it is producing miracles, that is, responding to worshipers, is not. When Robert Textor wrote his 1960 dissertation "An Inventory of Non-Buddhist Supernatural Objects in a Central Thai Village" (Textor 1960), he rather surprisingly ends it with a discussion of Buddha images and amulets. Are these "non-Buddhist"? In fact, they are, as he shows how they relate to other supernatural objects previously discussed for which no Buddhist connection is made. Textor's Thai villagers are in constant contact with miraculous Buddha images, with which they make contracts, express vows,[19] ask questions, and predict the future.

### The Image of the Buddha as a Personality

Let me return now to the human character of the Buddha images mentioned at the beginning of the paper. I want to argue that if one treats the image as having a human character, it also has to do with the image as object, and has little to do with its form as the Buddha or to its Buddhist nature, except, as we shall see, in a negative sense. I mentioned that the Phra Jinaraja was known for its ability to predict the outcome of health problems. Some twenty years ago I was living in Bangkok and I faced a life-threatening disease. While the medical tests were being evaluated in Bangkok, my wife and I went to Phitsanulok to worship Phra Jinaraja and, knowing of his reputation and on advice from Thai friends, to ask him the outcome. What were my motivations? What did I see in this image of the Buddha? Was I asking the Buddha my questions, in the sense of Buddha Sakyamuni? I do not think so. I was asking this particular image, this particular object. Otherwise, I could have directed my questions to some distant Sakyamuni directly through prayer, or used another Buddha image in Bangkok, including the copy of the Phra Jinaraja at Wat Benchamabopit in Bangkok itself. I am opening up again here, of course, the central question of this essay: what is the relationship between the image and the Buddha?

The Emerald Buddha would kill the false swearer, and I mentioned, rather obviously, that this is not in keeping with the Buddha's nature. Nor would be the Emerald Buddha's taste in duck's eggs. Many Thais would suggest that these idiosyncratic, and often un-Buddha-like, characteristics are due not to the Buddha image itself, but to supernatural beings who guard the image. These beings, called *phi* in Thai, are of a very large class of predominantly threatening spirits and ghosts. When the Emerald

Buddha was brought to Thonburi by the founder of the present Chakri dynasty in 1778, he also brought another Buddha image, Phra Bang, and the two images were for a period housed together at Wat Phra Kheo in Bangkok. There followed a series of national catastrophes. The cause of these problems was found to be the personal dislike that the two images' *phi* felt for one another. When the images, and thus their *phi* guardians, were separated,[20] the problems ceased.

The chronicles are often not clear about who is making such personal decisions. Returning to the sixteenth-century *Jinakalamali*, for example, it says that when King Tiloka first attempted to bring the Emerald Buddha to Chiengmai from Chiengrai (as mentioned above), "On account of its [that is, the Buddha image's] aversion to being brought along the highway it performed a miracle by becoming extremely heavy" (Jayawickrama 1968:145). The image wanted to go to another city, and was indicating its intentions. There is no mention here of a *phi* making the decision, and it is phrased as if the image is deciding. But there is no reason given for the image's desire to go to one place or another. Most incidents, including the happenings and movements of the Buddha images, are not given any cause, logic, or reason in the chronicles: things simply happen.

When M. C. Subhadradis Diskul refers to the incident in his history, he attributes the decision to the guardian *phi* (Diskul n.d.:18). To my mind, the desire to explain such a human characteristic of a Buddha image as a decision to take one fork in the road over another (for no apparent reason), or such personal antipathy and rivalry as that between the Emerald and Phra Bang Buddhas, and so forth, as due to supernatural beings separate from the Buddha, is due in part to the discomfort Buddhists feel attributing human character traits to the Buddha.

And correctly so. Can we speak of the Buddha having a personality? The Buddhist texts, monks, and scholars argue relentlessly against the reality and importance of a person's personality, and most particularly that of the Buddha. Peter Harvey in "The Nature of the Tathagata" says "The death of a Tathagata is simply the cessation of the dukkha-khandas. No real satta or atta or 'I am' is destroyed, as such things do not exist" (Harvey 1983:50). The choice of this quotation is almost at random, so many others could be used, and while the nature of the personality in Buddhism can be argued in some technical detail by scholars, a particular personality of the Buddha does not take form in textual stories of his life nor in his artistic representations.[21]

Buddha images, however, do have unique personalities. The attribution of these personality traits to the *phi* is one way of avoiding their attribution to the image and thus to the Buddha. I doubt, however, that most worshipers attempt to keep the icon isolated and inert. They must approach the image as they would a person, and thus as having a personality, the possession of which for an image gives it miraculous power. The kindness, goodness, and reverence of the historic Buddha is probably indicated by the image, but if a question or issue is raised by the worshiper, it is the image that is being addressed and that responds.

## Conclusion

I have attempted in this essay to address the issue of the agency of the miraculous Buddha image. What gives the image power to perform miracles? Who is providing the image this power? Central to these questions has been the nature of the interrelationship between the Buddha and the image of the Buddha, since one source for an image's miraculous ability, indeed the most obvious source, would appear to be the Buddha himself. Yet we see that the relationship is not simple or direct. While the Buddha performed miracles, which are frequently depicted in the art, there does not appear to be any necessary connection with an image performing miracles. The image, for example, often does not perform the same miracles the Buddha was said to perform, or, as with the Emerald Buddha, the image may perform miracles that we know the Buddha would never perform.

Even the performance of miracles by the Buddha is an issue for many scholars, who maintain that the Buddha was nothing more than a teacher, the miraculous and extraordinary aspects of his life being a (later) corruption stemming from popular beliefs that led to his deification. If the Buddha did not perform miracles, and his purely human nature is an essential element of true Buddhism, then much of the Buddhist art in the South and Southeast Asian traditions cannot be considered true or accurate Buddhism, since it is replete with the miraculous. As indeed are the texts, and the attempt to strip the texts of the legendary to reveal the true historical Buddha has been the focus for many scholars. How successful their attempts have been appears to me largely to rely on predetermined notions of the Buddha as a modern man, but it is interesting that it does not work to pry apart the historical from the legendary in the artistic depictions of the Buddha's life.

Nevertheless, Susan Huntington has introduced an interesting twist to the issue of the historical nature of the early Buddhist reliefs usually identified as life scenes by suggesting that most are illustrations of contemporary (that is contemporary with the making of the sculptures) sacred places and events. Huntington's argument is new insofar as it rejects the notion that the Buddha is present (although not in anthropomorphic form) in these scenes, and thus, that they are not life-scenes at all. That some represent sacred sites is, of course, not a new argument, although most scholars have felt, like Dehejia, that they indicate simultaneously both site and life-scene (Dehejia 1992). When Nancy Falk wrote "To Gaze on the Sacred Traces" in 1977, she suggested that the illustrations of sacred sites on stupas might, with the ritual of circumambulation, be "in effect a mini-pilgrimage," thus emphasizing the notion of place (Falk 1977:283. n. 5). But why are the places sacred? For Falk, it is because "the traces seem to have preserved the miraculous power of the Master" (Falk 1977:283), and thus their illustrations would, presumably, partake of this power. As far as I can see, Huntington's historical snapshot interpretation proposes that the illustrations of places and events are of interest to Buddhists because they teach them the importance of worship.

Interestingly, Falk does not include Buddha images as one of the sacred traces. She cannot speak of them since her list of traces is only of objects and places directly connected to the Buddha's bodily presence.[22] This relationship between object or place and Buddha, one created by contact with the Buddha's body, does not normally apply to the image.[23] The agency for its miracle power must come from another source. Indeed, my argument has been that the power may in important instances not be directly connected to the Buddha, but may reside in other categories entirely. I have suggested two, that of the object nature of the image and of its personality. I do not imply that these are the only two, only that the power of images may not relate to Buddhist doctrine. The cult of the miraculous Buddha images may have to be written in categories of knowledge other than those of traditionally understood Buddhism.

## Notes

1. The dates of Sakyamuni's life have always been uncertain, but the recent scholarly tendency is to move them somewhat later than the traditionally accepted dating, placing his death as late as 400-350 B.C.E. See the papers written for the 1988 symposium on the Buddha's date published in Bechert 1991.

2. See my other article in this book "Expected Miracles: The Unsurprisingly Miraculous Nature of Buddhist Images and Relics."

3. The eight major scenes from his life are themselves often called the *astamahapratiharya*, or the Eight Great Miracles. It may be, however, that the grouping together of these eight scenes is a late development in Indian Buddhism, dating to the Pala period, with its first artistic occurrence around the eighth century C.E. See Leoshko 1993/94.

4. The interest in Indian culture and religion as a source for discovering mankind's pristine religious origins is in large part what motivated the scholarship of the earliest Orientalists, whose description of India continues, however incorrectly, to dominate even scholarly thinking. See, for example, Neufeldt 1980.

5. The Kalupahanas identify the first attempt as Nanamoli 1972.

6. Only wooden architecture existed at the time, with fired brick not appearing until the second century B.C.E. The mud stupas would only exist today if they had been enclosed later by larger brick or stone stupas.

7. The Piprahwa reliquary and inscription has elicited the most arguments for being interred in a stupa at the time of his death, but Härtel believes it can date only from the second century B.C.E. (Härtel 1991:75).

8. The earliest extant Buddhist monuments may date to the time of Asoka (r. ca. 272-231 B.C.E.), and would include stupas. That there were stupas earlier than those built by Asoka is assumed, however, as Asoka is said to have opened stupas to remove their relics, as well as enlarged one already existing stupa. [See the various references (as page 23) in Mitra 1971.] Other than the Asokan stupas, the only other extant Buddhist monument dating from this period is the pillar set up at Sarnath by Asoka which is topped by a wheel (assumedly the *dharmacakra*). If we are talking about early Buddhist iconography, therefore, we have only two symbols to name, the wheel and the stupa. It is very difficult, however, to know how they were understood at this point, specifically in relationship to the Buddha. Mireille Bénisti has argued that even the reliefs on the fence of Stupa II at Sanci, dating to about 120-100 B.C.E., have nothing about them that can be defined as specifically Buddhist in iconography (Bénisti 1986). By this she means that there is nothing depicted at Stupa II that needs be interpreted in terms of Buddhism, rather than in terms of pan-Indian religious symbolism. This would make the reliefs from such sites as Bharhut, Bodhgaya, and Amaravati examples of the earliest Buddhist iconography, including life scenes, all dating to about the early first century B.C.E.

9. I have argued this position in detail in Brown forthcoming.

10. The complexity of these issues cannot be explored here, but it seems to me that the argument for an aniconic period of art would not be in terms of the symbols being the Buddha (such as the Bodhi Tree being the Buddha), nor of the symbol "replacing the Buddha," but that the symbol indicated his presence in particular contexts. The most obvious argument for the existence of an aniconic period is very simple: there are no figural images of the Buddha in early Buddhist art. The reasons for this, what it means, and so forth are open to discussion, but that it happened is a fact at this point.

11. In some sense this raises questions similar to those asked regarding the life-scene reliefs, only applied to the geographical places themselves. For example, what does it mean that after two hundred years of Buddhism, no anthropomorphic imagery of the Buddha existed, whether in the reliefs or at the sites themselves?

12. Von Glasenapp 1966. His book makes, I feel, a curious argument for the Buddha's non-theistic character. Basically he says that the Buddha cannot be a god (or, I should say the "God") because the Buddha did not create the world nor rule it. His notion of a god as a being who must have complete single-handed power over every area of human activity is clearly based on the monotheistic Judeo-Christian-Islamic conceptions of God, although he seems unaware of his Western-centric orientation. It has no authority, as far as I can see, for defining divinity in the Buddhist tradition. Here, by the way, is von Glasenapp on the issue of miracles: "The form of Buddha, together with all the many miracles with which it became adorned in the course of the centuries, may be compared with a statue

overloaded with countless garments and ornaments, but which is itself not contained in the drapings but possesses a true, original core to which one may still penetrate provided one does not get sidetracked by the many elaborations" (p. 65). In short, he is a believer in the true-core approach of the Kalupahanas and Nakamura, in which there is no place for miracles.

13. These three panels have a number of inscriptions. Those for the middle and lower panels identify the figures as deities.

14. They are dressed and look exactly the same as the deities in the middle and lower panels, and while I feel they are most likely deities, their identification is uncertain.

15. Perhaps she would prefer for the figures to be the contemporary first century B.C.E. audience worshiping at Bodhgaya, but this is simply not what is being represented.

16. Alexander Cunningham, who first undertook excavations at the ruined site of Bharhut in the nineteenth century, was told that a box had been found in the center of the stupa mound and, given to the Raja of Nagod, had been lost (see Barua 1979:2).

17. As will be mentioned just below in Suryavarman's oath, the jewel was associated with the "sacred fire." At Angkor Wat (twelfth century), a relief depicts the sacred fire being carried on a palanquin. The scene, inscribed in Khmer as *vrah vlen* ("the sacred fire"), shows a curious dome-shaped form surrounded as if by a tiny pillared fence on the palanquin. While it is not at all clear what exactly is being depicted, Bosch points out in passing that there is a jewel on top of the dome ("couronne" d'un *ratna* sur un coussin de lotus") (see Bosch 1932:10; also see for illustrations). While Bosch does not refer at all in his article to the "holy jewel," he discusses and illustrates a second similar dome-like form (he calls it a *linga*) in a relief from the Bayon that has an even more pronounced jewel on top (see Bosch 1932, fig. 2). In addition, at Angkor Wat the group carrying the sacred fire is in the relief preceded by a group of ascetics, one of whom is identified by inscription as the *rajahotar* or "royal sacrificer" (see Bosch 1932, fig. 1 and *Le Temple d'Angkor Vat* 1932: Pls. 548, 549, and 568). Might this then be the "brahmans and acaryas" mentioned as well in Suryavarman's oath? In other words, one may argue that the holy jewel is represented, along with the sacred fire and court brahmans, in the Angkor Wat relief.

18. By 1956, when Helen Bruce witnessed the changing of the clothes, the ceremony had become reduced to a procedure involving no water and the simple cleaning of the image "with a pure white cloth." Bruce does not describe it in any detail, but my impression is that it had become more a "Buddhist," less a royal, ceremony (Bruce 1960:44).

19. When vows are not fulfilled, the Buddha image can punish the person, for example by sickness, recalling the Emerald Buddha's similar ability.

20. The Phra Bang image is today in Luang Prabang, the capital of Laos. (The capital is, of course, named after the image "City of Phra Bang.")

21. See, for example, Werner 1988 and Griffiths 1994. Particularly appropriate here is Griffith's comment on p. 94 that "... early Buddhism was resolutely aniconic in its presentation of Buddha as a body of magical transformation [that is,

*nirmanakaya*]. Just as Gautama understood as such a body, is not understood as a center of identity with character-traits, intentions, volitions, fears, hopes, and goals, so also he is not depicted in the early traditions as a person but rather as a significant absence ...."

22. Her category "traces" is not completely clear to me. She lists four types of traces: bodily relics, objects once touched by the Buddha, sites visited by the Buddha, and "just traces," such as footprints (pp. 282-283). All appear to me to be directly connected with the Buddha's bodily presence. In a footnote she divides the stupa into three types: "*sariraka*, for the bodily relics; *paribhojika*, for objects used; and *uddesika*, 'commemorative,' for the holy sites" (p. 283). This largely Theravadan categorization is interpreted differently by A. B. Griswold, who places the sites of the Eight Great Events under that of *paribhogacetiya* ("reminder by association"); it is copies or illustrations of the sites that would be a *uddesikacetiya*, a category of "indicative reminders" that includes Buddha images (Rajanubhab 1973:vi).

23. There are instances when relics were placed within images. In fact, the Emerald Buddha is said in the chronicles to have the Buddha's relics inside, although there is no evidence of which I am aware that the actual image is not solid stone.

# 4

# Divine Delicacies:
# Monks, Images, and Miracles
# in the contest between
# Jainism and Buddhism

*Phyllis Granoff*

### Introduction

Rivalry between Jains and Buddhists is a common theme in medieval Jain narrative literature. In didactic stories and biographies of famous monks we often hear of Jain and Buddhist monks who, in quest of royal favour, battled each other in learned debates in the courts of famous kings. Monks also engaged in contests of magic powers at the courts of powerful rulers; in some cases the ability to speak forcefully in a debate was itself a magic power granted the rival monk by some deity, and the Jain had to use his own rituals to subdue that deity or propitiate a more powerful deity and secure his victory.[1] If the stories have any basis in reality, competition between the two groups was by no means limited to the monastic community. We also meet Buddhist and Jain laymen who vie with each other to win the hearts of beautiful maidens. In one such story a Buddhist disguises himself as a Jain to marry a Jain girl and finally comes to realize the truth of the Jain teachings; in another story, a Jain converts to Buddhism to marry a beautiful Buddhist girl, only to realize later that the conversion was a mistake, even if the marriage was not.[2] Buddhist story literature from a relatively early period also tells us of a strong rivalry between the Buddhists and the Jains. Indeed the *Pratiharyasutra* of the

*Divyavadana* describes a contest of supernatural powers held between the Buddha himself and a group of rival teachers, who included Mahavira. Most of these contests between the Jains and Buddhists in medieval Jain literature take place between individuals, although their outcome may well determine the fate of the entire religious community. In these contests the outcome is never really in doubt; a Jain monk, severely beset by an opponent in debate, nonetheless triumphs in the end. There are a few contests, however, in which the battle is waged for the hearts of the entire Jain monastic community and in which the spectre is raised that the Jain side may indeed lose. The participants in this very threatening contest are usually an individual on the Buddhist side, and the entire Jain samgha on the other side. These contests involve food and the supernatural preparation and distribution of food. Typically, a Buddhist monk or a Buddhist reborn as a demigod favourable to the Buddhist side makes and distributes marvelous food to the Jain monastic community. This results in mass conversions of the Jain monks to Buddhism and threatens the very existence of the Jain samgha. Extraordinary means are needed to stop the distribution of the food and to wean the Jain monks back to the harsher life of the Jain samgha.[3]

The stories about food miracles and the conversion of Jain monks to Buddhism that are told in medieval Jain literature reflect at once the common stereotyping of Buddhist monks as gluttons that was so prevalent in Jainism and Hinduism, and a keen awareness on the part of the Jains that their own monastic rules were far stricter than the rules that prevailed in the Buddhist community, and therefore possibly less attractive to both potential and actual members of the Jain monastic community. The Jains seem to have felt that the Buddhists, with their more comfortable monastic life, represented the greatest challenge to the survival of the Jain monastic community. Both Jainism and Buddhist shared a rejection of the Vedic sacrifice and, in later times, of the practice of making blood offerings to deities, particularly the blood offerings to clan goddesses so prevalent in the medieval period. Both emphasized nonviolence and self-control. In fact, others saw them as so similar that they constantly confounded the Jains with the Buddhists in their writings. It is no wonder then that the Jains feared the allure of the Buddhist monastic life, which, all things being equal, they saw as less difficult and filled with deprivation, and thus potentially seductive to would-be Jain converts and actual Jain monks.

In this paper I examine some Jain stories about Buddhist food miracles. The paper has essentially two focal points. It is intended as a small step towards understanding medieval Jain and Buddhist attitudes towards miracles in general and their conceptualizations of the agents of those miracles, human or superhuman, and the to us inanimate agents of the painted or sculpted image. While the Jain information about food miracles comes from didactic stories and biographical narratives, we are fortunate in having a very different type of source for Buddhist attitudes towards the magical preparation of food. The Jains may have told stories about Buddhists who could magically produce rich food, but the Buddhists from their side gave actual rules for rituals which accomplished the preparation and distribution of sumptuous foods through supernatural means. In their stories the Jains credit the Buddhist food miracles to human or semidivine agents, humans reborn as demigods. On the other hand, Buddhist rituals included in a medieval Tantric manual, the *Manjusrimulakalpa*, chapter 11, require the intermediary of a painted image of the Buddha and a mantra, which they also consider to be a form (albeit non-corporeal) of the Buddha.

In my analysis of the Jain stories and the Buddhist rituals I shall attempt to understand why humans, humans reborn as demigods and painted images and mantras are all interchangeable in the performance of these food miracles. I shall argue that the modern scholar in many cases makes a false dichotomy in singling out an image as the agent of miracles. To the Jain or Buddhist there is no such thing as an image in many ritual or religious contexts; there is the Buddha or the Jina, the human or the suprahuman being, through whose powers the miracle is performed.[4] This suggestion in turn raises another question. What was the status of painted or sculpted objects in general in Jainism and Buddhism? To what extent was the painted likeness regarded as totally different from its subject and to what degree was it seen as the subject itself? Were images of the Jina or Buddha that are described as the Jina or Buddha himself, or that function as the Jina or Buddha himself was said to function, categorically different from other images or likenesses? I hope to address this question at least briefly, even if I cannot answer it completely at this stage of my research. I shall cite material from Jain and Buddhist story literature in my discussion of general attitudes towards the arts and artists.

A second major focus of this paper will be to examine how the Jains might have gone about composing the stories of Buddhists who magically produced food that are the starting point of this paper. Again, I shall be suggesting that when Jains singled out food miracles and made the Buddhists the agents of the miracles, they were responding to actual Buddhist claims in Buddhist texts. I shall further suggest that even the details of the Jain stories betray a close knowledge of Buddhist claims and that the Jain stories were carefully crafted around Buddhist beliefs and attitudes towards food.

I begin the paper with a translation of a Jain story about food miracles, which is followed by an analysis of Jain stories about Buddhists making food in supernatural ways. I consider in the analysis Buddhist attitudes towards food and how these contrast with Jain attitudes. I go from there to a discussion of the ritual for making food in the Buddhist *Manjusri-mulakalpa*. In my discussion of the *Manjusrimulakalpa*, I shall emphasize the fact that the painted Buddha of the mandala really does nothing different from what the Buddha himself was said to have done in his show of super-natural power to the heretics in the *Pratiharyasutra* of the *Divyavadana*: he glows and enables the sadhaka to fly, for example. In a third section I con-sider further evidence from Jain hymns in support of my hypothesis that in many cases an image, particularly a miracle-working image, is not an image but the Jina himself. The hymns I shall discuss were composed by monks on the occasion of their pilgrimage to famous Jina images. Many of these hymns tell us in passionate and emotional language that the singer of the hymn has at last seen the Jina himself. Moreover, we are told that seeing the Jina brings marvelous results, from the healing of leprosy to the promise of final release. The modern scholar knows of course that it is the image of the Jina the monk/author of these hymns is seeing; nonetheless in his own words the monk speaks fervently of seeing the Jina and not of seeing his representation in stone. The evidence in these sections of the paper, then, asks us to reconsider our own conceptualizations and cate-gories: all of these accounts, from the stories of food miracles done by gifted monks and humans reborn as demigods in the Jain texts, to the rituals in the *Manjusrimulakalpa*, done through the aid of the Buddha as painted image and mantra, and the miracles of the hymns performed through the agency of the Jina as sculpted form, are telling us the same thing. The power to save and to heal, to astound and amaze, belongs really to unusual humans or divine beings: to the Buddha or the Jina, Manjusri and other gods, existing either as sacred word or image, or living being, and to gifted monks, both in their mortal bodies and after death in their rebirth as demigods.

Finally, in a fourth section I consider some attitudes towards images and paintings in general in Buddhist and Jain story literature. I shall argue there that there is at least some limited evidence that images and painted likenesses other than those of the Jina and Buddha--in other words, non-religious images and those made in a totally secular context--could at times function exactly like their subjects. Even when they were not seen as the exact functional equivalents of the subjects they represented, they could still affect their viewers deeply, for the evidence indicates that the mark of a well-made image or picture was precisely its ability to present itself as the real thing and be taken by a spectator for the real thing. The images and the painted likenesses of ritual, then, functioning as the Buddha or the Jina, and seen by the fervent devotee as the Jina or the Buddha, may not be unique. Perhaps they can tell us more than we have realized about Indian attitudes towards art objects in general.

### The Story of Surastra from the Mulasuddhiprakarana

The story of Surastra is told twice in the commentary to the *Mula-suddhiprakarana*. The first time it appears in the context of the *samyaktva-dusana*, "things that detract from the right faith." The story is given there as an example of the fault of *kutirthikaprasamsa*, "praising ascetics who follow a false path." The story is then referred to in the discussion of the *chindikas* or "temporary lapses from the faith" and the reader is simply asked to supply the story in full from the earlier section. In this case it is intended to illustrate the temporary lapse of faith made in order to survive in the forest. I give here the story in full.

There is on the continent of Jambudvipa, in the midst of the land of Bharata, the most beautiful of kingdoms, Saurastra, nestled on the shore of the ocean. It had many villages, all neatly arranged, and in it reigned peace and prosperity, for there was no danger from the many arrogant hostile kings who had all been subdued. All of its subjects possessed whatever wealth they desired and were fine and outstanding citizens.

And in that kingdom was the town named Girinayara, built right at the foot of Mt. Ujjinta. And listen now to the qualities of that town, which was like so many different things in this world, if only you know how to turn and twist the words that I say, for the likeness lies in the town and these different things all being described by the very same adjectives. The town was like the greatest of kings, for such great kings give refuge to many while the town had many houses; it was like a host of powerful enemies, for such heroic foes possess great valour while the town possessed great riches; it was like a painting, for a painting has many colours while the town had people of all stations; it was like a poor family, for a poor family always has many children while the town had many residents; it was like the ocean, for the ocean has much water while the town had many merchants; it was like a music composition, for a piece of music has many different notes while the town had many lakes; it was like a bad king, for a bad king has many lazy hangers-on while the town had many bazaars filled with wares; it was like the apocalypse, for when the world is to be destroyed the sun blazes to make an inferno, while the town was filled with heroes.

There dwelt the pious Jain layman Jinadasa, who understood the nine entities taught in the Jain doctrine and who spent his wealth in making gifts to the poor and to those monks and nuns who were worthy of charity. Jinadasa thought often about the nature of reality and the pain and vanity of the cycle of rebirths, just as these things were taught in the

Jain texts, and he was known everywhere for his conduct, which exemplified the virtues of the Jain layman. He never listened to the religious texts of other religions, which he knew to be false, and he rigorously observed the vows incumbent upon a Jain laymen--the five *anuvrata*, not to harm any living creatures, not to lie, not to steal, not to violate his marriage vows, and not to be attached to material possessions--and the four *siksavratas*, which involved particular rituals. Thus he agreed at certain times to restrict his activities to a small area; to meditate and fast, and finally to make gifts to Jain monks and nuns. He scrupulously observed all these excellent religious practices, and he understood completely the true nature of worldly existence. Jinadasa and a cloth could be described by the same word, only for the cloth the word meant that the material was made up of threads, while applied to Jinadasa it meant that he possessed every excellent virtue. Jinadasa also gave no opportunity for carelessness, the enemy of religious behaviour, to overcome him. He always observed the commands of the Jina and never praised an undertaking that was in any way contrary to what the Jain scriptures enjoin. He had destroyed in himself every trace of false belief and was ever eager to listen to the Jain teachings; he gave comfort to creatures in need and was indeed the best of Jain laymen.

Now one day when famine struck the land and Jinadasa found himself unable to support himself, he set out for Ujjain with a caravan. Somehow along the way he was careless and lost the rest of the caravan. All of his food that he had brought along for the journey was with the caravan and he had nothing. Unable to find any other caravan to join, he joined up with a group of Buddhist monks. The Buddhist monks told him, "If you carry our provisions and our bundles we will give you something to eat." Knowing that one must sometimes stray from the true Jain path when caught in the midst of the forest, he agreed and began to carry their things. And those Buddhist monks gave him rich food, sweets and the like, for that is what they normally eat. For it is said by those heretics,

> A soft bed, something to drink as soon as you rise, dinner at
> noon and tea in the afternoon, grapes and sugar at night, and
> finally liberation: this is what the Buddha has taught.

And again,

> Having eaten a tasty meal and settled into a comfortable bed
> in a comfortable building, the monk meditates without any
> discomfort.

Now once after he had eaten all this rich food he fell ill with severe indigestion, vomiting and diarrhea. He experienced incredible pain, and suffered terribly, for there was no remedy for his sickness. Knowing that he would die, he sat up straight and began to call out with the formula of praise all Jains recite:

> Praise be to the arhats, praise to the siddhas, praise to the
> ganadharas, praise to the upadhyayas, praise to all the sadhus.

The arhats, siddhas, and sadhus, and the doctrine proclaimed by the Omniscient Ones--may these four things ever bring me peace and well-being.

These are the most noble things in all the world and I take refuge in them in word, thought, and deed.

I renounce doing harm to living beings; I renounce stealing and lying, fornicating and being attached to possessions. I renounce attachment to my body, and in thought, word, and deed, I renounce all food.

In this way, reciting the sacred words of praise and accepting upon himself the sacred rite of voluntary renunciation of all food, he abandoned his rotten body and was reborn as a god in the heaven Saudharma. Instantly he found himself in a new body, radiant and handsome, in a heavenly realm that was exceedingly bright. He rose from his couch, a thrill of joy coursing through his body as he surveyed his divine splendour. As he heard his servants shouting to him, "Victory to the king! Victory to the king!" he began to ponder, "What was it that I did in my previous existence that has resulted in my enjoying such wealth and splendour?"

And then, using his supernatural knowledge, he looked about and he saw his own body, which the Buddhist monks in keeping with their own custom had covered with red robes and shoved to one side. Now his supernatural knowledge was not quite perfected, since he had just been reborn in the realm of the gods, and so he mistakenly began to think, "Aha! I was a Buddhist monk in my past birth, for see how my body lies covered in the red robes of the Buddhist ascetic. Clearly this teaching of the Buddhists is very powerful, for it has led me to be reborn in my present marvelous state. I must devote myself now to honouring the Buddhist monks."

And with these thoughts in mind, he went to Ujjain. He greeted the Buddhist monks with the utmost respect. And every day he reached his bejewelled arm into the Buddhist monastery and fed the monks there with exquisitely prepared and delicate divine dishes. Everyone began to sing the praises of the Buddhist doctrine, "See, see! May the Buddhist doctrine be ever victorious, for it has such great powers!"

The Jain monks and nuns were in terrible distress. Just at that point the Jain monk Dharmaghosa in the course of his wanderings arrived in Ujjain. The Jain lay devotees all went out to pay him their respects. And after they bowed down to him, they told him everything that had happened. They declared, "If, our lord, you allow such an insult to the Jain doctrine, then to whom shall we turn in our distress? Blessed One! You must do something to enhance the prestige of the Jain cause, for there is no one but yourself who is equal to this great task."

At that the monk used his heightened knowledge and he came to know who was feeding the Buddhists divine food. He sent one of his own disciples to him and instructed him in this way. "When the Buddhist monks offer you food from his hand, you must grab that hand. First recite the sacred formula, praise to the arhats, and then say this: 'Come to your senses, supernatural being! Come to your senses! Do not be deluded!' " The disciple agreed to do exactly as he had been told and set off to the Buddhist monastery. The Buddhist monks, seeing that Jain monk approach and proud of their supernatural powers, went right up to him and said, "Come, come with us so that we may give you some divine food made by the gods." And the Jain monk went right to that place where the hand was serving food. When the hand was about to give the Jain monk food at the instruction of the Buddhists, the Jain monk grabbed the hand with his own hand. He first recited the Jain formula of praise and then said, "Come to your senses, supernatural being! Come to your senses! Do not be deluded!"

Now when he heard these words, the supernatural being realized at last the true state of things through his own supernatural knowledge, and he knew exactly what he had been in his previous life. He confessed his wrongdoing and, assuming his true form, he said to the Jain monk, "I am at your service." He let out a loud laugh and then went away to find the Jain master. And then, a crown upon his head, his cheeks touched by the long jeweled earrings that dangled from his ears, his chest hung with necklaces and chokers and chains of gold and pearls, his soft arms gently waving, adorned with every kind of gorgeous armlet and bracelet, his fingers ruddy from the rays of gold emanating from all the rings on them, his body covered with a diaphanous silk that was free from any trace of dust and hung with gently tinkling bells, he touched his forehead to the ground and bowed at the feet of the Jain monk Dharmaghosa. With his hands folded in reverence and held over his head, he spoke to the monk with these words: "Blessed One! Today you have shown me your great favour. Without you I would have continued to sink, deluded, into that ocean of rebirths, that terrible ocean of rebirths that is limitless and filled with the most awful sufferings." And having said these words, he went to all the Jain temples and conducted great festivals there and, filled with devotion, he danced there in ecstasy. And he proclaimed to all the world, "This doctrine that has been taught by the King of the Jinas is capable of putting an end to the cycles of rebirth. All of you, devote yourselves to this faith. What more need I say?"

And in this way many people were led to embrace the Jain faith. And that god, praising and praising the Jain teachings, rose up to the heavens and reached the realm of the gods.

Let this be a lesson that one should never praise false teachings.

This remarkable story tells us of a Jain who willy-nilly becomes a Buddhist and moreover supports the Buddhist monastic community by providing them with supernatural food. The food miracle so amazes the local populace that they desert the Jains in droves and the Jain monks and nuns are left without any support. The miracle thus aids the entire

Buddhist samgha and threatens the existence of the Jain samgha. If there is a story type about food miracles, this much would seem to be paradigmatic for it: a food miracle is performed by a Buddhist on behalf of the Buddhist samgha. But the agent of the miracle is not any ordinary Buddhist; it is a Jain who has become a Buddhist for false reasons.

The story of the food miracle that is part of the biography of the monk Arya Khapatacarya offers a close parallel to this account of the deluded Jinadasa. In this biography, a disobedient Jain monk reads a magic spell from a Jain text and obtains the knowledge of how to transport objects through the air. He uses the knowledge to make bowls of food cooked in the homes of wealthy merchants fly through the sky to him and he feasts on the rich food. The Jain monks find out about his trick and are outraged. They demand that he stop. The monk leaves the Jain community and becomes a Buddhist. He causes the begging bowls of the Buddhist monks to fly through the air to the homes of the rich and return to the monks full to the brim with delicacies. The Buddhist monks, unlike the Jain monks, find nothing amiss in this, and welcome the former Jain into their fold. It is not long before the miraculous food transport wins numerous converts for the Buddhists, and the Jains, in danger of losing their basis of support among the lay community and their monks to the Buddhist monastic community, turn to Arya Khapatacarya for help. Arya Khapatacarya employs some counter-magic to destroy the flying begging bowls. When their contents crash down on the heads of the bystanders, the Buddhists lose much of their newly won popular appeal![5]

From this brief account it should be readily apparent that here, too, we have to do with a Jain turned Buddhist for false reasons. In this case, the Jain monk has read a magic book forbidden him and learns how to perform a supernatural feat. He becomes a Buddhist not because he is attracted to the Buddhist doctrine, but out of anger and gluttony. In both stories the food miracle threatens the existence of the Jain community and must be stopped with counter-magic, counter-spells, or counter-magical objects.

These two stories include many themes familiar to readers of medieval Jain narrative literature. Reading magic books in secret is a familiar topos, and monks are repeatedly warned in the biographies told of them of the danger of magic books and magic spells.[6] Buddhists and Hindus who die and become demigods are also a frequent scourge of the Jain community in the story literature.[7] These stories may thus be seen as typical and conventional examples of medieval Jain narrative literature, but it would be a mistake to conclude from this that they are therefore nothing more than pieces of inventive fiction, constructed by the Jain community as yet one more weapon with which to degrade and belittle their opponents. In fact, I think it is also necessary to read these stories as solidly grounded in the reality of claims and counterclaims made in the Buddhist texts themselves and as reflecting the Jains's close familiarity with actual Buddhist assertions in their story literature and ritual practices described in their ritual handbooks. Artful fantasies, these stories are nonetheless a close reflection of the religious milieu in which they were told and circulated.

Each of the accounts in fact contains one telling detail that suggests that the stories may in fact be oblique references to Buddhist claims. In the account of Jinadasa from the *Mulasuddhiprakarana*, the demigod not only makes food for the Buddhist monks; he also serves it to them in an unusual fashion. He reaches his preternaturally long arm into the monastery and dishes out the delicacies. There is a monk in the Buddhist story literature known for his long reach in grasping the *salaka*, the stick that enables him to take part in a feast prepared by a lay devotee for the Buddhist monks. This is Purna, who is pronounced by the Buddha to be the "foremost of those who grab the sticks," in the *Etadaggavagga* of the *Anguttaranikaya*, and to whom one of the longer *Avadanas* in the *Divyavadana* is devoted. Purna's story is told in some detail in the Manorathapurani, the commentary to the *Anguttaranikaya* (*Divyavadana* 2:15-34; *Manorathapurani* 1: 280-286). It is significant that Purna's unusually long reach enables him to attend a feast that is surrounded by supernatural events. If we look at the account of Purna in the *Manorathapurani*, we hear about the pious lay devotee Maha-subhadda, who was the only Buddhist in her family. She fasts and purifies herself, and then standing on the roof of her mansion throws some flowers into the air with the wish that they might reach the Buddha, who was staying in a distant city. She prays fervently that the flowers will be magically transported to the Buddha and that they will form a perfect canopy over his head. Furthermore, the Buddha is to know that this is a sign that she invites him and five hundred monks to receive alms from her. The flowers are then transported through the sky to form a canopy over the Buddha as he is teaching the Dharma. The Buddha understands their import at once and in his mind he accepts Subhadda's invitation. The next morning, as soon as the sun comes up, he tells Ananda that today they will be traveling a long distance for their alms. Ananda is to give the *salakas* only to monks who are already arhats and not to any of the rank and file. Ananda announces all of this to the monks, and Purna is the first to put out his hand to receive the stick. Ananda rebukes him, telling him that the Buddha has specifically said that the sticks are not for ordinary monks like Purna, but only for those with more highly developed spiritual potential. Ananda returns to the Buddha to ask what he should do, and the Buddha replies only that he should give a stick to anyone who requests it. Ananda assumes that there must be a reason why the Buddha has not explicitly forbidden him to give one of the sticks to Purna. As Ananda returns to Purna, Purna suddenly masters the fourth stage of meditation, which brings with it the ability to perform certain supernatural feats. Purna floats up to the sky and from there extends his arm all the way back down to Ananda on earth.

The account of Purna in the Sanskrit *Divyavadana* likewise emphasizes the fact that only monks with supernatural powers can partake of the feast in question. The invitation in this version comes from the layman Purna, who is the main subject of the *avadana*. Purna has returned safely from a sea voyage and decides that he will use the fabulously valuable sandalwood he has acquired to build a residence for the Buddha. He and his brothers then agree to invite the Buddha for a meal. Purna stands on top of the palatial residence he has built for the Buddha and faces in the direction of Sravasti, where he knows the Buddha is staying. He throws some flowers and incense in the direction of the Buddha and offers his worship. The text then goes on to say that because of the power of the Buddhas and the gods to perform miracles (*buddhanam buddhanubhavena devatanam ca devatanubhavena*), the flowers take on the shape of a pavilion and are wafted to the Buddha in the Jetavana. The incense takes on the shape of a cloud and is transported to Jetavana, while the water Purna had offered in his worship looks like a slab of cat's-eye gemstone as it makes its way to the Buddha. Ananda knows how to read supernatural signs and realizes that this is all part of an invitation from some devotee. He asks the Buddha from where the invitation has come. The Buddha explains that the invitation has come to them from the distant city of Suparaka. The Buddha then tells Ananda that he should summon the monks and tell them that only those monks who can travel the vast distance to Suparaka by the next day should take a *salaka*. Ananda returns to the company of the monks and tells them what the Buddha said. The monk Purna Kundopadhaniyaka is among those present, and he immediately tries to take one of the sticks that would admit him to the feast. Ananda rebukes him, saying that he lacks the magical powers (*rddhi*) that would enable him to traverse the long distance to Suparaka in the time required. Purna Kundopadhaniyaka is ashamed he does not have magical powers and he exerts himself with all his might. The text then says, "Before Ananda could give a stick to a third monk, Purna stuck out his arm that was as mighty as the trunk of an elephant and grabbed that stick." Purna's long reach is supernatural; it is what he achieves through his acquisition of magical powers or *rddhi*. It is also what allows him to partake of the wonderful feast that is being prepared for the monks.

Although in these stories of the monk Purna Kundopadhaniyaka the food is not magically prepared, this entire episode of a feast prepared for the monks is replete with supernatural events. To begin with, the invitation itself is supernatural, and then the monks must use magical means to travel to the feast. In fact, the Buddha makes clear that only monks with magic powers are invited. Purna gets to participate in the feast because he is able to perfect his magic powers and reach his arm an unnaturally long distance to grab a ticket for himself. The long reach of Purna is the sign that he has the magic powers that are the condition for the invitation.

It seems to me that the Jain story of Jinadasa, the demigod with his long reach preparing a magic feast for the Buddhist monks, recalls this other story of a long reach that led to participation in a feast made for the Buddhist monks. While Buddhists seem to show little awareness of Jain story literature, I have argued elsewhere that Jains by contrast seem to know well select parts of the large corpus of Buddhist *avadanas* and *jatakas*, which they took great pleasure in mocking (Granoff 1990c: 225-239; Granoff 1992a: 1-42; Granoff forthcoming c). In the Jain story the feast turns into a fiasco, as the host renounces the Buddhist monks and turns back to the Jains.

There is another point in the Jain story of Jinadasa that may also recall and make fun of other actual Buddhist claims and practices. Jinadasa, it is to be remembered, joins the Buddhist monks when he is lost in the woods. The Buddhist monks are also travelers. They feed Jinadasa with the rich food, which lead to his untimely death. Despite the fact that the Buddhist monks and their rich food have a very specific context in the story, namely, a journey through the dangerous jungle, the narrator of the story generalizes from the specific and tells us that Buddhist monks in fact always eat such rich foods, which were of course forbidden to Jain monks. What makes such an accusation against the Buddhist monks work is its very semblance of probability. The *Mahavagga* 6.22, *Pancagorasadianujanana*, tells of the wealthy landowner Mendaka, who feasts the Buddha and monks on milk products, in classical India the standard examples of rich and luxurious food (*Mahavagga*: 257-259). The monks at first hesitate to partake of the rich milk dishes, but are persuaded to do so. Mendaka then asks the Buddha to explain what the monks are allowed to take as provisions on a journey. He prefaces his question with the remark that in many cases the way through the jungles is dangerous and it is often difficult to find food or water in the jungle. The Buddha responds to this question first by saying that he allows the monks to eat five dishes made from milk products, and then he goes on to say that he also allows them to purchase provisions for a journey. In this section of the monastic rules, then, eating rich foods made of milk and taking along provisions for a journey are somehow indirectly tied together.

If we return to the Jain story, it may not be accidental at all that the Buddhist monks offer the unfortunate Jain layman foods so rich that he cannot digest them while they are on a journey through a dangerous jungle. In fact the Buddhists allowed their monks to carry provisions on a journey, and the passage that allowed them provisions also dealt with permitting the monks to eat what the culture considered to be rich foods: ghee, fresh butter, milk, yogurt, and cream. The Jain story may only exaggerate what was actual Buddhist practice; I suggest that it is precisely this exaggeration of what Buddhists themselves said and possibly did that would have made the Jain satire so effective.[8] Finally, in connection with Mendaka's offering, it is worth noting that Jain texts explicitly forbade the eating of some of the very substances Mendaka offers--in particular, *navanita*, which I have translated as "fresh butter." The *Yogasastra* of Hemacandra, though late, provides an overview of Jain attitudes towards various religious and secular practices. In the section on foods, Hemacandra explicitly forbids the eating of *navanita* for both monks and nuns and all lay devotees (*Yogasastra* ch.3 vs. 34-35).

The magic feast in the biography of Arya Khapatacarya is also not without hints of allusion to Buddhist stories. While in the Jain biography a Jain monk, rebuked for wrongdoing, turns to the Buddhists in anger and makes their begging bowls fly through the air, filled with sweets, in the biography of the Buddha that is included in the *jatakas*, a monk magically transports a bowl filled with sumptuous delicacies from King Suddhodhana to the Buddha (*Jatakas* vol.1, 87). The monk causes the bowl to fly up into the sky. He then ascends into the sky himself, and the two, monk and bowl, fly together to the Buddha.

I would like to suggest that the Jain storyteller chose his details carefully. It is not simply convention that it is a Buddhist (false Buddhist though he may be in both of the stories) who makes a magical feast for Buddhist monks; nor is the way in which the feast is given to the monks arbitrary. Jains chose the long reach of the demigod precisely because Buddhists themselves told stories about marvelous feasts and the magical ability to stretch one's arm a vast distance that was a prerequisite for attendance at the feast. Jains told a story about a Buddhist monk who could make begging bowls fly through the air precisely because the Buddhists told about monks who could perform this feat. What we have in these stories, then, is something more pointed than just stories told to ridicule an opponent. These stories in fact are part of a dialogue, a debate, and, written in the style of all such debates in classical India, they contain, in this case, scarcely veiled but nonetheless precise references to the opponent's own claims.

In keeping with this line of argument, I would like further to suggest that the very fact that in their anti-Buddhist stories the Jains seem to focus on food miracles almost to the exclusion of other miracles also reflects something about actual Buddhist emphases in their own texts. There is a telling story in the *Mahavagga*, the *Rajomallavatthu*, which is intended to explain why Buddhist monks are allowed to eat certain foods, but which also makes very clear a fundamental contrast between Buddhist and Jain attitudes towards food as a ritual gift (*Mahavagga* 262 and 6.11: 237). In this account the Buddha comes to Kusinagara with a large retinue of monks. The Mallas hear of his arrival and order all of their clansmen to honour the Buddha, proclaiming a heavy fine for those who refuse to do so. Rajo Malla, a companion to Ananda, goes to greet the Buddha and is praised by Ananda for his display of respect. Rajo explains to Ananda that he is not particularly keen on the Buddha at all, but fears that he will be punished by his clansmen if he does not comply with their order to honour the Buddha. Eventually Rajo is made to see the greatness of the Buddha and in his fervent devotion he asks the Buddha to accept only the offerings that he gives and to reject offerings from anyone else. The Buddha explains that he must accept all offerings; he is happy to accept Rajo's offerings as well, but he cannot refuse to accept the things that his other devotees may give him. Now at that juncture the citizens of Kusinagara were preparing a great feast for the Buddha and his monks. Rajo is too late to make his contribution to the feast in the normal way, and so he decides that he will look over all the dishes and offer the Buddha and the monks something that has not been brought by any of the other donors. He notices that there are no greens and no cakes made from flour and asks Ananda if he might be permitted to contribute these items. Ananda consults the Buddha, who gives his permission, but the monks hesitate to eat Rajo's gifts, for they have never eaten these things before. The monks eventually are persuaded to eat Rajo's gifts, and the occasion becomes the precedent for the Buddha's permitting the monks to eat greens and cakes as they wish.

The point of the story that is relevant for the present discussion is not merely its depiction of fervent devotees vying with each other to make donations of food to the Buddha and the monks. Jain stories were also told in which laymen vie with each other for the honour of feeding the Jina, particularly for the honour of offering the Jina food to break a fast.[9] Both Jain and Buddhist piety could express itself through the desire to be the one singled out by the Jina or Buddha as the giver of food. In the Jain accounts the emphasis is increasingly placed on the mental attitude of the donor: in one popular story that was told repeatedly in the medieval didactic story collections, two merchants vie with each other for the honour and merit of offering Mahvira food to break his fast. The story takes an unusual turn when we learn that the devotee who had prayed fervently to be allowed to make an offering is passed over by Mahvira. But in fact he reaps even greater merit than the person who actually makes the gift of food to the Jina. The point of the Jain story is unambiguous: the special quality of a gift is in the giver: a gift not given but intended can entail even greater merit than a gift actually made. The substance of the gift is truly immaterial.[10]

I believe that the Buddhist story of Rajo Malla implies a very different emphasis on the act of giving; it locates the special qualities of the gift not in the intentions of the donor, unlike the Jain stories, but in the uniqueness of the substance given. If, in the Jain story, the devotee who cannot fulfil his desire to make a gift of food to the Jina is satisfied by the rewards of his mere desire to make a gift, in the Buddhist story the devotee is somehow allowed to gain merit by finding a new kind of material to give. He satisfies his desire to show his love of the Buddha by making a gift of a unique type of food. Rajo, having been denied his request to be the only one to offer food to the Buddha and the monks, reformulates that desire and fulfills it by asking to offer some type of food that no one else has ever given to the Buddha and the monks. The special quality of the gift becomes vested in the substance of the gift and not the mind of the donor. It is worth noting that the *Mahavagga*, 6.19, *Sihasenapativatthu*, is fully aware of Jain criticisms of Buddhist food practices. In this interesting passage, a Jain, Sihasenapati, is drawn to the Buddha and prepares a feast for the Buddha and the monks. The Jains are distraught at the loss of a lay follower and parade around the streets accusing the Buddha and the monks of eating meat that has been deliberately prepared for them. The Buddhist reply is telling; instead of rebutting the charges directly, the Buddhists shrug off the accusation by saying that the Jains are always looking for some reason to abuse the Buddhists! In the end, however, the Buddha promulgates a rule prohibiting the monks from eating meat that has been prepared specially for them.

A story in the *Mulasarvastivadavinayavastu* (134-135), although not as explicit as this *Mahavagga* passage, nonetheless hints that the Buddhists were well aware of the criticism leveled at them by their rivals that they were overly interested in food. This story is also a Buddhist food miracle account. The Brahmins and wealthy citizens of Nagarabinda are arguing whether the Buddha and his followers have great desires (*maheccha*) or modest desires (*alpeccha*). A Brahmin Vairattasimha stands up and agrees to put the Buddhists to the test. He invites the Buddha and his followers to a feast of *guda*--brown sugar or molasses. We are told that he has five hundred pots of guda. He starts to serve the Buddhists from one pot and then something remarkable happens. "The Buddha magically caused that one pot to serve all of the assembly of monks and to remain full after they were all served." (*yavadbhagavata tathadhisthita yatha bhiksusamghasya carita, avasista purnvasthita*)   At this Vairattasimha loudly proclaims that the Buddha and his followers have small desires indeed. He then invites to dine members of other non-orthodox religious groups--*tirthya*, a term that includes the Jains as well as other non-Brahmanical groups.  He serves them guda and they eat vast quantities. Some even stuff pots full of the sugar and take them along with them. The language with which Vairatta-simha upbraids them is important. He shouts at them, " It is you, deluded men all of you, who have great desires, and no one else. The ascetic Gautama has small desires. And his followers too have small desires; they do not have great desires." (*Yuyam eva mohapurusa mahecchah. Sramanas tu Gautamah alpecchah. Alpeccha vasya sarvakah.*) I take the *eva* after *yuyam* to be particularly significant; it implies to me that these were the very accusers of the Buddhists; the story is really about the conflict between the Bud-dhists on the one hand and the Jains and possibly other  groups on the other hand. It is worth emphasizing that this could almost have been a Jain anti-Buddhist story, but for the conclusion in which the Brahmin Vairattasimha becomes even more devoted to the Buddha.  After all, the story does not say that the Buddhists did not eat their fill of brown sugar, but only that they covered their tracks with a miracle, making the pot stay ever full, no matter how much was removed from it!

Another passage in the *Mahavagga*, the *Tarunapasannamamattavatthu*, 6.12, is also relevant to the present discussion. The passage concerns the consternation of one donor, Tarunapasanna, who has prepared a sumptuous feast for the monks. Unfortunately for the host and the guests, the monks have already eaten and cannot eat very much of Taruna-pasanna's grand banquet.  The donor becomes angry at the monks and later wonders if by his anger he has spoiled the merit he had hoped to acquire from his gift. The Buddha assures him his merit is great, and then further sets out the rule that the monks must not eat elsewhere on a day they have been invited for a meal. That Buddhists monks were supposed to eat heartily, a familiar accusation from the Jain side, seems readily acknowledged in this chapter of the *Vinaya*.[11]

The Buddhist preoccupation with food is clear throughout the various *Vinaya* texts.  Indeed special powers of digestion are attributed to the Buddha and to monks of an advanced stage of spiritual preparation.  In the *Mahavagga*, 6.13, *Belatthakaccanavatthu*, a lay devotee offers *guda* to the Bud-dha and the monks.  He has a lot left over and asks the Buddha what he should do with it.  Ultimately the Buddha explains to him that he should throw it out, casting it into a nearby body of water, since, the Buddha tells him, only the Buddha and his disciples have the power to digest brown sugar properly. No other creature in the universe can do so. This recalls the plight of Jinadasa in the Jain story from the *Mulasuddhaprakarana*; while the Buddhist monks seem to subsist fine on their rich fare, the unfortunate Jain layman suffers from fatal indigestion.

A passage in the *Mulasarvastivadavinayavastu, Bhaisajyavastu*, speaks in a similar vein of the remarkable powers of taste that the Buddha possesses. Circumstances have so conspired that the Buddha and the monks are left without proper food for the three months of the rainy season. A king has offered to feed them and indeed promulgated an edict in his kingdom that anyone else who offers them food is to be punished by death. The king does not fulfil his promise and the only one who dares to violate the king's edict is a horse trader, who chances to come to the city with his horses. But all he has to offer is coarse barley. The Buddha and all but two of his five hundred monks agree to eat the barley with him. Sariputra explains that he suffers from gas, or *vata*, and so cannot possibly eat barley for three months. He prepares to go to Mt. Trisanku, and Maudgalyayana, Sariputra's attendant, goes with him. There they are fed by the gods on divine nectar, while the other monks and the Buddha must eat barley. Ananda cries when he sees the Buddha eating such coarse food, and the Buddha asks Ananda if he would like to try a grain that has lodged between the Buddha's teeth. The Buddha gives Ananda a grain to try and explains to him that a Buddha has special organs of taste. Even when a Buddha eats the most ordinary and unpalatable food, it is immediately transformed into a feast of subtle flavours.

Jain stories offer a stark contrast to this Buddhist belief in the transformation of coarse fare into ambrosial feast. The *Yogasastra* of Hemacandra, *trtiyaprakasa*, verse 24, emphasizes the opposite point: that even rich and delicious food, even the drink of immortality, all end up as urine and feces, no different in fact from coarse grains or water. A story in the *Satrunjayakalpa* makes the same point, albeit in a more humorous way. There a prince graphically learns that tasty sweets produce farts that smell foul. And from that he comes to understand the corruption of the body (*Satrunjayakalpa* 68-69).

The *Mulasarvastivada* story further underlines the importance of food in these texts as the Buddha explains why he has had to eat the coarse barley for three months. Eating food of such poor quality is explained as the result of past bad karma; once in a previous birth the Buddha had been a Brahmin who had abused the monks of the Buddha Vipasyin, saying that they did not deserve the rich rice and condiments they had received, and should eat coarse barley instead. Only the two ascetics who were to become Sariputra and Maudgalyayana had not joined in reviling Vipasyin and his disciples, and so they have now been spared the unpleasantness of eating coarse barley for three months and have been fed on divine nectar by the gods (*Mulasarvastivadavinayavastu* 23-34). While fasting and eating coarse food are uniformly regarded as a virtue in the Jain tradition, a form of worthy penance, here in the Buddhist text they are regarded as without positive value, merely a painful deprivation, a form of suffering incurred on account of a past wrongdoing.[12]

Finally, in concluding this discussion on attitudes towards food in Jain and Buddhist literature, I would like to note that it was not only non-Buddhists who would question the liberal Buddhist attitude towards food reflected in a number of texts, such as those cited here. The *Milinda Panha* often seems relentless in its questioning of Buddhist practices, and it should come as no surprise that in the 42nd dilemma it directly questions the assertion made in some texts that the Buddha himself often ate heartily, while at the same time he admonished his followers to eat moderately. The text solves the dilemma by saying that aspirants should eat sparingly, while such ascetic practices are not necessary for the Buddha, who has already achieved his great goal (*Milinda Panha* 2:4-8).

It seems to me that the passages I have cited from the *Mahavagga* and the *Mulasarvastivadavinayavastu* together make abundantly clear an attitude towards food in the Buddhist community in which rich and abundant foods could at times be spoken of as the natural reward due the Buddhist monks, and as certainly the fit food for the Buddha himself. I would argue that it was just such an emphasis on food that was picked up and satirized by the Jains in a wide range of didactic stories. The Buddhist accounts, like the Jain caricatures of Buddhist practices, all seem to agree in emphasizing the special nature and quantity of the food given to and eaten by the Buddha and the monks. The story of Rajo Malla, indeed all of the Buddhist texts I have been discussing, are also consistent with the later material, which actually describes rituals for making feasts. In the next section I further consider the evidence of Buddhist ritual texts for an understanding of Buddhist attitudes towards food. I hope that these texts will support my contention that the Buddhists did indeed emphasize the nature of food as a ritual gift and that the Jains in their stories were mocking actual claims made by their Buddhist rivals. In this section I shall also begin to address directly the question of the agent of all these miracles associated with food: human, divine, or artifact.


## Making magic food: The Manjusrimulakalpa

The *Manjusrimulakalpa*, chapter 11, contains a ritual for making food. The ritual is introduced after a brief discussion on how important it is for the *sadhaka*, the one who performs the rituals of this text, to eat properly. The text states that the *sadhaka* must procure his food through begging. Having collected his alms, he is to return to the monastery where he offers some of his food to the Buddha. The text is very careful to state in verses 114ff. that the aspirant should not offer too much of his food to the Buddha, however; it is very important that the aspirant have enough for himself to eat. A person tormented by hunger and thirst will not be able to perform the rituals the text enjoins. The text continues, explaining that in the past the Buddha Kasyapa taught a mantra that caused great clouds filled with the most delicious food to appear in the sky. Living beings were all able to eat and drink to their hearts' content. Sakyamuni, who is the narrator of the *Manjusrimulakalpa*, adds that he was present at that miracle. Presumably that is how he now knows the mantra that he is about to teach, a mantra that will free all living beings from hunger and thirst. He says that if an aspirant is unable to beg for his food, he should go onto a mountain and recite the mantra six hundred thousand times over. He should spread out a cloth on which the mandala of Manjusri has been painted. (Instructions for having the cloth made and painted have been given in earlier chapters.) He is then to worship and give offerings. In the middle of the night a dark cloud mass will appear and the aspirant must not fear. The clouds will clear and a divine damsel, beautifully adorned, will call out to him. She will give him all the food that he desires.

Food is important elsewhere in the *Manjusrimulakalpa*. In addition to this section, which prescribes a ritual to procure divine food, chapter 25 has a lengthy discussion on the importance of proper eating if one is to succeed at the rituals in the text. The food the *sadhaka* eats will determine the nature of the dream that he has, and the dream in turn presages either the success or failure of the rituals. More fundamentally, the type of food a person eats is said to determine the personality of the eater and the type of mantra and ritual to which he is suited.[13]

Like most of the rituals in this text, the ritual for making food in chapter 1 requires the use of a painted mandala. The painted mandala is the central object of worship and the single most important ritual implement in the *Manjusrimulakalpa*.[14] The various rituals, intended for different purposes and suited to aspirants of different characters and dispositions, nonetheless share a common description. After a *sadhaka* worships the painted *mandala* in the way enjoined, usually by constructing a fire altar and making offerings into it, rays of light come out of the central painted figure of the *mandala*, who in most cases is Sakyamuni, but who may also be Manjusri or another figure. The *sadhaka* is next enjoined to grab ahold of the cloth. Having done so, the *sadhaka* flies up at once to heavenly realms, where he sees Manjusri and various Tathagatas and

Bodhisattvas. He remains in the heavenly realm for thousands of *kalpas* and the cloth remains there with him. The *sadhaka* gains numerous magic powers, including the ability to manifest himself in a myriad of different bodies.[15] The worship of the painted *mandala* in several places in the text involves the *sadhaka*'s grasping of the cloth and using it as a kind of flying carpet, which transports him to heavenly realms. It also involves the acquisition of magic powers on the part of the *sadhaka*.

Traditionally, both the ability to fly and the acquisition of magic powers had been associated with the Buddha and certain of his distinguished disciples. We have seen above how the arhats in the Buddhist story of Purna were able to get their feast because they had perfected their spiritual practices to the extent that they possessed magical powers. Presumably this was also the case with the Buddhist monk who could make the bowl of food fly to the Buddha in the Buddha biography included in the *jatakas*, noted earlier. In other Buddhist stories the Buddha himself can make a person fly, much as his painted image is said to do in the *Manjusrimulakalpa*. Thus we read in the *Pratiharyasatra* of the *Divyavadana* that when the Buddha was summoned by Uttara Manava into the presence of King Prasenajit in order to match supernatural powers with other teachers, the Buddha caused Uttara Manava to fly through the sky back to the king (*bhagavata tathadhisthito yathottaro manavas tata evoparivihayasa prakrantah*).[16] The language of the *Divyavadana* offers a striking parallel to the language of the *Manjusrimulakalpa*. In chapter 8, in the description of the ritual worship of the painted mandala and its results, we are told that the *sadhaka* becomes "*sarvabuddhabodhisattvadhisthita*," something I would translate as "imbued with the powers of all the Buddhas and the Bodhisattvas," just like Uttara Manava, who was "imbued with power by the Buddha so that he was able to go there, flying right through the sky."

The *mandala* of the *Manjusrimulakalpa* is in fact performs the very same miracles as the Buddha in the *Pratiharyasutra*: it glows with light and enables the sadhaka to fly. Just as the Buddha in the *Pratiharyasutra* of the *Divyavadana* could directly imbue one of his disciples with magic power, so does the painted *mandala* confer upon the aspirant the magical strength and abilities of the Buddhas and Bodhisattvas. The painted Buddha of the *mandala* is the exact functional equivalent of the living Buddha of the *Divyavadana*.

In addition, the *Mulasarvastivadavinayavastu, Civaravastu* provides a remarkable parallel to the *mandala* as flying carpet in the *Manjusrimulakalpa*, and further supports the identification between painted Buddha and living Buddha that I am proposing. In the *Civaravastu* the Buddha tells certain disciples to hold on to his robe, so that they may fly up with him into the sky (*Mulasarvastivadavinayavastu* : 193-196). The Buddha tells Ananda, for example, to grab onto a corner of his robe. As soon as Ananda does so, the Buddha uses his magic power (*rddhi*) to fly up with Ananda into the air. The Buddha transports the physician Jivaka to the Himalayas by the very same means. Clearly, holding on to a corner of the Buddha's robe or holding on to a corner of the painting of the Buddha are closely related acts; each imbues the devotee with something of the Buddha's powers.

Besides these suggestive passages from other Buddhist sources, there is also ample evidence from within the *Manjusrimulakalpa* itself to suggest that in this text no distinction is made between the painted likeness and the extraordinary being, divine or human, that it represents. While in many passages the painting is the only agent of the miraculous results of the *sadhaka*'s worship, in other cases a deity comes and does what the painting is said to do elsewhere. Thus in chapter 10 the *sadhaka* performs his rituals in a boat. The boat flies heavenward, where the *sadhaka* sees Manjusri. Manjusri himself then touches the *sadhaka* directly and as soon as he is touched by Manjusri he gains magical powers, exactly as elsewhere an aspirant is said to gain magic powers after touching the cloth. Manjusri and the painted likeness of Manjusri are here functionally identical: Buddha and painted Buddha have the same miraculous powers. Similarly in chapter 14, we hear how Buddha Ratnaketu comes directly and touches the *sadhaka*, at which the *sadhaka* instantly becomes the lord of seven realms.[17] At one point in chapter 11, the *sadhaka* performs his oblations in front of the painted *mandala* and in the middle of the night he sees Manjusri directly. Manjusri gives him a boon; the *sadhaka* gains long life, magic powers, and the ability to fly (*Manjusrimulakalpa*: 77). It is worth noting that these are the very same results the *sadhaka* was said to have gained from touching the glowing cloth painting in chapter 8. The text in fact seems to attribute these powers either to the Buddha or Bodhisattva directly or to the painted cloth, without any obvious distinction.

It is not only painted image and Buddha or Manjusri that are functionally identical in the *Manjusrimulakalpa*. The text tells us unambiguously that the mantra is also the Buddha, or the deity which is its presiding deity. Thus we read, *esa bhagavan sarvajnah buddhair mantrarupena vyavasthitah*, "This is the blessed Buddha, the Omniscient One, who exists now in the form of the mantra."[18] The text explains in verses 10-12 that there are both fleshy and incorporeal forms of the Buddha and that there is no difference between them (*Manjusrimulakalpa*: 223). For the *Manjusrimulakalpa*, it would seem, image, word, and living Buddha are all equally the living Buddha.

To return to the ritual for producing food, the context in which the use of a painting for the food ritual is prescribed reinforces the hypothesis advanced here that the painting is the Buddha and that painted image and what it represents are functionally identical for the text. It also offers an explanation of why the text might have made such an equivalence between painted likeness and subject.

The ritual for making food is legitimated by a story of the past with which it is introduced. We are told that the magic food was first made by the Buddha Kasyapa, in times long past, and that Sakyamuni was a direct witness to that miracle. Leaving aside for a moment the issue of the identification of the mantra with the Buddha, the authenticity of the ritual is here assured by the very constancy of the mantra; Sakyamuni, having been present at the initial event, has received the direct transmission of the mantra. The text is at pains here to assert that a past event continues into the present in all its efficacy. I would like to argue that the text regards Buddha or Bodhisattva and painted Buddha or painted Bodhisattva as identical also as a means to insure the persistence of power. The painted image, as the Buddha, enables the powers of the Buddha to continue to work in the world, just as the mantra, either as the Buddha himself, or as something passed on in a direct line of transmission, can persist and work its powers long after the Buddha's disappearance. The presence of the Buddha is repeatedly assured in these rituals, then, through a number of devices: through the continued transmission of the mantra, which is also said to be a form of the Buddha; through the painted image which acts in exactly the same way as the Buddha himself, glowing and causing the aspirant to fly as the Buddha himself is repeatedly said to do; and finally by that act of magic flight itself, in which the devotee is literally transported to heavenly realms where he may see a host of Buddhas and Bodhisattvas, from whom he may also get magical powers.[19]

### The presence of the Jina: The evidence of some Jain hymns

This paper began with Jain stories about food miracles and progressed to a discussion of the agent of those miracles, human and human reborn as demigod in the Jain stories, painted image of the Buddha in the ritual text. I have tried to show that in fact the stories, Jain and Buddhist, with their human agents, and the ritual text, in which a painted likeness is necessary for the ritual, are in fact consistent with one another. Painted likeness and the person it represents are one and the same for the text; indeed, painted likeness, sacred word, and Buddha are all the Buddha. In this section I would like to offer some evidence from medieval Jain hymns which make clear that seeing the Jina image is equivalent to seeing the Jina and able to bring about the same miraculous results. There is a substantial literature of pilgrimage hymns poems written by monks on the occasion of their visit to a famous Jain pilgrimage site and viewing of a famous image.[20] In these hymns, monks sing fervently of their joy and expectations on seeing the Jina.

The fifteenth century monk Somasundara wrote many such hymns. I cite here only a few of his verses to the famous image of Parsvanatha at Stambhana.

> Today my eyes are cleansed, for I have the good fortune to see your body, which is a vessel filled with every marvelous quality, and which is like a scythe that cuts down the grasses of all my grave sins.
> Today I have seen you, all aglow, with all your wondrous qualities.

As Somasundara tells us, he has seen the Jina himself as he beholds what we would designate as the Jina's image.

In a similar vein another medieval monk sang of Mt.Ujjayanta,

> May that Glorious Mt. Ujjayanta endure forever in all its splendour! For on that mountain the first Lord of the Jinas himself dwells in a magnificent temple, as magnificent as the temples on Mt. Astapada, made by the chief of ministers, the Glorious Vastupala.

To the poet/devotee, then, the Jina is alive and present here in his temple.[21]

The medieval Jain, like the Buddhist of the *Manjusrimulakalpa*, could and did speak of image and what it represented as if they were one. This brings us finally to some conclusions about who or what performs miracles. We shall see in the next section that there is evidence from traditional Jain and Buddhist stories that all "images" or "likenesses" could potentially act as their subjects; in these stories it is in the very nature of an "art object" to be that which it represents.

### The artist as magician and the art object
### as specially empowered object:
### Some evidence from Buddhist and Jain literature

The Jain *Prabandhacintamani* of Merutunga includes a brief account of a potter, Punyasara, whom chance makes king (*Prabandhacintamani*: 11 and Tawney 1901:179-180.) In many ways the central theme of the story is the relationship between a likeness and the real thing; the story eventually concludes that the likeness in fact can be just as real--if not more real--than that which it represents. A king is out riding when his horse bolts; he is carried away by his horse. The king dies and his minister is left to ponder what should be done. He fears anarchy if the people learn that the king is dead, and so he decides on a stratagem. He finds a potter who looks exactly like the king and dresses him in the king's garments, making him king in the dead ruler's place. Time passes and the minister eventually finds that he must lead the army in battle against a rival king. He leaves the potter-king behind, and no longer watched over by the zealous eyes of the minister, the potter reverts back to being a potter. He summons all his potter friends and they make clay animals and other clay objects and play with them. When the minister comes back and sees the potter-king playing with the clay toys he is furious. But reality is more complicated than the minister had assumed. At the potter's commands painted soldiers rush at the minister and bind him. The potter-king is persuaded by the minister's pleas to free him and the minister acknowledges the potter's greatness, saying that only great merit acquired in a previous life could have enabled the potter to make painted figures that come to life. Thus the story concludes, with the likeness of the king, the potter, fully confirmed as a true king, and the clay and painted army a fully functional, indeed extraordinarily effective, real army.

The story of clay soldiers coming to life recalls a more famous story told of an even more famous king in Jain literature, king Satavahana. The *Prabandhakosa* (66-74) of Rajasekhara includes a long account of King Satavahana, who also makes a clay army that fights better than any real army. Satavahana is born to a Brahmin woman who has been raped by Sesa, king of the snakes. When the signs of her pregnancy become obvious, her two brothers cast her out, each one suspecting the other of being the father of her child. From a very early age Satavahana shows signs that he is a future king. His mother supports him by working as a servant in various homes. The child amuses himself with his friends by playing king and giving the other boys toy horses, elephants, and chariots for their use. Once again, likeness implies an essential reality: the child plays at being king because it is his nature to be king; he gives his companions toy equipages as a king gives his retinue real horses and chariots. The child spends much of his time in the shed of a potter, where every day he makes clay soldiers, elephants, and chariots. He also manages to settle a dispute between brothers contending over an inheritance, something that is the usual duty of a real king. While the mother and child thus pass their time, unbeknownst to them an astrologer happens to inform the king of Ujjayini, Vikramaditya, that Satavahana will become king in the city of Pratisthana. Fearful and jealous, Vikramaditya conspires to kill Satavahana. He sets out for Pratisthana with a full army, much to the surprise of all the citizens of Pratisthana who have been living at peace with their neighbours. King Vikramaditya sends a message to the child Satavahana, informing him that he is the object of Vikramaditya's wrath. Satavahana is unmoved; he goes on playing with his clay army. His mother, however, does not share his composure, and at the advice of her brothers, who have somehow figured out the divine paternity of their nephew and returned to help her, she goes to seek out the snake who had fathered her son. The snake gives her a pitcher of the drink of immortality and tells her to sprinkle the clay army with the liquid and later use it to consecrate the child Satavahana as king. The woman does as she is told; the clay soldiers come to life and Satavahana is made king.

While in this story the clay soldiers do not come to life without the aid of the elixir of immortality, I think it would be a mistake to assume therefore that they are lifeless replicas of soldiers and horses that are then imbued with life from an external source. In fact, the story seems to imply the contrary by adding that the child too is to be sprinkled with the elixir as a royal consecration ceremony. The story thus treats the clay army and the future king quite similarly: both the clay army and the child must be sprinkled with the divine elixir before they assume their full functioning as king and army. In the case of the child, we do not therefore assume that the sprinkling of the child turns an ordinary man into a king. We have known all along that there is something special about the child and future king. The circumstances of his birth, first of all, have prepared us for the fact that the child will be unusual, and we have seen how he plays king and how a Brahmin skilled in reading signs has predicted that he will be king. We have also seen how he functions as a king, although he is but a child. He is able to settle disputes where other kings have failed. The child is thus king by nature and by birth. I think we are invited to draw a similar conclusion with regard to the clay figures: these are not merely dead likenesses that are brought to life by the divine elixir, but latent living beings who manifest their true powers when sprinkled with the divine liquid.

These two stories of clay soldiers come to life invite us to reconsider our own conceptualizations in which we rigidly dichotomize between the subject of an art work and the art work itself. In these two stories painted and sculpted soldiers fight and do whatever their living counterparts can do. In an important sense, the likeness is its subject, for Jain and Buddhist philosophers alike could define the existence of an object as its ability to perform a given function.

There are other stories that suggest that making an image or a painted likeness is a special kind of act, requiring special abilities on the part of the artist and producing a product that has special status. Again from Jain story literature, the *Brhatkathakosa* of Harisena, story number 20, tells of a sculptor who was unable to finish the image of the Jina he was sculpting because he was himself ritually impure. Every morning when he goes back to work the sculptor finds that the image he is working on has fallen over. Every day he finishes it anew, and every night the same thing happens. Eventually the king who has commissioned the image becomes furious. The sculptor seeks the advice of his guru and agrees to renounce drinking liquor, eating meat and honey and certain fruits and rich milk products, and to abstain from sex, until the image is finished. Having made this vow, the sculptor is able to complete the image.

While this account of the sculptor of the Jina image in the *Brhat-kathakosa* deals with a religious image, it leads us neatly into a discussion of some Buddhist accounts that indicate more broadly that the special behaviour of the artist was important in all artistic creations, not just in the fashioning of religious images.[22] The *Mulasarvastivadavinayavastu* (99-102) contains an account of the rivalry between Sariputra and Maudgalyayana, a rivalry that is a contest to determine which of the two monks has the greater *rddhi* or magic powers. Sariputra defeats Maudgalyayana and the Buddha then explains to the assembled monks that this was not the first occasion on which Sariputra has defeated Maudgalyayana; in many past births he had also defeated him with his greater powers as an artisan, *silpakusalena*. Even before we consider those stories of the past, the first thing to notice is that a contest in *rddhi* is equated here with a contest in *silpakausalya*, skill at making art objects. In the stories that follow, the term *silpa* will include painting, making mechanical contrivances, carving ivory, and magically producing or preventing rain, magically stopping the sun from rising, and causing an opponent's head to split open. Clearly, "art" is a category that is far broader than we might have thought.

In the first story of the past Maudgalyayana appears as a maker of mechanical devices, a *yantracarya* living amongst the Yavanas. Sariputra is a painter who happens to find lodgings with the *yantracarya*. In an odd display of hospitality, the *yantracarya* decides to trick his guest. He fashions a mechanical doll that he gives to the painter as a servant. The painter is duly taken in; assuming the doll to be real, he becomes furious at her when she will not answer his questions and grabs her a little too violently; she falls apart. Humiliated, the painter decides on his revenge: he will humble not only the *yantracarya*, but the king as well. He paints himself on the town gate, hanging by a rope, and quite unmistakably dead. This time the *yantracarya* is fooled; he runs to the king and asks the king to come see the dead man before he performs the last rites. The king comes, and the painter creeps out from his hiding place and puts them all to shame. His is proclaimed the greater skill in artistry.

In this story there is no question that the painting and the painted are totally different and to mistake one for the other is to be foolish. Nonetheless the story also makes clear that skill in artistry is the uncanny ability to deceive, to paint or sculpt so realistically that the beholder does not realize that the painted or sculpted likeness is not the real subject but only its representation. The best art is on the edge of the border between imagination and reality.

In a second contest between Sariputra and Mahamaudgalyayana the two are both painters who argue with each other over which of the two of them is the finer painter. Unable to decide, the king gives them both the same commission. They are given six months to paint a wall surface. The two painters each retire behind curtains to do their work. At the end of the six months the painter who will be reborn as Mahamaudgalyayana pulls back his curtain and reveals his painting. The king is astonished and praises his work. The second painter then pulls back the curtain behind which he has been working; the king's shadow or reflection (*chaya*) falls on the blank polished wall surface.[23] The king is even more astonished, and praises his painting in even more lavish terms. The painter explains that he has not really painted anything; the king has just seen his delicately prepared wall surface and his own shadow. It is this painter who is then pronounced to be the superior artist.

This story, I think, makes two separate points. The first is obvious: to paint a wall one must prepare the wall surface with great care. The second point is more subtle and is connected with the judgment of the work of the two painters: the painting that is the best painting is in reality nothing more than the shadow or reflection of the subject. A person's shadow is inseparably connected with that person and shares mysteriously in his or her essence, while in most discussions a reflection has no reality separate from the object that casts the reflection. In this story the best painting, then, belongs inextricably to its subject and is not something apart from the essence of the subject that is being depicted.

This story of the painting as shadow is also important in the present discussion in that it recalls the account of the first painting of the Buddha that is given in the *Rudrayanavadana* of the *Divyavadana*. (*Divyavadana* :466; Osamu 1967:24-25).[24] Bimbisara wishes to give his friend Rudrayana a special present in return for the set of jeweled armor Rudrayana has given him. He approaches the Buddha who tells him to have a likeness of the Buddha painted on a cloth as a present for Rudrayana. Bimbisara summons all the painters of his realm, but they are unable to capture the complete likeness of the Buddha. So overwhelmed are they by every inch of his body that they cannot even look at him in his entirety, to say nothing of painting him. Eventually the Buddha solves the problem by causing his shadow to fall on the blank cloth. He then tells them to color in the shadow.[25]

It seems possible that both of these stories of shadow-paintings imply something about the relationship between painted likeness and subject. Like the shadow, the good painted likeness is not just a painted likeness, but contains within itself something of the essential nature of its subject. In the story of Bimbisara's painted Buddha, no one could in fact paint the Buddha. The reality of the Buddha is there said to escape human conceptualizations and to be beyond the range of all painterly skill. The successful painted likeness of the Buddha is his natural reflection, the shadow of the Buddha, and as such it embodies all of those marvelous attributes of the Buddha that had escaped human conceptual and artistic abilities. If we generalize from this account of the painted Buddha back to the contest between Sariputra and Mahamaudgalyayana, the judgment of the skill of the two artists seems to be making the same statement about all painting: painting succeeds where it stops being painting. The best of painting is a subtle form of the painted subject itself and not just a human artifact. Painted form now looks more and more like the potter-king's toy army: a good piece of art is not a lifeless inanimate object, but is something far closer to the living reality it represents, something which at any moment may cross the boundary between image and reality and become what it truly is.[26]

We see this boundary crossing in another contest between Sariputra and Maudgalyayana in a past birth. Here the two future disciples of the Buddha are two sages, rsis, who vie with each other by showing their supernatural abilities to control natural forces. When one of them, Sankha, the future Mahamaudgalyayana, slips in the mud, he becomes angry at the rain god and curses him not to rain again for twelve years. Brahmadatta, the king of Varanasi, is distressed by the drought that afflicts his subjects, and after failing to convince Sankha to rescind his order to the rain god, he turns to another rsi, Likhita. Likhita, the future Sariputra, causes the rain god to rain. Sankha has his turn to take his revenge on Likhita, when Likhita bows down at his feet one day. Sankha grabs him by his matted locks. Likhita screams at him that Sankha's head will split into pieces when the sun rises. Predictably, Sankha prevents the sun from rising and the world is plunged into darkness. When King Brahmadatta and all the citizens beg Sankha to allow the sun to rise, Sankha explains to them that if he does so his head will split into pieces. Likhita finds a way out of the dilemma. He tells Sankha to make a clay head of himself and Sankha does as he is told. When the sun rises the clay head shatters.

In this contest between the two sages we see how the object that has been made, the clay head, takes the place of that which it represents. Like the clay and painted soldiers which carry out the same function as the real soldiers, this sculpted head can fulfil the rsi's curse just as well as the real head would have done.

The last story in the *Mulasarvastivadavinayavastu* account of the contest between Sariputra and Mahamaudgalyayana also gives us some insight into traditional Indian attitudes towards art objects. In this story Mahamaudgalyayana is an ivory carver and Sariputra is a painter. The ivory carver comes to the home of the painter, who lives again in the land of the Yavanas. He is carrying with him some ivory beads. Not finding the painter at home, he gives the beads to the painter's wife and tells her that they are rice grains she should cook. She cooks them and cooks them, using up her entire supply of fire wood, but they still do not become soft. When the painter comes home he realizes at once what is going on, and he tells his wife that her rice will not turn soft unless she cooks it in fresh soft water. He sends the ivory carver out to fetch the water, but not before he has painted a well and a bloated corpse of a dog next to the well. The ivory carver is taken in, and before he tries to draw water from the well, he covers his nose so that he will not have to smell the putrid dog corpse. But he drops his water pot and it breaks. And so we hear, the ivory carver was beaten by the more skilled painter.

This story recalls the earlier account of the painter and the *yantracarya*, in which the painter defeated the *yantracarya* by painting himself hanging dead on the city gateway and making the *yantracarya* believe the painted likeness was real. It also bring to mind another famous story of artificial water that an unsuspecting person takes to be real, the story of Duryodhana at Yudhisthira's new palace in the *Sabhaparvan* of the *Mahabharata*. I conclude with a few remarks about the *Mahabharata* story, for it makes clear that the attitudes towards art works that we have seen exemplified by the Jain and Buddhist stories cited here were in fact pan-Indian.

In the *Sabhaparvan*, chapter 43, we see Duryodhana in the palace that the danava architect Maya has built for Yudhisthira. At first Duryodhana sees a pond made of crystal and mistakes it for real water. He lifts up his clothes so as not to get wet, much to his subsequent embarrassment (43.3-4). He then sees a real pond with crystal clear water and crystal lotuses and, not wanting to make the same mistake again, he assumes that it is artificial and falls fully clothed into the water (43.5-6). Next he bangs into a glass door that is really shut tight, and then he deliberately walks around to avoid a second door that is in fact wide open (43.9-10). As the text tells us, these are just a few of the many examples of how poor Duryodhana was deceived by appearances (43.11). The artistry of Yudhisthira's palace is just what we might have expected from the stories we have studied thus far: the consummate skill of its superhuman architect lies in his ability to deceive the beholder, to make the beholder take representation for represented. Good art challenges the boundaries between imagination and reality.

Jain story literature also includes accounts of artists whose creations could deceive the unsuspecting. The *Brhatkalpabhasya* alludes to an incident in which a famous Jain monk, Padaliptacarya, made a mechanical statue of a king's sister. The statue could move and blink its eyes. Some Brahmins rush to the king and accuse the Jain monk of having somehow gotten control over the king's sister. The king demands proof and when he is shown the mechanical likeness of his sister, he is immediately taken in. He assumes the likeness to be the real thing and is furious at the monk. Padalipta explains that it is only a likeness, after all, and the king is mollified.[27] The text adds that mechanical contrivances such as the one Padalipta made were particularly popular among the Yavanas. There are a number of similarities between this story of Padalipta and the account of Sariputra from the *Mulasarvastivadavinayavastu* cited above. Like Sariputra, Padalipta was famous for his magical powers. He is the archetypical wizard in the early Jain tradition. The attribution of these deceptively lifelike images to a monk who is essentially a thaumaturge suggests strongly that such art objects were unusual creations.

Perhaps the most famous Jain story of an image meant to deceive, however, occurs in the biography of the Jaina tirthankara Mallinatha told in the eighth chapter of the *Nayadhammakahao*. In an effort to dissuade her six princely suitors, the princess Malli has a building constructed with six smaller structures in it. These six structures all face yet another structure, which has latticed walls. Malli then has a statue of herself made of gold, an exact likeness in every way. The statue has an opening in it and Malli puts the leftovers from her meals into this opening. When the young men come courting, Malli tells her father to usher each one into one of the surrounding buildings on the pretext that he is to be the lucky bridegroom. While each prince gazes in longing at the image of Malli, believing it to be the princess herself, Malli opens the statue to let the fetid odor of the rotting food escape. With this ruse she teaches the princes about the corruptibility of the body and dissuades them from their desires for her.[28]

The stories considered here all hint at an attitude towards created objects in which the boundaries between the real and the artificial may well break down. While an investigation into portraiture in classical India would surely take us beyond the scope of this paper, suffice it to say that there is still further evidence from literary descriptions of art works and from the actual works themselves to support the conclusions I have tried to derive from the Buddhist and Jain stories considered thus far. This evidence concerns two types of art: Tantric ritual paintings and funerary portrait sculptures.[29]

The *Manjusrimulakalpa* (45) in its description of how to paint the *mandala* includes the instruction that a likeness of the *sadhaka* should be painted into the *mandala*. He is to be depicted just under the Buddha Sakyamuni, with his gaze fixed reverently on Manjusri. This suggests that the painted *mandala* in fact repeats the actual act of worship that the ritual involves. The ritual act takes place twice: with the *sadhaka* offering worship to the painting in the ritual itself, and, in the painting, with the *sadhaka* offering worship to the deities.

Ritual paintings in which a specific *sadhaka* can be identified are known in medieval Jainism. A painting of the *Cintamani Yantra* in the collection of Agarchand Nahta includes an inscribed portrait of the Jain monk Taruna-prabhacarya, one of whose works has been dated 1354 C.E. The painting is a *mandala* of Parsvanatha.[30] Another painting, a *Suri Mantrapata*, has a portrait of the monk Bhavadevasuri and probably also dates to the 14th century C.E. The existence of such paintings associated with Tantric ritual and the instructions of the Tantric Buddhist *Manjusrimulakalpa* suggest that these paintings are not static icons, frozen depictions of objects of worship, but are somehow themselves the act of worship in which they also figure as object.[31]

The evidence concerning funerary images and their worship is both more abundant and clearer in the conclusions it allows us to draw. While portrait statues of donors were made throughout the medieval period, funerary statues seem to have received particular attention and were often accorded regular worship.[32] The evidence is widespread and comes from all over India, throughout the medieval period. For example, from the northwest, the royal cemetery at Bikaner houses statues of all the deceased kings that were said to have been worshiped daily (Aravamuthan 1931:13). An inscription from the twelfth century C.E. in the Siva temple of Kala-hasti, South India, describes the donation of an image of the donor's late brother with an endowment for its perpetual worship (Aravamuthan 1931: 38). I have argued elsewhere that in the Jain tradition, according to the accounts given of the first images and temple the first Jain images of the tirthankaras or Jinas were in fact funerary images, and the first temple was a funerary monument (Granoff forthcoming c). Funerary monuments for Jain monks who have died the pious death of voluntary starvation similarly include likenesses of the monk being honored (Settar 1989).

The nature and status of these funerary images are suggested by the fact that the images are accorded worship. Stories told of images of the deceased help us further to understand how such images were viewed. My reading of these stories is that the statue of the deceased was indeed regarded as the deceased in some ritual contexts, much as, as I have argued above, paintings of the Buddha or images of the Jina could be regarded, and indeed as all art objects could well be regarded. I consider here two stories in which images of a deceased person figure. The first suggests that the image of the deceased could stand in for the deceased person in a particular ritual, and must therefore in some sense have been regarded as the deceased person himself or herself. The second suggests that there were in fact many contexts in which the image of a deceased person could be understood as the person himself.

In the Jain *Prabandhakosa* there is a long biography of the ministers Vastupala and Tejahpala. At one point in the account (114-115) we hear how Vastupala was honored in a religious ceremony. All of the community, monks, nuns, lay men and women, gathered to pay their respects. Now a certain sculptor had made a wooden image of Vastupala's late mother. The image may have been intended to be life-size, for the text tells us that it was newly made and very large. The minister looks carefully at the image and then bursts into tears. He tells the gathering that it is his great sorrow that all this honor has come to him after his mother's death. Had she been alive she would have performed certain elements of the ritual with her own hands. This episode in its depiction of Vastupala's grief over his mother's absence stresses clearly that the image of Vastupala's mother is not the functional equivalent of the living mother, as I have argued above the painted Buddha was the functional equivalent of the living Buddha. Nonetheless it makes clear that portrait statues of the deceased could serve in rituals as substitutes for the deceased person. In some way or another, to a greater or less extent, they embodied the presence of the deceased. The following story told of the funeral statue of a South Indian philosopher suggests the very real way in which artists and devotees might attempt to insure that the statue did embody the essence of the person it depicted.

The story is told in some of the traditional biographies of Ramanuja that when he was dying he allowed an image of himself to be made and transferred his life force into the image. On the day that the image was consecrated Ramanuja began to feel terribly weak. The statue was eventually housed in a shrine erected over his remains. The image is said to have been fashioned of clay, red earth, and pieces of the garment that he was wearing on his death bed. Similar stories are told of death-bed portraits of other famous teachers in the lineage; in one case the portrait statue was cast from the metal obtained from the teacher's drinking vessel (Aravamuthan 1931:62, 65).

Robes and bowls belonging to the teacher have a long history in India as relics; among the earliest Buddhist stupas, for example, are those that were said to have enshrined portions of the objects that the Buddha used.[33] Incorporating relics which were parts of the saint into his funerary statue, was a way of perpetuating the deceased saint. The statue is the person represented and is literally composed of that person's body.[34]

The account of the statue of the deceased that is present in a ritual, and stories about the existence of statues of the deceased made from relics of the deceased, together, I believe, strengthen our contention that in certain contexts images or likenesses are the subject they depict. The following episode from a story in the *Civaravastu* of the *Mulasarvastivadavinayavastu* (177) provides further literary evidence that at least in some cases statues of the dead were regarded as the deified dead themselves. In this story we learn that the town gatekeeper of Vaisali has died and been reborn as a demigod (*amanusyesupapannah*). He tells the townspeople of his rebirth and further instructs them to make a place of worship for him, appropriate to his new status as a demigod or *yaksa*. He further instructs them to hang a bell around his neck; when anyone comes who wishes to do harm to the townspeople, he promises to ring the bell to warn them. The townspeople agree to do as he says and they have an image made of the *yaksa*; they install the image on the town gate and the demigod/image indeed fulfills his promise: when someone comes to take away one of the women of Vaisali, in direct violation of their custom that no woman shall marry outside the town, the bell rings loudly, warning them of this affront. There is no doubt in this text that the demigod on whom they hang the bell is the image that they have made.[35] It is worth noting that earlier in the same story, we learn how there was an image of the Buddha and a monastery or vihara in a certain garden. The narrator adds that this is why the elders say that the Buddha sojourned in the garden of Gopa and Simha in Vaisali. All of the evidence given above allows us, I believe, to interpret this remark as implying that it is the image that is the presence of the Buddha in his temple (Schopen 1990).

In concluding this section of the paper, I would like to suggest that the stories about art objects and artists considered here help us to conclude two things: one, that in certain religious contexts likenesses were not merely likenesses but were their subjects; two, that it was not just religious images that could be seen directly as the reality they depict. In fact, from the stories retold here, it seems possible that in traditional India all artifacts were potentially more than "made" objects. To the extent that they were fashioned by skilled artists, who like the Danava or demon artist Maya have something supra-human about them, all art objects partake of the essence of their subject. If they have the power to deceive it is not just because they are well-made, but because they are so closely tied to the very nature of what they represent. Potentially all clay soldiers are real fighters, and the true painting bears the imprint of the essence of its subject. In some rare cases that potential was merely heightened and made actual by incorporating the very body of the subject, his relics, into the image as its raw material.

Returning to our food miracles with which we began, if the stories tell us that the agents of these miracles are humans or divine beings, then it seems natural that at least some painted and sculpted representations would also be capable of performing the very same miracles. For it is generally accepted that the best of all art *is* its subject.

## Conclusions

This paper examined stories and prescriptive texts dealing with one type of miracle, the miraculous preparation and serving of food. The paper began as an effort to analyze medieval Jain and Buddhist attitudes towards the agents of such miracles: human, divine, or artifacts. The agent of food miracles in the stories, Buddhist and Jain, was consistently depicted either as a human being of unusual powers, or as a divine being, which includes those human beings who have died and been reborn in a godly realm. With the Buddhist ritual text we moved from the sphere of telling to that of doing; the agent of the food miracles, however, remained substantially the same: extraordinary human or divine being. The only difference is that in the ritual text the divine being (or extraordinary human, depending on one's view of the Buddha) was present in the ritual either as a mantra or a painted likeness. The language of the *Manjusrimulakalpa* makes it clear that its miracles are performed equally by painted likenesses and by the Buddha or Manjusri directly; they are functionally equivalent. The conclusion seems hard to escape that the painted likeness does what the Buddha or the Bodhisattva does precisely because it indeed is the Buddha or the Bodhisattva. At the very least, the fact that the same miracles are performed by the Buddha and his monks in the story literature indicates that the miracles are not unique to a painted likeness; they are not specifically "image miracles" at all.

A brief look at some medieval Jain hymns confirms in fact the stronger conclusion, that painted likeness or sculpted image in some contexts is the Buddha or Jina himself. For the poets/monks of the hymns address a sculpted image of the Jina as the Jina himself and not as a sculpted likeness. To the devotee of these hymns--and, I would argue, of the Buddhist ritual text as well--the painted or sculpted image is in fact the Jina or Buddha, and we are to understand that it is the Jina or the Buddha, extraordinary human or divine being, who performs the unusual acts of all our texts: stories, hymns, and ritual manual.

The interpretation I have given here is also consistent with what we know from other types of texts. For example, the fourteenth-century *Vividhatirthakalpa* of Jinaprabhasuri, a collection of stories told about various pilgrimage places important in the Svetambara tradition, does sometimes attribute miraculous happenings to a particular temple or its image. But more often than not it takes pains to explain that it is the superintending deities of the image that are responsible for those unusual goings on (Cort 1990). The agent of a miracle must be human or divine. One lesson that I think we are to take away from the Jain stories about food miracles and the Buddhist ritual text, then, is that human, semidivine, painted likenesses are all one in these supernatural banquets, and to the extent that they can all be agents of the same types of miracles, it is because they are all equally alive, all equally human or divine.

The question must of course remain as to whether or not these traditions also recognize certain categories of miracles which are specific to images or painted representations and which may be spoken of as "image miracles," implying that only images can be the agents of such unusual occurrences. By contrast, it may be helpful to consider a group such as the Vaisnava followers of Vallabha, for whom the activities of Krsna in his various manifestations as images to be worshiped are central to the self-definition of the group and the way in which they assign status to devotees. In the accounts of Vallabha and his followers, miracles are attributed to Krsna's images or *svarupas*, which only make sense as something unique to images: after the death of a devotee, for example, the unworthy sons will find that the image is gone from the family temple, although all the other things required for worship have been left untouched. Krsna has fled the impious boys and will appear suddenly in the home of a pious Brahmin lady, eventually to end up in the hands of Vallabha's son, Vitthalanatha.[36] Other images, for example the one worshiped by the devotee Narayandas, also finally come to the home of Vitthalanatha, and it is difficult not to read into these movements of Krsna's images a deliberate attempt by the community to consolidate religious authority in the hands of Vallabha's son (*Caurasi Vaisnava ki Varta*: 114). It is tempting to suggest that "image miracles," where they occur, are politically motivated and serve to legitimate the authority of specific groups.[37]

In addition I have tried in this paper to frame another question, whether all art works are thought to be capable of acting and doing things, or whether only images and painted likenesses of deities were seen as the deities themselves. As a tentative answer I have suggested that Jain, Buddhist, and Hindu texts all indicate that art works could be seen as having a special ontological status. If they are not seen as quite the same as what they represent, neither are they seen as just lifeless representations. Any successful art object has the same latent powers as its subject and can in some contexts function exactly like the real thing. Religious images are only one special class of such artifacts, and I would like to propose that if they are the Jina or the Buddha, it is not only because of the rituals of consecration of an image in which the Jina or Buddha is made to reside in the image; it is also because of their nature as art objects, which often cross the dividing line between image and reality.

A second focus of this paper has been the nature of Jain stories about Buddhist food miracles. Why did Jains single out food miracles as something that Buddhists performed to the detriment of the Jain community? Through reference to specific passages in Buddhist texts I have tried to suggest that there were fundamental differences between the Jains and the Buddhists in their attitudes towards food and that this difference in attitude may have motivated the Jain stories. Even more specifically, I have argued that the Jains in their stories may have been exaggerating and making a mockery of actual Buddhist claims. If the Jains singled out the Buddhists as the nefarious agents of miracles connected with food, I have tried to show that they did so precisely because the Buddhists themselves placed such great emphasis on monks' eating and receiving rich foods as gifts. In addition, the Buddhists themselves told stories of the miraculous preparation and presentation of food; to mock them, then, would have been natural for their opponents. The Jains in their stories, then, simply turn what were originally Buddhist miracle stories around, and in so doing they show how the miracles ended up not in Buddhist triumph but in Buddhist humiliation. Much remains to be done on this topic, both on the question of Jain and Buddhist attitudes towards food, and on the question of how much pure fantasy and how much reality underlay stories like the food miracle stories discussed in this paper.

I hope that this paper will stimulate further thought on all of the issues upon which it has touched. For surely we need more work on all of these questions. What were "miracles" in traditional Indian religions and who or what was capable of performing them? What may we learn from the polemics we find in medieval Indian didactic stories; how much in these stories was based on a rival's claim and how much was fantastic distortion? What were traditional Indian attitudes towards artists and their works and how are we to understand religious art in the broader context of such traditional attitudes? For all of these questions Jain, Buddhist, and Hindu stories provide rich material that remains to be studied.

## Notes

1. I have studied and translated some of these accounts. For the debate between Haribhadra and his Buddhist rivals see Granoff 1988. I have translated two versions of the biography of Mallavadin in a volume that I edited (Granoff 1990b:166-170). I have translated the biography of Bappabhattisuri from the *Prabandhakosa* of Rajasekharasuri (Granoff 1994b) and translated and discussed in detail the biographies of Jinaprabhasuri in Granoff 1992a.

2. Several such stories occur in the *Brhatkathakosa* of Harisena. See specifically stories 54 and 68. Another such story occurs in the commentary to the *Mulasuddhiprakarana*, written by Devacandrasuri in 1089-1090. The story in question illustrates one of the *chindikas* or "temporary lapses of faith." I have translated and discussed the story in Granoff 1994a.

3. I began to study some of these stories of food miracles in Granoff 1994a. I have translated the biography of the monk Arya Khapatacarya from the *Prabandhakosa* in Granoff 1990b: 153-156. This biography includes a food miracle performed by a Jain monk who has gone over to the Buddhists. This renegade monk causes the begging bowls of the Buddhists to fly through the air to the homes of wealthy householders and return to the Buddhist monastery, full to the brim with delicacies. A second story I have translated is the one from the *Mulasuddhiprakarana* commentary that I translated in Granoff 1994a and that I give below.

4. Compare these comments with the remarks made by Gregory Schopen 1990. I have also argued elsewhere (Granoff 1993: 66-94) that the language of the *puranas* makes clear that medieval religious images in Hindu temples are in fact the God they represent, in concrete physical form, and not abstract symbols or aids to meditation.

5. I summarize here my translation in Granoff 1990b: 153-157. I have discussed this biography in some detail in Granoff 1989a: 67-99.

6. For some comments on this *topos* see Granoff 1991a: 82-85.

7. See for example the biography of Varaha, who becomes a Vaisnava monk and on his death returns as a demi-god to torment the Jains, and the biography of Arya Khapatacarya, in which a Buddhist monk named Vrddhakara dies and returns as a demi-god to harass his former Jain enemies. I have translated both biographies in Granoff 1990b.

8. It is worth noting that elsewhere in the *Mahavagga*, 6.21, Mendaka and members of his family are associated with certain miraculous powers, *iddhanubhava*, several of which have to do with the preparation and distribution of food. Mendaka's wife and daughter-in-law, for example, have only to sit beside a pot and the food in the pot will never diminish while they are there. The food miracles here are not associated with Buddhist piety; Mendaka only later approaches the Buddha. Despite the real contrast between Buddhists and Jains in their attitudes towards food, medieval Jainism does know a food miracle similar to Mendaka's. See Dundas forthcoming:14 on the ability of Gautama to ensure that a little food given to many suffices for all and is never exhausted.

9. See the story from the *Mulasuddhiprakarana*, translated in Granoff 1990b: 115-117, and the accounts translated and analyzed in Balbir 1982.

10. See the story of the two merchants translated in Granoff 1990b: 115-117.

11. The same theme is to be found in the *Suttavibhanga, Pacittiya* XXXIII (*Vinaya Pitaka*, vol. 4: 77).

12. It is worth noting that both the *Divyavadana* and the *Mulasarvastivada-vinayavastu* tell a story with a very different thrust. Mahakasyapa has just come from some forest retreat; his hair and beard have grown long and his robe is disheveled. Anathapinda has invited the Buddha and the Buddhist monks for a feast and given the order that the Buddhists are to be fed first and only then can members of other religious groups be served. When Mahakasyapa comes to the gate the gatekeeper does not recognize him as a Buddhist and turns him away. He takes this as an opportunity to let the poor have the chance to make merit and seeks alms among the needy. When the God Indra realizes what great merit a poor woman earns from giving Mahakasyapa alms, he decides to disguise himself as a poor weaver and seek the same chance for merit making. Mahakasyapa comes to the weaver's home, thinking him to be among the poor and miserable, and Indra gives him divine nectar to eat. Mahakasyapa realizes the weaver is Indra and upbraids him for depriving the poor of a chance at merit making. Indra is unmoved; he ascends to the sky and pours nectar into Mahakasyapa's bowl as the monk goes on his begging rounds among the poor. This is the reason, the story concludes, why the Buddha permitted the monks to cover their begging bowl, so that nothing undesired should be allowed to fall into it. The story is particularly important for our discussion in that Mahakasyapa is clearly the exception; he dwells in the forest and does not even look like a Buddhist monk. He also does not act like one in seeking his alms among the poor while the other monks feast at Anathapinda's. The story may be found in the *Nagaravalambikavadana* (*Divyavadana* 51) and *Mulasarvastivadavinayavastu, Bhaisajyavastu*: 52-54. Gregory Schopen, in a personal communication, remarks that the *Divyavadana* and the *Mulasarvastivada* are clearly the same text; one, probably the former, has taken the passage from the other. He cites Sylvain Levi in an article in *T'oung Pao*, 8, 1907, pp. 105-122.

13. On the significance of food in Indian religious thought see Olivelle 1991. The *Annadakalpatantra* has a concise statement of the centrality of food in its opening verses, *vinannena na kutrapi srstisthityadi jayate/ annad bhavanti bhutani iti catharvani srutih/ /7* "Without food there can be no creation, maintenance, or destruction of the world." The *Atharvani Sruti* declares, "All creatures originate from food."

14. On the painted mandala see Lalou 1930. On the date of the text see Matsunaga 1985. I am indebted to Gregory Schopen for both these references.

15. I have taken this from chapter 8. Similar descriptions may be found in chs. 9, 10, and 14.

16. Last line on p. 96 and top line of p. 97.

17. With this can be compared earlier statements in the same chapter, vv. 90 ff, in which the *sadhaka* is said to grab ahold of the blazing painting and fly upward to become the lord of all the siddhas. Touching the painting or being touched by a god have the same result.

18. V. 8, p. 223. I read "*buddha*" for "*buddhair*," but the meaning of the verse is clear in any case. Reading the instrumental would give something like v. 14, in

which it is said that this mantra proclaimed by the Buddhas is in fact the Omniscient One himself, visible on earth.

19. This interpretation is different from the explanation offered by the tradition itself for the making of images of the Buddha. The Chinese *Anguttaragama* speaks instead of the longing of the Buddha's devotees to see the Buddha, who was preaching to his mother Maya in heaven. This sense of intense personal longing also pervades the account of Upagupta's seeing the Buddha (or Mara disguised as the Buddha, as the case happens to be) in the *Asokavadana*. For a summary of some of the stories told to account for the first images of the Buddha, see Osamu 1967, ch. 1.

20. I have discussed some of these hymns in detail in Granoff forthcoming b.

21. Compare Schopen 1990. I have continued to work on the language of medieval Jain hymns and the theme of "seeing the body of the Jina." I am preparing a paper, "Medieval Jain Accounts of Mt. Satrunjaya: Visible and Invisible Sacred Realms," that will include a more detailed discussion of some of this material.

22. I have examined further Jain stories and prescriptive texts that describe the importance of the special qualities of the sculptor in making Jina images in Granoff forthcoming c.

23. *Chaya* means both "shadow" or "reflection," although its most common meaning is certainly "shadow." The story considered below in which the *chaya* must be colored in suggests that "shadow" is more appropriate, while in the present context one might suspect that the finished wall surface was so shiny as to be capable of accepting a reflection. *Chaya* is also used to mean a likeness or portrait. The other common word for "image," *pratibimba*, has a similar range of meanings. I acknowledge the fruitful discussion I had with Robert Sharf on this issue.

24. Gregory Schopen informs me that there is a closely related story in the *Adhikaranavastu* of the *Mulasarvastivadavinayavastu*, p. 63ff in the edition of Gnoli. He also mentioned Hackin 1914.

25. On the translation of the word *chaya* here as shadow see n. 23. There is a remarkable parallel to this story about the origin of the Buddha painting in Greek myth, in which a young girl, anxious to keep her lover with her, paints in his shadow that has fallen on the wall (Barasch 1992: 212 ff).

26. Compare the remarks of Faure 1991: 170ff. For example, Faure states that certain portraits were not merely "realistic," " they are *real*, pointing to no reality beyond themselves. At first glance, the metaphoric logic of Western representation, in which one thing stands for another, seemed apt to describe the two-tiered structure of Buddhist cosmology. This metaphorical logic, however, was replaced in ritual practice by the logic of metonymy and synecdoche, in which the shadow or trace becomes as real as the body, *is* this very body."

27. The story is cited in the *Abhidhanarajendrakosa* (V.1176) and is from *Brhatkalpabhasyacurni* 1238. It is worth noting that the verse occurs in the context of a longer section on occasions when a monk might be tempted to masturbate. Jain texts on the behavior of monks consider images as dangerous because they are sexually arousing. The *Nisatha Sutra*, ch. 16, contains a detailed section on the subject that deserves fuller study as revealing of certain attitudes towards art.

28. In addition to what this passage tells us about portrait statues, it is also of great interest for our understanding of secular and sacred architecture in classical India. The six structures Malli has built are called *gabbhaghara*, and in a lengthy discussion of this and some of the other architectural terms Roth 1983 shows clearly that the *gabbhaghara* was simply an inner building or room positioned in the center of other rooms or pavilions, where whatever was held to be most important could be kept secure. Scholars who work on the symbolism of the temple following Kramrisch have tended to see in the *gabbhaghara*, which they translate misleadingly as "womb chamber," the point of emanation of the Godhead. The fact that the *gabbhaghara* was simply a normal part of the palace and meant generally an inner room suggests how much we are in need of rethinking current understandings of sacred architecture. See Granoff forthcoming b.

29. Since writing this paper I have done considerably more work on portraits in medieval India. I have presented some of my findings under the title "Portraits, Likenesses and Looking Glasses: Some Literary and Philosophical Reflections on Representation and Art in Medieval India," at a conference sponsored by the Jacob Taubes Center held in Heidelberg, Germany, February 1997.

30. It is illustrated in Chandra 1949: fig.175 and discussed on p. 46. The other paintings I mention are also discussed in this volume.

31. Little is in fact known about Jain Tantric worship. I have tried to study the Jain tantric worship of Sarasvati in connection with my analysis of the biography of the monk Bappabhattisuri, who was said to have been a devotee of Sarasvati and to whom is credited a Tantric ritual manual for the goddess. See Granoff 1994b.

32. A convenient if somewhat outdated reference work for portraits in India is Aravamuthan 1931. There is also a recent thesis by Kaimal 1988. For further bibliography see Desai and Leidy 1989. In fact there is far more evidence for portraiture in traditional India than this catalog indicates. See Granoff 1992d and n. 29 above.

33. See Faure:1991, ch. 7 on relics in Buddhism. Faure makes a distinction between "bodily relics" and "contact relics," and he cites Schopen 1987: 193-225 as stressing that relics were regarded as not different from the Buddha himself.

34. While these are the only cases I know in which relics were said to have been incorporated into a portrait statue of the deceased, the practice was certainly widespread in East Asia and may have been far more common in India than our state of knowledge indicates. On the practice in East Asia see Faure 1991: 171.

35. There is a rich tradition in India of stories like this in which deceased individuals are reborn as demi-gods and interact closely with the community in which they once lived. The most common paradigm for the origin of clan deities in Jainism, for example, is the account of a woman who has met an unusual death and is reborn as a goddess. See Granoff 1989c: 195-217. I have translated the account of the Jain Goddess Ambika from the *Vividhatirthakalpa* in Granoff 1990b: 183-185. In this story, a pious woman commits suicide to save her honor and is then deified. Stephen Inglis cites an interesting variant of this larger pan-Indian tradition, in which wronged women die and are transformed into clay images (Inglis 1988: 159). This reinforces what I have tried to establish in this section of the paper, namely that gods and their images in some contexts are to be regarded as identical. Inglis also notes that people may serve as vessels for the gods (in rituals involving

possession by the deity) just as clay images can be the locus of the deity. Again, I would like to see in this ambiguity the same lack of boundaries between images and imagined that I have tried elsewhere in this paper to establish.

36. See the account of Devakpur in the *Caurasi Vaisnavan ki Varta*:123. I am indebted to the late Alan Entwistle for providing me with a copy of the text.

37. I take this suggestion from the paper of Koichi Shinohara on the biographies of the Chinese Buddhist monk Zhuli, included in this volume. In this paper Shinohara argues that the movement of certain Buddhist images was closely connected with political motives. The paper was delivered at the March, 1993 meeting of the Association of Asian Studies, Los Angeles. I would like to see Shinohara's theory generalized into a hypothesis about "image miracles" that also explains something of the nature of similar stories in medieval India.

# 5

# Miraculous Abhiseka: Miracle and Authority in a South Indian Non-Brahmin Lineage

*K. I. Koppedrayer*

### Introduction

Traveling through the Tamil countryside of the Tanjavur District of South India, one is often told wondrous stories of the deities of many temples that punctuate the landscape. Whether of Siva, Visnu, the Goddess, local deity, or whatever, the stories tell of miraculous images. Commonly the stories return to the time of the *nayanmar* and *alvar* hymn-singers, and weave the cherished past of these saints into the present. Yet, as compelling as the stories of these saints are, there is much Tamil religious lore that looks to more recent times for its moments of both miracle and history. This paper will deal with one such story which involves an image of Siva, a Cokkanatha linga, that for the past four hundred years or so has been located in the Dharmapuram Adhinam. The Dharmapuram Adhinam is an important Saiva Siddhanta centre,[1] and its very existence is tied to its relationship with Cokkanatha. The account of how Cokkanatha got to Dharmapuram calls up a couple of miraculous events which stake out a place for the Adhinam not only in its religious world of Saiva devotion, but within a social arena of contending rights and obligations. Not only are these events awe-inspiring for people associated with Dharmapuram, the narrative that continues to invoke them constitutes a mighty powerful declaration of authority. But as is often the case surrounding miracle, such declarations and claims are not unambiguous.

To explore the claims made by this story, I present my material as follows. I start with a description of the Dharmapuram Adhinam, paying some attention to the range of activities of the centre and to its internal organization. I start with this introduction to Dharmapuram, rather than with the miracle story, for several reasons. This discussion situates the image in the web of religious, social and economic activities that surround it. Further, it gives context to the miracle story by highlighting the importance of Cokkanatha to Dharmapuram, as well as indicating the kind of authority--religious and otherwise--that is implicated in the narrative. This description also indicates how much rests on the relationship between Dharmapuram and Cokkanatha. Then I turn to the story of how Cokkanatha came to Dharmapuram, and consider the claims it forwards and the ways they are presented. Embedded in this story is an explanation of the origin of the Dharmapuram Adhinam, for the story of how the image came to Dharmapuram is the story of the religious journey of the sixteenth century Gurujnanasambandhar, whose spiritual descendants make up membership of the Dharmapuram Adhinam. Gurujnanasambandhar's arrival at Dharmapuram marks the beginnings of the religious centre, but the story, as it continues to be told, underwrites the present as much as the past. In my discussion I first tease out the religious meaning attached to the miracle story, noting how that meaning relates to the Adhinam's present circumstances. I draw upon material from another related religious centre for further understanding of the worldview that informs this story. Like Dharmapuram, this second centre is also a Saiva Siddhanta centre.

I then explore how Dharmapuram's story reveals the way the members of Adhinam see themselves in relation to other lineages, and I suggest that the assertion of religious authority is contained within recognized social relations both defining and enmeshing the groups involved. I also suggest that the centrality of miracle in this story manages to question the very claims it fosters. With those remarks I consider what constitutes miraculous power and what miracle means when it is considered as an event grounded in shared expectations and shared understandings.

## Dharmapuram Adhinam

Dharmapuram is a small settlement situated on the south bank of the Kaveri river, a few kilometers east of Mayilatuturrai and about thirty kilometers south of Citamparam. The Dharmapuram Adhinam is a religious institution headquartered there;[2] it is a Saiva *matha* (Tamil *matam*; religious centre) that traces its history back to the late sixteenth century, when the ascetic Gurujnanasambandhar took up residence at Dharmapuram and gathered disciples around him (see Figure 5). In the centuries that followed, the religious centre has greatly grown and developed into a large and somewhat powerful institution in Tamil Saiva South India. Among its various functions today, the Dharmapuram Adhinam is a landlord, temple administrator, teaching centre, and monastic centre of sorts. In its capacity as landlord and temple administrator, the Dharmapuram Adhinam has control over an extensive network of land endowments which support not only the Adhinam's administration, but also the maintenance of rites in some twenty-four Saiva temples (Anon. 1981). At present, twenty of these temples, including the well-known Siva temples at Sirkalli and Vaitisvarakoil, are completely under the Dharmapuram Adhinam's administration, making the Adhinam in effect a temple overlord. At the four other sites, among these the large temples at Citamparam and Madurai, the Adhinam administers endowments for *kattalai*, endowments which support a specific *puja* or other rite within the temple.[3]

Such arrangements render the Dharmapuram Adhinam a power broker of some importance in South Indian temple politics, all the more so since it possesses considerable wealth in its own right.[4] Yet, notwithstanding its rather extensive involvement in land management, and other such endeavours, the Dharmapuram Adhinam is first and foremost a religious brotherhood organized around a lineage of initiated ascetics. In that respect the Dharmapuram Adhinam resembles a secret society whose members share a body of secret knowledge.

That knowledge relates to the worship of the *sivalinga* in the form of Cokkanatha, the name of the portable image of Siva (or Sundaresvara) from the Minaksi temple of Madurai. The *cokkanatha linga* housed at Dharmapuram was the personal deity of Gurujnanasambandhar, whose story we will turn to shortly. Since he was the founder of a line of disciples originating at Dharmapuram, his personal deity is also the tutelary deity of the ascetic lineage that makes up the Dharmapuram Adhinam (see Figure 6).[5] The lineage at Dharmapuram is ritually defined by its own unique practices, the most important of which centres around the worship of Cokkanatha. Though the members of the Dharmapuram Adhinam are Saivas and they regard themselves as Saiva Siddhantins, that is, as members of a Tamil Saiva tradition based in part on the teachings of the Saiva Agamas, their religious, sectarian, and corporate identity is derived from the *parampara* (teaching lineage) to which they belong. As Sanjukta Gupta notes (1979:122), a *parampara* is defined by a traditional line of teachers who in turn determine the shape of the tradition followed, "the complicated variations in ritual performances arising from the theological and metaphysical background of the *parampara*, and the personal attitude and idiosyncrasies of the eminent teachers of the line." In Dharmapuram's case, a series of rites of initiation determines formal membership in the lineage and establishes ritual competence; the initiations follow Agamic specifications, reflecting the pattern of qualification and application presented in the *Agamas* and in the *paddhati* texts such as the *Somasambhupaddhati* (Davis 1991:89-100; Brunner-Lachaux 1977). These same initiations provide the rules governing the succession of leadership within Dharmapuram's lineage.

In addition, caste membership, which is rooted in kinship ties, has historically played a crucial role in determining who was eligible for initiation into the lineage. The traditional history of Dharmapuram (Kalyancuntara Tecikar 1970; Celvakkanapati 1984) emphasizes the *velala* parentage of the preceptors of its lineage. At present, initiates of the Dharmapuram Adhinam come from five highly specific caste groupings which make up what are known in South India as the Saiva castes. These are the *pillai, tondaimantalam mutalaiyar, saiva cettiyar, karkarta velala*, and the *tecikar* or *otuvar* group, all of which are considered by their members to be high-ranking, but decidedly non-brahmin, castes. Today at Dharmapuram it is expected that the head of the lineage will come from the *karkarta velala* grouping, the same caste grouping of Gurujnanasambandhar (see Figure 7).

Dharmapuram is thus a non-brahmin institution, or, perhaps better put, a *velala* institution. It, like several similar *velala* lineages, follows a tradition of three initiations--*samayadiksa, visesadiksa, nirvanadiksa*--with a special fourth rite--*acaryabhisekam*--administered to those destined to become preceptors. The *velala* lineages' teachings derive final and unique form from what is transmitted personally from guru to disciple; as noted above, however, the manner of transmission through initiation, and indeed the rites that are central to the lineages' working, are Agamic-based. The effect of the initiation rites is to bring about a transformation in the individual, who by the receipt of *nirvanadiksa* shares an identity with Siva. This transformation occurs as the preceptor, who has prepared both himself and the initiate, draws out the initiate's soul (*atman*) and removes from it its binding obstructions (*pasa*). The preceptor then joins the initiate's *atman* with his own which through his preparations has become pervaded with Siva's essence. This union and the ensuing acts of the preceptor give rise to a new, completely pure body created out of the subtle elements that is able to experience fully the joining with the essence of Siva. The guru then gives the *pancaksara* (root mantra) to the initiate, who is transformed and united with Siva. *Nirvanadiksa* has another significant effect. The individual who has received *nirvanadiksa* becomes fully qualified to undertake the worship of Siva. To that end, the initiate is presented with a personal *linga* and instructed in the practice of worship.

At Dharmapuram, these initiations are administered by the head of the Dharmapuram Adhinam to both the ascetics (*tampiran*), who make up the Dharmapuram Adhinam's order, and to some lay members--both men and women--who lead ordinary lives outside the Dharmapuram Adhinam, though not all lay people who frequent the Dharmapuram Adhinam have taken initiation. Women can receive all three levels of initiation (and possibly *acaryabhiseka*), but only men can be members of the spiritual lineage. The lay people who frequent the Adhinam usually come from families that have had a long history of association with this particular institution, and though there are shifts of loyalty from Dharmapuram to other *velala*-led institutions, such as the nearby Tiruvavatuturrai Adhinam, the general rule seems to be that a relationship with an ascetic lineage such as Dharmapuram's is part of a family's inherited tradition. The ritual activities of lay members are limited to the performance of their own personal worship and to the attendance at, and hence vicarious participation in, the Dharmapuram Adhinam's activities as conducted by members of its ascetic order. In part, this restriction relates to the qualification of celibacy, usually lifelong celibacy (*naistika-brahmacarya*), required of the members of the order.

For any initiate, each stage of initiation carries with it duties and obligations. In a strict sense, all the ascetic members of the Dharmapuram Adhinam who have received *nirvanadiksa* are qualified to undertake the worship of Cokkanatha, but in practice only those to whom *acaryabhiseka* has been administered are considered competent, for they alone can be designated as successors to the *gurupitha*. *Acaryabhiseka* entitles its recipients to initiate others; as the name indicates, the rite qualifies one to be a preceptor. This unction rite transforms the initiate into the preceptor by letting the preceptor's *atman* (which in turn is pervaded by Siva's essence) pervade the *atman* of the initiate. Only a preceptor, that is, only one who possesses the power to initiate others into the mysteries of the lineage, can head the lineage. The title used to designate this head is *Gurumahasannidhanam*, a term indicating the "sacred presence of the guru" (Yocum 1990: 250).

Once a member of the Dharmapuram Adhinam ascends to the *gurupitha*, which signifies the seat of authority of the lineage, he is considered *to be* Gurujnanasambandhar. In fact, any signature he might affix to any document, legal or otherwise, is that of Gurujnanasambandhar, notwithstanding his initiated name. When in the mid-1980s I asked the present head of the lineage about his relationship with Gurujnanasambandhar, he simply tapped his seat and responded, "I am." Members of the Dharmapuram Adhinam maintain that the rite of *acaryabhiseka* transfers the essence of the guru from the preceptor to the initiate. They maintain that because he has received this rite, the present Gurumahasannidhanam, who is the twenty-sixth in succession from Gurujnanasambandhar, is infused with the nature of Gurujnanasambandhar, who established the *matha* at Dharma-puram in the late sixteenth century. They hold that the present Guru-mahasannidhanam, like each of his predecessors, is one and the same as Gurujnanasambandhar. That he must maintain the worship of Cokkanatha acknowledges this equation.

The status of the head of the Dharmapuram Adhinam is a metonym of the teachings. As the heir of the *parampara*, the present Gurumaha-sannidhanam is the most recent initiate in the line of teachers; as Guru-mahasannidhanam, he is considered the embodiment of the first guru of the lineage, and its potential for perpetuation. He is both foremost disciple of the first guru and the living presence of the first guru. In his status as the guru's disciple, he is bound by vows of obeisance to the guru. His pos-ture is one of servitude, as the guru-disciple distinction is always maintained. Yet, on account of the *acaryabhiseka* that transfers the essence of the teacher from one to the other, his presence is infused with that of the first guru: he is *guru, par excellence*. He is completely pervaded by grace and his very touch grants release.

## Worship of Cokkanatha

It is part of the institution's tradition that Cokkanatha has been worshiped daily at Dharmapuram from Gurujnanasambandhar's time to the present. That daily cycle of *puja* is vital; without the continued worship of Cokkanatha, the Dharmapuram Adhinam would, quite literally, cease to exist. If the Dharmapuram Adhinam would fail to keep up its tradition, it would no longer have any justification for its existence, and the Hindu Religious and Charitable Endowments Board--the agency of the state government that controls religious institutions--would have the right to take over the other functions of the Dharmapuram Adhinam. Here I want to emphasize that the Dharmapuram Adhinam's very legitimacy as an institution depends upon its transmission of ritual knowledge. According to *The Tamil Nadu Hindu Religious and Charitable Endowments Act, 1959 (Tamil Nadu Act 22 of 1959)* (Murugan:1983), a *matha's* reason for existing is to perpetuate its religious tradition (6:13, 11). This legal interpretation of a *matha* is based on views held during the colonial period. For example, the turn-of-the-century jurist, P.R. Ganapati Iyer wrote:

A place of worship is a necessary adjunct of a muth [*matha*] as the object of a muth is not merely the propagation of a system of religious doctrine, but also the propagation of the worship of God according to a particular cult. The worship though intended for the inmates...[is] also intended for the general public. At time of worship it is not possible for the head of a muth, or his disciples, to exclude the public. No muth can exist without a place for worship (1918:270-1).

Although, as I noted above, there is a long history of other functions, such as the administration of temple *kattalai*, the current South Indian legal understanding of a *matha* focuses on the cultic activity of the centre. If there is a breakdown of usage, a *matha* abrogates its purpose and thus forfeits its autonomy. Once there is proof of the lapse of tradition, the Hindu Religious and Charitable Endowments Board then can make a move to bring the *matha's* functions, such as the administration of temples, under its control (5:58, 57-58). In the case of the Dharmapuram Adhinam, the established tradition of the institution is its unfailing worship of Cokkanatha. The head of the Adhinam (who is also head of the lineage) must ensure the continued worship of Cokkanatha in order to maintain the viability of the tradition that informs the Adhinam's existence. Obviously with the wealth that the Adhinam controls in the form of lands and endowments, there is much more at stake than spiritual concerns, and there are individuals in high places who see centres like Dharmapuram as useless--and parasitic--relics of the past.

In sum, with its complicated relations with other groups in South India, the Dharmapuram Adhinam is a large and complex institution,. The compound which houses the institution at Dharmapuram covers an area about two hectares in size, not counting the cultivated lands and ryots' living quarters that extend out around the Adhinam proper. Within the compound are the buildings, temples, samadhi shrines of previous head of the lineage, a clinic, the schools and colleges, co-operative store, stables, residences of both employees of the institution and initiated members of the lineage, gardens, and so on. Yet, at the heart of this complex is the *matha*, the building which houses the shrine of Cokkanatha. The chamber where Cokkanatha is kept and where the present head of the lineage conducts the daily rites opens onto a large hall (*pujamandapa*) accessible to anyone who wishes to attend the rites. All visitors to the Dharmapuram Adhinam who seek an audience with Gurumahasannidhanam in his reception hall (called *otukkam*, an area where Gurumahasannidhanam alternately receives visitors or sits in meditation) must pass through a pillared hall leading to the business hub of the institution. This hall brings the visitors directly past the *pujamandapa*, thus all visitors must pass by Cokkanatha, whatever their purpose is in coming to the Adhinam.

## Story of Gurujnanasambandhar

Everyone connected with the Dharmapuram Adhinam can--and often does--tell the story of how Gurujnanasambandhar came to worship Cokkanatha. Judging from the frequency with which this story is re-counted and the pleasure evinced during the telling, it is a much loved story. I will summarize it as it was often told to me, and as it is sum-marized both in paintings which adorn the walls of the *pujamandapa* (reproduced in Tarumai Kanakapiseka Vilamalar 1961) and in a publication (Arunachalam 1972) issued to commemorate the ascension of the present Gurumahasannidhanam to the *gurupitha* in 1972. As we will see later, the time of the release of that publication is not insignificant, as the publication marked both a public retelling of Gurujnanasambandhar's life and a reminder of the present Gurumahasannidhanam's continuity with Guru-jnanasambandhar.

In the village of Sri Villiputur in the far south of Tamil country, in what is now the Ramnad district, a pious couple, Subrahmanya Pillai and his wife Minaksi, belonging to the Saiva *karkata velala* community, longed for a son. Subrahmanyan and his wife led ideal householders' lives. They were devout followers of Siva and they spent lavishly on worship in the temple and in their home and undertook such acts as the feeding of devotees, as was the practice of the Saiva community. In due course, the grace of Siva shone on the couple and a son was born to them at an auspicious moment. They named the child Jnanasambandhar after the Tamil saint Tirujnanasambandhar, whose songs form the first three books of the Tirumurai, the Saiva Tamil canon. The child prospered and by the age of sixteen mastered the Tamil and Sanskrit Saiva Siddhanta Sastras.

The family deity of Subrahmanya Pillai was Lord Sundaresvara of Madurai. Daily Subrahmanya Pillai offered worship to Cokkalinga (the moveable image of Sundaresvara) in his home. The time came for Subrahmanyan Pillai to undertake a pilgrimage to Madurai to worship Lord Sundaresvara there. On that pilgrimage his wife and young son accompanied him. Once at the Minaksi temple, the boy was overtaken by rapture at the sight of Sundaresvara and Minaksi and refused to leave the temple when his parents returned to their home in Srivilliputur.

The boy remained at the temple experiencing some inner peace resulting from the grace of Siva. He followed the daily pattern of worship of Sundaresvara and Minaksi in the temple. The practices of Saivite ascetics engaged in their own worship, complete with *mantra, bhavana,* and *kriya,* captured his attention. As he watched their ecstasy he felt a desire to perform such worship himself, but having had no spiritual instruction, he had neither an image nor knowledge of the procedure of worship. He prayed to Sundaresvara. That night the Lord appeared to him in a dream and told him that he would find a coffer in the northeastern corner of the tank which in time he would be able to worship.

In the morning he found the coffer containing the Cokkalingam while bathing in the corner of the tank as directed. Overcome with joy he took it to the sanctum of the temple and praised Sundaresvara for his grace. But he still did not know how to perform *puja*. He again prayed to Sundaresvara, this time for a preceptor to instruct him. That night, again he had a dream in which Cokkanatha appeared before him and told him to proceed to Tiruvarur, where he would meet Jnanaprakasar who, hailing from a long line of disciples descending from Siva himself, would initiate him into *jnana*, *carya*, and *kriya* (supreme knowledge, practice, and worship). That same night Jnanaprakasar also had a dream in which Lord Tyagaraja, the deity of Tiruvarur, informed him of Jnanasambandhar's coming and instructed him to teach Jñānasambandhar the personal worship of Cokkanatha.

Jnanasambandhar set out for Tiruvarur, stopping at many important Siva temples along the way. Finally he arrived in Tiruvarur, bathed in the Kamalaya tank, entered the temple, worshiped Tyagaraja and his consort, and then began to make his rounds in the temple. In the meantime Jnanaprakasar had remembered that this was the day he was to meet his new disciple. He arose early, finished his personal worship, and then went to the temple, where he attended the worship. Then he went to the shrine of Siddisvaram and seated himself facing east in the presence of Daksinamurti. There he went into meditation and awaited the arrival of his disciple. When Jnanasambandhar arrived, Jnanaprakasar lifted him up with both hands. His very touch transported Jnanasambandhar into a state of ecstasy. Then Jnanaprakasar seated Jnanasambandhar facing north and gave him *diksa* and instructed him in Siva *puja*. In time he taught him the doctrines of *Civananacittiyar*, one of the canonical works of the Saiva Siddhanta tradition.

From then on, Jnanasambandhar stayed at Tiruvarur in the service of his preceptor. It was the practice of Jnanaprakasar to attend the *ardhajamapuja*, the midnight rite, accompanied by his disciples. One night, Jnanaprakasar sat in contemplation of Daksinamurti longer than he was accustomed to. When he emerged from the temple to return to his home, his torch bearer had fallen asleep. Jnanasambandhar quickly took up the position of the torch bearer to lead his master home. Jnanaprakasar was quite oblivious to this. When they arrived in front of his home he told the torchbearer to stop. Obeying this order, Jnanasambandhar stopped. When the other disciples dispersed, he remained standing, holding the torch, his mind focused only on the order of his preceptor.

That night there was an unusually heavy downpour of rain, but Jnanasambandhar remained in a state of *samadhi* induced by his devotion to his guru. Not a drop of rain touched either him or the torch. And the torch kept burning in spite of its oil being all used up. At daybreak the wife of Jnanaprakasar opened the door to sweep the walkway. When she saw Jnanasambandhar still standing untouched by the rain, holding the burning lamp, she ran to her husband. When Jnanaprakasar came to look at Jnanasambandhar, he recognized the realized nature of his soul, gave him his blessings, and told him the time had come for him to leave Tiruvarur.

In Arunachalam's words (35-6):

> My dear Jnanasambandha, you have now been given unparalleled spiritual evolution. You have grown into a great spiritual master who can shed spiritual lustre and disseminate spiritual knowledge and impart solace to suffering mankind. No longer need you stay with us. You may go forth, and stay at some suitable place you may like and there propagate the knowledge of God and give spiritual instruction to such mature souls as come under your influence....

Jnanasambandhar was reluctant to leave his master, but Jnanaprakasar then instructed him to go to Dharmapuram to establish his own *matha*, taking with him the image.

Once there, Jnanasambandhar erected a small hermitage for himself to the west of the temple. There he installed Cokkanatha and performed worship as he had been instructed. In due time he attracted devotees and disciples whom he initiated. The sages who were looking after the Dharmapurisvara temple came to realize his spiritual eminence. They bestowed upon him many of the esoteric sciences they knew and handed over to him the possession and administration of the temple. Giving him their blessings they departed.

## Design and Tradition

This story weaves together not only a history of the origins of the Dharmapuram Adhinam, but also a reflection on what the institution exemplifies. It forcefully installs the lineage of Gurujnanasambandhar at Dharmapuram by establishing its past and guaranteeing its future. This is done through Gurujnanasambandhar's relationship with his preceptor Jnanaprakasar. That relationship situates Gurujnanasambandhar, and hence the Dharmapuram Adhinam, in South Indian religious history, as

Jnanaprakasar, or Kamalaijnanaprakasar, as he is otherwise known, is a well-known figure of Tamil literature. But more than that, Gurujnana-sambandhar's relationship with his preceptor situates him fully in the sense of divine being that informs Agamic teachings. Three divine dream inter-ventions bring Jnanasambandhar and Jnanaprakasar together: Jnanasam-bandhar's dream of where he would find the image of Cokkalinga, his dream of where he would find his preceptor, and Jnanaprakasar's dream of finding his disciple. In each case, it is the deity in temple image form-- Sundaresvara, Cokkanatha, Tyagaraja--who makes manifest this knowledge.

In Jnanasambandhar's first dream, Sundaresvara makes manifest this knowledge in concrete form as well, in that the Cokkalinga Jnana-sambandhar finds in the temple tank is Sundaresvara in the form of a movable image. Reiterating South Indian theological views while at the same time reconfirming the Adhinam's reason for existence, this story recognizes the image as the deity, posessed with the agency of Siva. That agency finds reflexive expression through Jnanasambandhar, as his rela-tionship with Siva is rooted in his ritual understanding of cultic activities and in his ability to undertake *sivapuja*. The progression of dreams, from image to preceptor to preceptor and disciple, marks an adept's preparation and readiness for initiation into the divine mysteries, which involve not just knowledge, but also the active expression of that knowledge through ritual expression.

The progression also anticipates the three stages of initiations Gurujnanasambandhar' is to receive, from *samaya* to *nirvanadiksa*. Here, overlaid with cognizance acquired in the dream state, Jnanaprakasar, the preceptor whom Jnanasambandhar finds, is simply the agency of these mysteries, into which Jnanasambandhar has already been brought by Siva himself. With this foregrounding, the nature of Jnanasambandhar, who is son to be Gurujnanasambandhar, along with the knowledge he possesses and his ensuing role as preceptor and founder of a lineage, is irrefutable, as it is located within the divine, or within Siva himself, in the embodied form of Cokkanatha.

By letting several miraculous interventions in the form of dreams intercede, the narrative downplays the role of Jnanaprakasar, Gurujnana-sambandhar's preceptor. However, the identity of Jnanaprakasar is signi-ficant. As I noted above, Jnanaprakasar is the well-known Kamalaijnana-prakasar of Tamil literature; Kamalai or Kamalaya is another name of Tiruvarur; hence Kamalaijnanaprakasar indicates Jnanaprakassar of Tiruvarur. Himself the disciple of Palutaikatniya Jnanaprakasar, Kamalai-jnanaprakasar is credited with numerous manuals on Saiva ritual (such as the *Civapucai akaval*), two Tamil *stalapuranas* (*Maluvatippuranam* and

*Tiruvanaikkappuranam*), and a range of poetic works, among them the *Tiruvarurpallu*, a work in which outcaste farm laborers discuss Saiva philosophy (Zvelebil 1972:203-4,258). In addition to Gurujnanasambandhar, Kamalaijnanaprakasar had several other important disciples such as Nirampa Alakiya Desikar and Tiruvorriyur Jnanaprakasar, who in turn are known for their compositions and who were apparently stationed at different temple sites such as Tiruvorriyur and Tiruvaiyaru.

A couple of epigraphical records take note of Jnanaprakasar. An epigraph (A.R.E. 104 of 1911) from Sikkil in the Tanjavur district dated 1562-3 records that the *paradesi* (meaning either ascetic or someone from a different locality) Jnanaprakasar-pantaram of Tiruvarr was appointed supervisor of the accounts of the temples at Sikkil, Vatakuti, Votaceri, and other places under the order of Krishnamarasayyya, son of Ali[ya]-Ramarasayya. A later inscription from the Pudukkottai District (Pudukkottai, no. 955) records the construction of a *matha* of Jnanaprakasa-pantaram of Tiruvarur at the behest of Viru-Puchchaya Nayakar.[6] In light of this material, it seems that Gurujnanasambandhar's relationship with his preceptor not only locates him in Tamil Saivite history, but also situates him in a much larger network of Saiva preceptors and initiates that linked individuals, lineages, and temple sites together. The inscription from Sikkil provides material that anticipates one of the present roles of the Adhinam, namely *kattalai* and temple manager, and hence resource manager.

In other words, the reference to Jnanaprakasar in Gurujnana-sambandhar's story encodes historical antecedence to present-day organization and corporate activities of the spiritual lineage at Dharmapuram. While not unknown to the people who frequent Dharmapuram, as they are aware of epigraphical evidence that refers to Kamalaijnanaprakasar, this embedded reference to temple affairs and antecedent lineages is a muffled source of interest. It is not the preceptor of Gurujnanasambandhar who is important; instead, as the story of Gurujnanasambandhar is told and retold at Dharmapuram today, attention is drawn to the miracle that stands centrepiece in the account, namely Gurujnanasambandhar's remaining dry in the midst of the heavy rainstorm and his carrying of an ever-burning torch.

This is *the* miracle. Though Arunachalam takes special care to relate the many productive and wonderous deeds (40) attributed to Gurujnana-sambandhar after his founding the *matha* at Dharmapuram, the night watch is identified as the event of major significance. In part it may be because it might be understood as making an allegorical reference to verses found in the seminal Saiva Siddhanta work Civananapotam (Nallaswami Pillai 1949). These verses speak of the soul, though obscured by darkness, shining through and overcoming its bondage. Liberation comes, these verses say, through the agency of the guru who is none other than Siva himself. Arunachalam echoes (40) this doctrine when he notes that the miracles attributed to Gurujnanasambandhar were performed "not through the assertion of the ego, but through the absolute surrender of the ego to the divine will, and through divine intervention." The story reiterates this point by making note of Gurujnanasambandhar's willingness to serve as torchbearer, a task ordinarily reserved for low caste individuals.

Behind this story is not Jnanaprakasar, the human preceptor, but Cokkanatha, who by penetrating through Gurujnanasambandhar's sleep as a dream image, gave direction to Gurujnanasambandhar in both the discovery of his personal linga image and his preceptor. If Gurujnana-sambandhar has manifested a perfected soul in this event and given face to miraculous power, it is because of that special and moreover unique relationship he has with Cokkanatha. Such a relationship extends beyond Gurujnanasambandhar; it extends back to his family who were devotees of Cokkanatha and on to his spiritual descendants. Read this way, the miracle story is a polemic for the rites that undergird the very large and prosperous organization the Dharmapuram Adhinam has become.

## Tirumalikaittevar

Before I turn to another area of significance in the way the story of Gurujnanasambandhar is presented, I would like to draw attention to a very similar miracle story that is associated with the Tiruvavatuturai Adhinam, another Saiva *velala* centre located about twenty kilometers to the west of Dharmapuram. This story offers further insight into the belief system suggested in Gurujnanasambandhar's hagiography. Like Dharma-puram, the Tiruvavatuturai Adhinam is organized around a lineage of religious preceptors, the first of whom, Sri-la-Sri Namaccivaya, dates to the same time as Dharmapuram's Gurujnanasambandhar. Of the two places, however, Tiruvavatuturai is an older religious centre. The two institutions share many of the same functions of landlord, administrator, and Saiva Siddhanta centre, and historically have engaged in a sometimes amicable and sometimes hostile rivalry.

The story associated with Tiruvavatuturai relates to a saint who predates Namaccivaya by several centuries. The saint is the tenth-to-eleventh century Tirumalikaittevar, whose verses make up the eleventh book of the canonical *Tirumurai*. He came to Tiruvavatuturai to serve his preceptor Bhoganatha, and while there had many adventures (Koppe-drayer 1993). One is already familiar to us. It takes place upon Bhoganatha's return from the temple one night (Nananata 1962:24-5):

Bhoganatha's torch bearer had fallen asleep, so Tirumalikaittevar took the place of the torchbearer, unbeknownst to Bhoganatha. Before he set off for the *matha*, Bhoga, as was his custom, gave hot *prasadam* to the servant holding the torch.

When he arrived at the entrance of the *matha*, Bhoga, still unaware his own disciple, Tirumalikaittevar, held the torch, ordered him to halt. Bhoga then went inside. However, Tirumalikaittevar, obeying the order of his guru, stood at the entrance of the *matha* the whole night, holding the *prasadam* in one hand and the torch in the other.

At sunrise, the time of his morning *puja*, he miraculously obtained two additional hands to perform his personal *puja*.

The next night, the torchbearer arrived. By then, the *prasadam* had been transformed into raw pulse by the power of being in contact with Tirumalikaittevar's hand throughout the night. Tirumalikaittevar then scattered this pulse in a plot near the *matha* and it yielded a bountiful crop, even though there were famines throughout the land.

This story expands upon one of the miracle deeds cited in the *Arputa Nikalccikai*, a set of verses composed by the eighteenth century Tottikkalai Subrahmaniyamunivar (Minatcicuntaram Pillai:223).[7] What is significant here is that the story line reproduces the same statement about the miraculous power rendered through rigorous discipline, correct performance of *kriya* (ritual practice, into the mysteries of which Tirumalikaittevar was initiated by Bhoganatha), and obedience to one's guru. Like Gurujnanasambandhar, Tirumalikaittevar is noted in his hagiography for his careful undertaking of *sivapuja* as taught by his preceptor. The miraculous nature of the event is not the event itself, but what the event is rooted in, namely an exercise of devotion predicated upon the power of Siva present in the disciple.

The story of the power generated by Tirumalikaittevar's devotion is tied back to an embodiment of divinity in an image, which in a reflexive fashion is the source of the miraculous power. A four-armed image of Tirumalikaittevar in the form resembling a guru offering teaching, which in turn resembles the form of Siva as Daksinamurti, is installed over his *samadhi*, or tomb shrine, at Tiruvavatuturai. Daily in the midst of the morning *puja* cycle undertaken by the head of Tiruvavatuturai's lineage, the head priest of the adjacent Siva temple performs the *puja* at that *samadhi*.

It is the essence of Siva, embodied in Tirumalikaittevar's *samadhi*, but gained through Tirumalikaittevar's initiation at the hands of his guru, that is worshiped here. The image in this *samadhi* is unquestionably that of Tirumalikaittevar, but it is also an image of Siva himself, that is, Siva who pervades the guru who pervades the disciple. This infusion, captured in the image installed in the *samadhi,* was what was exercised and experienced when the hot *prasadam* held by Tirumalikaittevar was transformed into raw pulse. Interestingly enough, among other things this episode purportedly explains why the image of Tirumalikaittevar has four arms--so that Tirumalikaittevar could undertake his morning worship while not relinquishing either the *prasadam* or the torch he held for his teacher. The reflexivity of Siva, Tirumalikaittevar, guru, and cult image and the iden-tification of one agency with another (Tirumalikaittevar with his image with the guru with Siva) serve to decentralize the source of miraculous power. Such power does not rest in one place--in either the will of the devotee or the divine--but instead is manifest as the process of devotion.

The torch episode, marking a turning point in Tirumalikaittevar's life, suggests that the effect of this relationship has benefits reaching beyond a simple guru-disciple relationship. Not only was the *prasadam* from the temple transformed into raw pulse by being in contact with Tiru-malikaittevar's hand--itself a miracle of no small degree--but also it germinated to yield a bountiful crop in the midst of a famine afflicting the land. The effect of Tirumalikaittevar's devotion accrued to others. It extended beyond mere notice of Tirumalikaittevar's spiritual well-being to offer sustenance to others. Though not nearly as dramatic as Tiru-malikaittevar's bringing food into a land of famine, the story of Guru-jnanasambandhar's devotion to his deity and his guru likewise is under-stood as offering spiritual sustenance to his followers, the initiates of his lineage and their families.

### Miraculous Acaryabhiseka

In addition to a message about devotion, there is another dimension to the way Gurujnanasambhandar's story is told. The story recounts Jnana-prakasar's giving *diksa* to Jnanasambandhar, but in it there is no mention of his giving *abhiseka* to Jnanasambandhar, or anointing him as a preceptor. Instead, the miraculous event leads directly to Jnanasambandhar's transformation from student to preceptor,[8] and with it is a demonstration of a pretty powerful transformation. The torch image, the rain, suggest disciplic succession; the torch suggests eternal wisdom, and the rain the ablution, the purpose of which is not to drench the initiate but to instill grace. The ever-burning torch denotes the essence of Siva (*sivatva*) present in Jnanasambandhar. In the story, this event signals *abhiseka* of an un-impeachable sort: miraculous *abhiseka,* one that can withstand any challenge to its authority. It provides unquestionable evidence of Guru-jnanasambandhar's qualification as a preceptor. Nonetheless, the story nowhere mentions *abhiseka* administered at the hands of the preceptor, the human representative of the lineage. In a backhanded way, the account of miraculous *abhiseka* thus also acknowledges the difficulty involved in recognizing a lineage outside of *sivacarya* circles. An invocation of miracle certainly constitutes a mighty powerful claim to authority, but the very quality of miracle--its extraordinary, fantastic and astonishing nature--suggests there is something out of the ordinary going on.

An event that occurred relatively recently echoes this question of legitimacy. The twenty-fifth preceptor of Dharmapuram's lineage and predecessor of the present Gurumahasannidhanam "attained the fullness of Siva" (*civaneripuranam*, i.e., he died) while on pilgrimage to Kasi in 1972. At this time he had not nominated a successor. Rumours still circulate as to exactly what happened in what followed, but one account is that the *tampiran* of the institution gathered together at Dharmapuram in the hall facing the cell where the image of Cokkanatha is located. From this gathering the present Gurumahasannidhanam emerged as the new leader. His right to office, initially determined at this meeting, was validated in an *abhiseka* performed in the Jnanapurisvara temple at Dharmapuram, the temple that is said to house the *samadhi* of Gurujnanasambandhar. In a rite undertaken by the *sivacarya* who maintains the shrine, the present Gurumahasannidhanam received the unction that flowed from the *sivalinga* that is said to mark the *samadhi* of Gurujnanasambandhar. As it is believed that Gurujnanasambandhar "still dwells in this temple and continues to guide the successive heads of the Adhinam" (Arunachalam 1972: 58), Dharmapuram's present head received the seal of office from this *abhiseka*, as it flowed from Gurujnanasambandhar himself.[9]

Interestingly enough, a published account of Gurujnanasambandhar's life was published not long afterwards, the one that I have quoted from above. It is the practice of the Adhinam to release a book in commemoration of the annual rite of *gurupuja*, the lineage's celebration of the anniversary of Gurujnanasambandhar's death. In accordance with that practice, the present head of the lineage had Arunachalam's work released when he undertook his first *gurupuja* after his assumption of office (Arunachalam 1972: iv). Since only the head of the lineage can perform the rites as celebrated by Dharmapuram on this day, the present Gurumahasannidhanam's authority to undertake his first *gurupuja* was underwritten by the narrative of miraculous *abhiseka*.

Given the current status of the Adhinam as a *velala* institution, and the emphasis placed on Gurujnanasambandhar's *velala* background, and indeed the *velala* background of those who followed in his line, one might wonder: What does the story of miraculous *abhiseka* have to say about the lineage's status as a non-brahmin lineage? In the most recent *acaryabhiseka*, unction flowed from Gurujnanasambandhar, as it was his temple, the Jnanapurisvara temple, where the *abhiseka* took place. However, the rite was conducted by a temple priest, a *sivacarya*. Who thus was instrumental in the *abhiseka*? And, does the *sivacarya* in this recent event stand in any way for the preceptor of Gurujnanasambandhar, namely Kamalai-jnanaprakasar? Put another way, does *sivacarya* background figure at all in Kamalaijnanaprakasar's person? As I have heard Gurujnasambandhar's story told and as it is written up in Arunachalam's publication, the background of Jnanaprakasar is not specified. Yet, the story suggests that possibility when it makes reference to Jnanaprakasar's wife, who, as we recall, was the person who first spotted Jnanasambandhar that important morning. In South India it is understood, though not always enforced, that *sivacaryas* who are consecrated and who serve in a temple must have a living wife. Although, as Fuller notes (1984:31), there appears to be no sanction in any Agamic text for this requirement, he suggests a long-standing tradition that invokes a Vedic norm. The reference to Jnana-prakasar's wife suggests a status of *sivacarya*, and at any rate, her presence in the story indicates that he is neither celibate nor ascetic. This reference in fact seems to contradict what the temple inscription at Sikkil says when it labels Kamalaijnanaprakasar a *paradesi*, a term used to indicate an ascetic, though as I noted above, it may have the sense of someone from another locality.[10]

The paintings prominently displayed in the *pujamandapa* where members of the public stand to watch the worship of Cokkanatha are even more forceful in identifying Jnanaprakasar as a *sivacarya*. In the fourteenth painting of the series, the one showing Jnanaprakasar teaching Guru-jnanasambandhar in front of the Daksinamurti shrine, Jnanaprakasar is shown wearing a sacred thread, and with the *sikha* of a temple priest. In a painting which follows Jnanaprakasar is shown with his wife discovering Gurujnanasambandhar holding the ever-burning torch. This material rather publicly and prominently proclaims Dharmapuram's *velala* lineage as an offshoot of *sivacarya* tradition. Thus, as it is told here, the story of Gurujnanasambandhar's nightwatch is also an account of the beginning of a non-brahmin line. With this, the story may be telling us something about the historical development of religious expression in South Indian Saivism. We know from other sources that in the late sixteenth-century at the time of Gurujnanasambandhar, there were spiritual lineages made up of *sivacaryas* which had connections with what are now *velala* lineages.[11] What that meant then, and whether attitudes have changed, are more tricky questions to answer.

Later material produced by members of Dharmapuram's lineage suggest doubts regarding the legitimacy of a non-brahmin lineage. About a hundred and fifty years after Gurujnanasambandhar came to reside at Dharmapuram, one of his successors produced the *Varnasramacandrika* (Tiruvambalavanatecikar:1930). This text, which I have discussed elsewhere (Koppedrayer 1991), is a compendium of Agamic, *paddhati*, and other sources. It testifies to the legitimacy of a non-brahmin lineage by, among other things, arguing for the qualified right of *sudras* to be given *acaryabhiseka*, a right that seemed not really an issue as far as earlier Agamic material is concerned (Brunner 1962). According to a story attached to this text, a violent challenge to the sanctity of Gurujnanasambandhar's *samadhi* temple prompted the compilation of the *Varnasramacandrika* (1930:5-12; Koppedrayer 1991:304-6). A miraculous demonstration of power from the image in the *samadhi* took care of the challenge and convinced all involved of the propriety of such a lineage (305). The text and the story of the circumstances in which it was compiled indicate a certain degree of uneasiness with the extent of the lineage's ritual domain. The *Varnasramacandrika* marshals abundant textual support for the legitimacy of a non-brahmin lineage and for its ritual patterns. Like that text, and the story surrounding its production, the account of miraculous *abhiseka* resolves the question of transmitting authority to a non-brahmin group

In light of this material, the story of Gurujnanasambandhar's miraculous *abhiseka* is a bit more ambiguous than first meets the eye. It presents a dual message: as a miraculous event, it offers unimpeachable evidence of Gurujnanasambandhar's authority as a preceptor, yet the miraculous nature of the *abhiseka* highlights a breach in ordinary transmission. The very extraordinary dimension of the event hints at its suspect nature; miracle makes up for what ordinarily might be questioned. By so dramatically proclaiming Gurujnanasambandhar's spiritual qualifications, the story may inadvertently draws attention to other deficiencies, namely his non-brahmin status. Even the action that sets the circumstances for this miracle echo the dual message. Out of love for his preceptor, he acted as torchbearer when no other was available. In doing this, he exemplifies a perfect posture of humility and religious devotion, while the role he assumed smacked of low caste status. Yet, the torch he held before Jnanaprakasar was ever-burning. Here there is a hint that Gurujnanasambandhar's spiritual adeptness surpassed that of his teacher. The story may be making the sly claim that *velala* religiosity outshines *sivacarya* countenance, but at the same time it tells us that Gurujnanasambandhar needed recognition by that tradition to establish his own lineage. Nothing less than a miracle forces that recognition. Whether the historical Jnanaprakasar was really a *sivacarya* is less important than what he represents in this account, namely the source of structure given to *velala* religious expression and their Saiva experience. That source is Agamic, and at present it is associated, however reluctantly, with *sivacarya* tradition.

Told from the point of view of the *velala* lineage, their spiritual prowess is greater than that of their *sivacarya* counterparts from whom they have derived their institutional structure and authority. Divine intervention in dreams, a powerful and highly coveted vision of the godhead, led Gurujnanasambandhar first to the possession of his personal *linga*, and then to his preceptor, but he needed a preceptor to secure that vision. Nothwithstanding his unique relationship with Cokkanatha, his knowledge of, though not his ability to, worship Cokkanatha was gained from his preceptor. As I have stressed above, it is precisely that knowledge, and its transmission through structured rites of initiation and *abhiseka*, that is at the very core of the Adhinam.

The story of the miraculous *abhiseka* fosters a claim for religious authority while simultaneously suggesting some hesitancy about that claim. As Richard Davis notes in the introduction to this volume, miracles and the narrations of miracles are social acts that play upon a shared worldview and understanding of order. Contained within the notice of a miracle is a challenge to that shared understanding of order as well as an implicit acceptance of that order. The miracle story is as much acquiescence to a notion of authority as it is a challenge for authority.

## Conclusion

In this paper I have examined the relationship between an ascetic lineage and its cult object, noting that this relationship is predicated upon an understanding of a unique tie linking the group to its deity. I have suggested that a pattern of kin grouping strongly informs the internal organization of lineage which traces its origin back to a founding ancestor, Gurujnanasambandhar. His personal deity, Cokkanatha, is the tutelary deity of the lineage. The lineage's ensuing ritual tradition continually propagates Gurujnanasambandhar's special relationship with Cokkanatha. I have noted how Agamic conventions have provided a container for their religious expression. The ritual tradition both defines and is defined by the make-up of the lineage, and promulgates the miraculous nature of that special relationship; the identity of the group hinges upon the articulation of miraculous power which in turn is diffused to its members. They make up a corporate self, and I have noted where the boundaries of the ascetic lineage blur into the institution's larger *velala* community.

In discussing the story of Gurujnanasambandhar, I have explored the miraculous event that is central to his coming to Dharmapuram to found the ascetic lineage there. I have drawn attention to the multi-layering of the story, showing how it works through different levels of doctrinal, religious, and social meaning. The account of Gurujnanasambandhar's nightwatch simultaneously offers messages of the strength of devotion, grace, and religious authority, and those messages echo in the present ritual tradition at Dharmapuram. I have especially singled out the question of religious authority for discussion, noting how the story of Gurujnanasambandhar as it is presented today addresses the specter of a non-brahmin lineage in an Agamic context. Here I suggest the story of the nightwatch offers an example of miraculous *abhiseka* and in so doing manages to underwrite and yet subtly question the roots of the lineage.

Extraordinary and ordinary, this particular miracle story moves both inside and outside those boundaries. At Dharmapuram, this story frames and fills the public space where people can stand and gaze upon the worship of Cokkanatha. It is told there through the paintings that illustrate the story, but more than that, the real telling of this story is the undertaking of the worship of Cokkanatha. The claim that is asserted in the narrative echoes daily in the actions that are recognized because they are done. The miracle story frames these activities, but their daily undertaking asserts their authority even more.

## Notes

1. In the same region there are several other religious centres or *mathas* with very similar histories. These include the Tiruvavatuturai Adhinam, the Kasi Matha of Tiruppanantal, and the Suriyanarkoil Adhinam, all of which like the centre at Dharmapuram are non-brahmin centres. Much of what I present in my discussion to follow pertains in general to these other centres as well, though the particularities of each centre are of course different. See Koppedrayer (1990) for further discussion on the centres.

2. The term *adhinam* (Tamil *atinam*) figures in the name of several religious institutions in South India, but as far as I know, this term is applied only to non-brahmin Saiva centres, and even then not to all of the non-brahmin centres. Though related, the two terms *matha* and *adhinam* are not interchangeable. In Tamil usage, *matha* (*matam*) carries a connotation of place, though the term *matha* is often used as an umbrella term for a wide range of religious centres and rest houses. In contrast, the term *adhinam* designates an independent institution that has its own internal structure of authority. An *adhinam* also typically exercises some type of corporate authority over smaller, related centres.

In casual conversation any of the centres at Dharmapuram, Tiruvavatuturai, or Suriyanarkoil might be referred to as a *matha*, especially with regards to the site, the land, and the buildings occupied by the centre. It would, however, be unthinkable to refer, for example, to the outpost of Dharmapuram at Citamparam as an *adhinam*. In other words, every *adhinam* can be designated by the term *matha*, but not every *matha* can be called an *adhinam*, as very few *mathas* house an *adhinam*. In a rare attempt to define the term *adhinam*, F. R. Hemmingsford, the British District Officer in the Tanjavur District in the early twentieth century, believed (1901:232) the term to designate "central mutts [*mathas*] exercising control and supervision over subordinate mutts and other institutions such as temples." The term *adhinam* suggests "property" and is possibly derived from a centre's association with property through its administration of temple endowments. The term appears in conjunction with centres in the Tanjavur District only in the eighteenth century, nearly a century and a half after they were founded. By the mid-eighteenth century the term *adhinam* replaces *matha* in copper-plate grants to several of these centres. In a copper-plate grant in the possession of Tiruvavatuturai, dated 1711-12, the endowment is made to the Tiruvavatuturai Matha. In another copper-plate dated 1732-33, the endowment is to the *pantaram* (head) of the Tiruvavatuturai Adhinam. The adoption of the term *adhinam* perhaps reflects a broadening of the social roles assumed by these centres.

3. This role of the Dharmapuram Adhinam follows a long history of how temple structure in pre-colonial South India was maintained. There were different groups and agencies, such as the spiritual lineage of the Dharmapuram Adhinam, that acted as brokers in administering and maintaining support for the various activities that together constituted the temple institution, a radically decentralized institution. As is well known, an endowment, such as a *kattalai* making provision for a special service, was usually not a one-time gift of money, but a grant of income from land that would be remitted on an ongoing basis for eternity, or "as long as the sun and moon shone." Assurance of the continuity of the endowment was obtained by appointing an agent to oversee its management. For example, a copperplate from Tygaraja-swami temple of Tiruvarur (Iracu 1983:xl, 62-7) records a grant of income from a village made by Capayi Viceyarekunata Meykkan Kopalan of Pampavalanatu for ablutions and oblations to the deity of the temple for the merit of the Maratha king Tukkoji. This grant was placed in the hands of Aghora-sivapantaram, a member of a spiritual lineage who was designated as the *abhiseka-kattalai* of the temple. This office appears to have managed endowments for *abhiseka*, such as the one this grant records. In this and many other records, a representative of a religious lineage was named as the trustee of an endowment to ensure its future. In turn, certain rights within the temple devolved upon that group. From pre-colonial times to the present there have been numerous changes in administrative patterns, and along with these changes there have been disputes over what agency or group actually has authority over the endowments, and over the extent of such authority. Here is not the place to go into this discussion; suffice it to say that some individuals in South India today see the role played in temple affairs by Dharmapuram and similar institutions as a vestige of medieval practice.

4. Some of the wealth of the Adhinam has been directed towards the sponsorship of learning. Several schools in Dharmapuram and Mayilatuturai are run by the institution, including a *tevarampatacalai* and an *agamapatacalai*, centres for training Tamil temple hymnsingers (*otuvars*) and young temple priests. An Oriental College was founded in 1946 and a Saiva Siddhanta Research Institute in 1984. Both

institutes are housed within the Adhinam. Though founded fairly recently, the purpose of such centres of learning echoes a role the Adhinam has historically played in the dissemination of tradition.

5. The line of disciples at Dharmapuram is known as the *Tirukailasaparampara,* the "lineage of Mount Kailasa." This line is traced back to Siva in the form of Sri-kantaparamahesvara. From Siva, the line descends through Nandi to Canar-kumaramunivar, Cattiyataracani, Paranjyoti, to the four preceptors of the Saiva Siddhanta tradition, Meykantar, Arunanti, Maraijnanasambandhar, and Umapati. Dharmapuram shares these very early lineage roots with other *velala* lineages, such as the lineage of the Tiruvavatuturai Adhinam, which also identifies itself as a *kailasaparampara*

6. I doubt whether this inscription means that Jnanaprakasar was to live at this *matha* located a considerable distance to the south of Tiruvarur; rather the *matha* marked a place in this region where Jnanaprakasar's authority, either as a preceptor or as a *kattalai* administrator, extended. As it appears in this inscription, the term *matha* likely designates an outpost where either an initiated disciple of Jnana-prakasar's lineage resided or where there were resthouse provisions for followers of his spiritual lineage.

7. I came across the story in the 1961 introduction of the *Turaicaippuranam (Nananta:24-5),* a work that also dates to the eighteenth century. The *Turaicaip-puranam* provides a hagiography of Tirumalikaittevar, but it does not, however, include the torch story provided in the introduction of the 1961 edition of the puranam. In my time at Tiruvavatuturai and in my conversations with individuals in association with the Adhinam there, this story was not recounted to me, nor have I located another written account of it, though certainly such accounts may exist. Based on the scanty material I have available, it is hard to say whether the similarity between these stories about Gurujnanasambandhar and Tirumalikaittevar reflects a disputed claim to a miracle story, distant memory of a shared past, or something else altogether.

8. I am grateful to Richard Davis for pointing this out to me.

9. There is another story from Dharmapuram that provides precedent for this procedure. As the account goes (Arunachalam:55-8), Gurujnanasambandhar had appointed Anandaparavasa as successor and then entered eternal *samadhi,* but Anandaparavasa, instead of assuming office, did the same to the west of the *matha.* The *tampiran* thus gathered at the *samadhi* of Gurujnanasambandhar and prayed (56):

> Oh Lord, now that Anandaparavasa your nominee has also entered eternal bliss, what is to become of us? We pray, you appear again to us to help us, and to ensure a proper succession to the headship of Dharmapuram, and name a competent spiritual guru for us.

At this, Gurujnanasambandhar came out of *samadhi* and appointed another disciple, Satcitananda, now counted as the third of the line.

10. The term *pantaram* attached to Kamalaijnanaprakasar in the same inscription at Sikkil at present indicates non-brahmin. The term *pantaracanniti* is a title of office of leadership of the lineage of Dharmapuram and of other *velala* institutions. It was used in earlier copper-plate inscriptions and in more recent legal

documents to refer to the heads of the present *velala* spiritual lineages. Whether the term *pantaram* as it appears in the late sixteenth-century Sikkil inscription referred to non-brahmin status is difficult to say. We do have numerous inscriptions that indicate *pantara* were representatives of spiritual lineages. For example, an inscription from Avudaiyarkoil (A.R.E. no. 503 of 1925-26), a temple under the administration of the Tiruvavatuturai Adhinam at present, records a sale of land through the agent of Paratecimanttira Vamadeva Pantaram, for the requirements of worship to the deity of the temple. Another inscription from the same year (no. 504) records a gift of land to the same *pantaram* for the purposes of *gurupuja*, a central rite undertaken by members of spiritual lineages. However, I do not know whether the term *pantaram* here automatically meant non-brahmin.

11. The lineage of the present Suriyanarkoil Adhinam, located not far from Dharmapuram, was founded by a preceptor identified as a *sivacarya* (Anavarata-vinayakar Pillai: 1936:v), and his disciple was the great Sivagrayogin, also a *sivacarya*. He was also an ascetic, as indicated in the colophon of his *Saiva-sannyasapaddhati*, where he calls himself *ativarnasrami* (beyond *asrama* and *varna*). The preceptors who followed in Sivagra's lineage are, however, *velala*, and the Suriyanarkoil Adhinam at present is known strictly as a *velala* institution. Like many other Agamic-based writings, Sivagrayogi's works, done in the late sixteenth century, accept with qualifications the admissibility of *sudras* (which is how *velalas* are sometimes classified) to preceptorhood. This same Sivagrayogi was also closely associated with the Namaccivaya who founded the *velala* lineage of Tiruvavatu-turai, now the Tiruvavatuturrai Adhinam, shortly after Sivagrayogi took up residence at Suriyanarkoil. The lineage chronicles (Cuppiramaniyan 1928:43) of Tiruvavatuturai hint of a teaching relationship between Sivagrayogi and Namaccivaya.

Figure 1.   The Emerald Buddha at Wat Thai in Los Angeles. Bronze with green
paint. Modern. Wat Thai, North Hollywood, California. The Emerald Buddha is
the dark image at the top. Note the boxes of chicken eggs brought by worship-
pers (duck eggs being difficult to purchase in Los Angeles). The image is used at
the Wat Thai specifically to cast horoscopes. (Photograph: Robert L. Brown)

Figure 2. Prasenajit Pillar. Stone. From Bharhut (India). Ca. first century B.C.E. Indian Museum, Calcutta. (Photograph: Frederick Asher)

Figure 3. *Cakravartin* relief. Stone. From Jaggayyapeta (India). Ca. first century B.C.E. Madras Government Museum, Madras. The rectangular gem is mounted on a pillar to the proper left of the *cakravartin's* head. Note the streams of square coins that rain from the scalloped clouds at the top. (Photograph: Robert L. Brown)

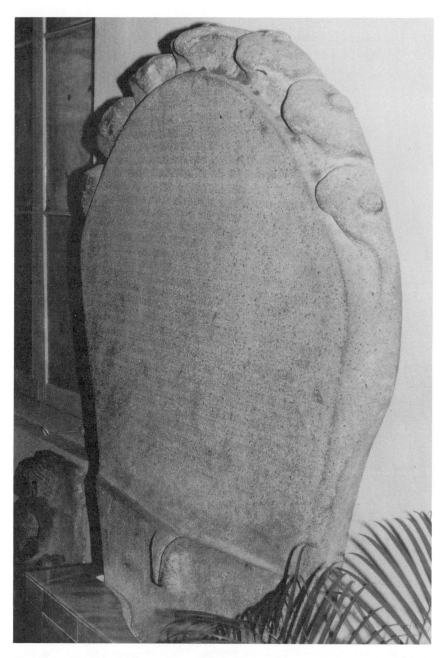

Figure 4.   *Naga* stone. Stone. From Sabokingking (Sumatra, Indonesia). Seventh century C.E. National Museum, Jakarta. (Photograph: Robert L. Brown)

Figure 5. View of buildings and temples of the Dharmapuram Adhinam, as seen through the eastern gateway. (Photograph: K. I. Koppedrayer)

Figure 6. Sri-la-Sri Canmukatecikar Nanacampantar Paramacarya Cuvamikal, the present head of the Gurujnanasambandhar lineage, and twenty-sixth in succession from the sixteenth century guru. Icon of Gurujnanasambandhar is in background. (Photograph: K. I. Koppedrayer)

Figure 7. Present head of the Gurujnanasambandhar lineage, bathing at the tank of the temple. (Photograph: K. I. Koppedrayer)

Figure 8. Shaka. Seiryoji, Kyoto. 985 C.E. Wood, 160 cm. (Photograph: Donald F. McCallum)

Figure 9.    Shaka. Saidaiji, Nara. 1249 c.e. Wood, 167 cm. (Photograph: Donald F. McCallum)

Figure 10.    Amida Triad. Tokyo National Museum. 1254 c.e. Gilt-bronze. Amida, 42.6 cm. (Photograph: Donald F. McCallum)

Figure 11.　Amida Triad. Toshadaiji, Nara. Kamakura period. Paper, 46.5 x 28.2 cm. (Photograph: Donald F. McCallum)

Figure 12. Amida Triad. Private Collection. Edo period. Paper. (Photograph: Donald F. McCallum)

Figure 13. Amida Triad. Private Collection. Meiji period. Paper, 14.5 x 10 cm. (Photograph: Donald F. McCallum)

Figure 14.    Amida Triad. Freer Gallery of Art, Washington, D.C. Kamakura period. Colors/ink on silk. (Photograph: Donald F. McCallum)

Figure 15.    Amida Triad. Seiganji, Tochigi
Prefecture. Muromachi period. Colors/ink on
silk, 89 x 37.6 cm. (Photograph: Donald
McCallum)

Figure 16.    Amida Triad. Hoshi Bukkyo Bijut-
sukan. Fukushima Prefecture. Edo period.
Colors/ink on paper. (Photograph: Donald F.
McCallum)

Figure 17.  Amida Triad. Private Collection. 1811. Clay, 5 cm. (Photograph: Donald F. McCallum)

Figure 18.　Shaka. Private Collection. Edo period.
Paper, 130 x 55.5 cm. (Photograph: Donald F.
McCallum)

Figure 19.　Shaka. Korenji, Kyoto. Kamakura period. Colors on silk, 133 x 53.2 cm. (Photograph: Donald F. McCallum)

Figure 20.    Shaka. Seiryoji, Kyoto. Momoyama
period. Colors on silk, 131.5 x 79.7 cm. (Photograph:
Donald F. McCallum)

Figure 21. Shaka. Royal Ontario Museum, Toronto. Edo period. Colors on silk, 58.4 x 23.7 cm. (Photograph: Donald F. McCallum)

# 6

## The Jina Bleeds:
## Threats to the Faith
## and the Rescue of the Faithful
## in Medieval Jain Stories

*Phyllis Granoff*

### The Context: Religion and the State in Medieval India

Medieval religious texts in India often link the prosperity of the state and all of its citizens with the proper and exclusive practice of a particular mode of religion. In an extension of an older concept that made the righteousness of the king more generally responsible for the wealth and happiness of his kingdom, such texts repeatedly assert that the king and all the citizens must worship correctly in conformity with the quite specific rules of the text in question in order to insure material prosperity for the kingdom. And so we hear that in the kingdom where an image of the right deity is installed with the appropriate rituals, the king has long life and his citizens flourish. There is no famine, there is no want; wealth and health await everyone. Conversely, where worship is not properly carried out or an image of the deity is installed in a ritually incorrect ceremony, disaster wreaks havoc on the ruler and his subjects.[1]

This close association of a correct mode of worship with the security of the kingdom would seem at least by medieval times to have been pan-Indian. Certain types of sectarian Hindu, Buddhist, and Jain texts all make such statements, sometimes couched in positive terms, but often uttered as dire predictions of what happens when a king or his subjects fail to follow the prescribed path. As a sectarian medieval Hindu example we

might consider the following quotations from a text of the Vallabha
Vaisnavas, the *Satsiddhantasamgraha* 140. 152.

> One should never dwell in the kingdom of a king who is not a Vaisnava.
> As a body is without eyes to see, as a woman is without her husband, as
> a Brahmin is without learning, so is the kingdom that is not ruled by a
> Vaisnava.
>
> (attributed to the *Brhannaradiya Purana*, ch. 23).[2]

Likewise, "When an image of Visnu is consecrated by someone who is not
a proper Vaisnava, the kingdom or its king will be destroyed." And elsewhere in the same text and in a similar vein, it continues, "If anyone should
worship without the proper mantras or at an improper time, then his
village will be destroyed and there will be a famine; the king and his
kingdom will be destroyed."

*Puranas*, with their sectarian emphasis, often display this kind of
rhetoric. They may also make more general statements such as those in the
*Visnudharmottara Purana* 3.38.27, where we are simply told that an image
with all the proper marks brings prosperity to the maker of the image and
to the king of the land in which he resides. In fact the ceremony for
consecrating an image in the *Visnudharmottara Purana*, 3.110, includes a
prayer to Visnu, informing the god that he has been made to reside in the
image in question and asking that the consecration of the image be
considered a proper consecration. The chapter then concludes with a
request that the god protect the *yajamana*, i.e., the donor of the image, and
the country in which the donor and the image reside. In these statements
we see clearly reflected a desire to connect the prosperity of the kingdom
and all of its subjects with the adequate observance of religious ritual; the
benefits of the installation of the image extend beyond the individual donor
to the king, the kingdom, and all its inhabitants.

In medieval Hindu texts images properly installed not only protect the
kingdom; they can also announce in unusual ways threats to the safety of
the king and his subjects. The *Visnudharmottara Purana*, 2.135, describes
how images may sweat, move, or even cry out. Such signs foretell the
destruction of the king and his kingdom. The same text, 3.117, describes
the festival in which a small image of a god is taken out in a portable shrine
and paraded around the city. The king and those he has appointed to be
in charge of the affairs of the city are to follow the image, along with the
court astrologer who is to watch for any unusual signs or portents. The
text then lists a number of possible unpropitious occurrences, most of
which pertain to the health and welfare of the king and the kingdom. For
example, if the flag staff breaks for no obvious reason, this portends the

death of the king. If the umbrella breaks, then the country will perish. If the break is slight, it is only the queen who will die. If the image itself breaks or falls, then all the citizens will be destroyed, while if the portable shrine falls, then the kingdom along with the king and all the subjects will perish.

In the *Bhagavata Purana*, 3.18.13, images of the gods shed tears when the demons are born and the kingdom is thereby threatened, while in the *Mahabharata* 6.2.26 and 6.108.11 images in the temple cry and shake and vomit blood, foretelling the terrible destruction in the impending battle. The *Brhatsamhita* of Varahamira, XLVI, 8, also provides an early statement that this type of unusual behavior of an image portends the destruction of the king and the kingdom. A much later text, the *Adbhutasagara* of Yogisvara Patra from Orissa, devotes an entire chapter to the subject of "*Devapratimadbhuta*," unusual manifestations associated with images of the gods. The *Adbhutasagara* is basically a compendium of puranic and agamic texts and the citations given in the chapter on images clearly attest to the fact that it was widely believed that images could portend the destruction of the king and his kingdom (*Adbhutasagara* II.5:27-33).

In some of the late royal chronicles of Nepal we find a number of reports of the very kind of unusual occurrences associated with images or temple objects that were considered by the *Adbhutasagara* to reflect ominously on the security of the realm. Many of the unusual manifestations in the Nepal chronicles were cases when an image or a ritual vessel was seen to exude blood; such incidents always called for rituals of propitiation to ward off the evil consequences that they signaled (Regmi II: 1966: 814ff.)

When we turn to Buddhist texts we find that Buddhist *sutras* often make the same claims as the Hindu texts make, although they tend to link the security and prosperity of the realm with the respect accorded a particular text or a more general ethical conduct as opposed to the stronger emphasis on images in the medieval Hindu material. Thus the *Suvarna-prabhasottamasutra* 15.73, declares, "There will be abundant crops everywhere in the continent of Jambudvipa and particularly in that kingdom where this sutra is recited," in chapter 12, a *yaksa* had promised to protect the person who recites the text; he then extends that benefit to the kingdom in which the reciter of the text dwells. Conversely we are told in chapter 13 that the king who does not behave as the text demands incites the anger of the gods and his kingdom perishes.

The *Maitribalajataka* in the *Jatakamala* dramatizes this Buddhist belief that the righteousness of the king protected his kingdom and all its subjects. Four *yaksas* decide to oppress a certain kingdom. Disguised as Brahmins, they come upon a cowherd out in the wilderness and are surprised by his lack of fear. The cowherd explains to them that he is protected by a special "charm," namely the righteousness of the king. Because the king observes the correct ethical and religious behavior no harm can come to any of his subjects. The *yaksas* will proceed to test the king, who vividly demonstrates his virtues by his willingness to give up his very life to the *yaksas*.

While I shall argue in this paper that Jains were less committed to linking support for Jainism with the prosperity of the kingdom, evidence that Jains shared the pan-Indian association of religion with the protection of the state is not entirely wanting. In the *Paumacariya* of Vimalasuri, the earliest of the Jain *Ramayanas*, we hear how the images in the temples weep when Ravana, king of the Raksasas, sets out to do battle against Laksmana and Rama--a portent that foretells the king's death. Later in the same text we are given a full account of the city of Mathura and its various trials and tribulations. We learn how the city was once devastated by plagues that were caused by a supernatural being who was angry at the citizens. The plagues begin to cease when seven Jain sages visit Mathura. Following their instructions the king erects temples to the Jinas and installs Jina images. He also erects images of the seven Jain sages whose visit had begun the process of healing. We are told that the citizens then followed suit and that whoever had an image of the Jina in his home was freed from the threat of plague. The king finally places Jain images in all the four cardinal points, surrounding his kingdom, like a protective wall. At that the kingdom and the capital city become secure: prosperity reigns again and no one suffers from any ailment (*Paumacariya* 1968: chapter 69.50-53; chapters 87-89).

In a similar vein, a late medieval Jain ritual text, the fourteenth century *Vidhimargaprapa,* also asserts:

> The king grows in might and makes all the corners of the sky glow with the bright glare of his glory; his merit increases greatly, when an image of the Jina is properly installed in his kingdom. Installing an image of the Jina with proper ritual care puts an end to disease and plague; it puts an end to famine; it brings happiness to everyone in the world when done with true devotion (*Vidhimargaprapa* 1941: 103).

The *Brhacchantistotra,* which is to be recited after bathing the Jina, after installing images, on the occasion of making pilgrimage, and at other important rituals, includes several verses that pray for the safety of the king and his kingdom, as well as for the welfare of the Jain community. The hymn is to insure that no harm comes to anyone associated with the rituals performed, and its benefits extend to the king and all of the citizens of the kingdom in which Jain worship is carried out.[3]

In addition, in the stories that they told of their famous monks, Jains as much as any other religious group in medieval India stressed the importance of a close relationship between monks and kings, and praised in fulsome terms the conversion of a king and his subjects to Jainism. The accounts of the founding of the Capotkata dynasty in Gujarat closely link the king Vanaraja with the Jain monk Silaguna, to whom the king offers his kingdom as soon as he is crowned (Tawney 1901: 18-19).[4] We also see that the monk Siddhasena is celebrated in the Jain tradition not for his many real gifts in philosophy, but for his alleged miracles that led to the conversion of kings and their retinue. Similarly Bappabhattisuri is honored for his close relationship with the King Ama, while the monk Hemacandra is best known as the one who converted King Kumarapala to Jainism. In fact under Hemacandra's tutelage Kumarapala initiates various practices that make the kingdom act as if it were indeed a Jain kingdom, although no mass conversion to Jainism is described in any of the traditional sources.[5]

Medieval Jain texts on monastic rules likewise underscore the importance of a monk's securing the favor of the king. These texts do not describe Jainism as a state religion or as integral to the protection of the state, but speak instead of the importance of royal favor for the prosperity of the religious community. In stressing the necessity of securing royal patronage, medieval texts on monastic rules even allow that a monk may violate normally accepted norms of behavior in an effort to please a king. Thus the *Vavahara Bhasa* tells us that a monk may postpone the obligatory ritual of confession if he is engaged in performing some major task in the service of the faith, which includes the instruction of a king (Caillat 1975:128). In addition, the conversion of a king is considered to be so momentous an event that major penances may be abbreviated for the monk who has succeeded in winning a king for the faith. For example, the *Vavahara Bhasa* 2.243-254 enjoins that when a monk has committed a very grave offense and is expelled from the community of monks, he may still be accepted back into the community upon the performance of a specified ritual. This ritual sequence involves the errant monk's presenting himself before the religious community as a layman--an act of great humility and humiliation, one might suspect, for the repentant monk. It is this key step that may be eliminated if the errant monk has succeeded in converting a king (Caillat 1975: 180).

The *Curni* to the *Nisitha Sutra*, another important text of monastic rules and exceptions, allows that a monk may perform black magic to secure the favor of a king, in direct contravention of a more general rule that forbids such practices to the monks (*Nisitha Sutra* 1982:162, v. 490). Chapter four of this text explicitly warns monks against the company of kings who might disturb the monks' religious practices; in addition the text notes that others may be jealous of a monk's preferred position at the court and cause him trouble. As an exception to this general proscription against a monk consorting with a king, the text then notes that this rule does not apply when a monk's being at court might secure some advantage for his own religious group. The same exception is then made to apply to local rulers and petty chieftains as well as kings (*Nisitha Sutra* IV. 1566 ff; Sen 1975: 284 ff).

While the monastic texts such as these all speak from the vantage point of the community of monks and nuns and thus stress the gains to be made for the religious community from involvement with the state, they nonetheless attest to a continuing interest in political centers of power on the part of the Jain religious community. In addition, the *Vidhimargaprapa* and the medieval stories about the conversion of kings indicate that Jains by no means entirely rejected the common Indian model of a sectarian group seeking royal patronage or the pan-Indian rhetoric of promising to bring prosperity to the realm if their religion was followed. Jainism, too, like Hinduism and Buddhism, could speak of itself as the state religion in certain texts and contexts.

Religion in all of these texts, which themselves cross various genres and religions, is consistently depicted as a matter of great concern not only to religious leaders, who as ritual specialists must see to it that worship is correctly carried out and images are properly installed. Religion is equally portrayed as a matter of vital importance to lay leaders, particularly those in power, who are responsible for the well-being of the state. Its importance for secular leaders is underscored by the clear message that no amount of secular wisdom alone can insure the well-being of a kingdom that is not ritually secure.

There is no question that religious groups, seeking coveted royal patronage, had a strong weapon in their repeated assertion that they were necessary to a king, as necessary if not more necessary than the more secular tools of kingship. They could turn this weapon against new religious groups, as a biography of the Assamese Vaisnava leader Damodara indicates. According to the *Gurulila* of Kavi Ram Ray Das, Brahmins hostile to the new Vaisnava movement protested to the king that the Vaisnavas were a threat to the realm precisely because they refused to worship the Goddess Kamakhya. The king has no difficulty in understanding the nature of the danger; worship of the goddess is the key to his own safety and the safety of his kingdom (Goswami 1924:800).

Royal chronicles, inscriptions and poems eulogizing kings in their turn reflect the widespread acceptance of this belief that royal power depends upon a king's close association with a particular deity and its worship; the king must pay special attention to this deity, which is regarded as the tutelary deity of the royal clan. A clear example of the concern for establishing the legitimacy of dynastic rule by reference to divine favors can be found in a poem like the *Navasahasankacarita* of Padmagupta, a tenth-century poem that celebrates the founding of the Paramara dynasty. This text does not describe the real historical battles that the Paramaras fought as they came to power; instead it concentrates on stories of magical conquests of supernatural realms, and accounts of daring exploits that culminate in the prince's winning of a supernatural bride and his acquisition of an image of a god. The Siva linga that the prince is given by his father-in-law, a Naga king, has its own impeccable pedigree and we learn how the linga was transmitted, like the hereditary kingship itself, from Visnu to the sages and then to the Naga king. When Sahasanka returns to his capital city of Dhara, his first two acts are religious acts: he visits the Mahakala temple to pray to Siva, and he installs the linga in a new temple. It is only then that he can begin to rule.

Medieval inscriptions often begin with a statement that the power of the particular dynasty which is being eulogized is a product of special divine favor. Thus a Kadamba inscription, for example, opens with a statement that the kings of the dynasty are consecrated to their royal position through the power of their meditation upon the mothers of Lord Karttikeya (Fleet 1877: 30). Calukyan inscriptions, which closely follow the Kadamba inscriptions in their rhetoric, describe that royal lineage as nourished by the seven mothers, the *sapta matrkas*, protected by Svami Karttikeya and further aided by Narayana. The opening epithets in Calukya inscriptions state that the Calukyas subdued all the other kings in the world through the power of their boar insignia, which they had obtained through the divine favor of the God Visnu (Vijayamurti 1952: 103).

The late medieval kings of Mysore were devoted to Mahisasuramardini as their clan goddess, while the Kolhapur kings worshiped Mahalaksmi. In an interesting vignette, a nineteenth century text describing the travels of the head of the Visistadvaita monastery, the Sri Brahmatantra Parakala Mutt, describes how the monk was invited to the kingdom of Kolhapur by its king. The king and the monk showed each other respect by worshiping each other's tutelary deities: the king worshiped the monk's Hayagriva, while the monk worshiped Mahalaksmi (Desikacharya 1949:26). The medieval practice of stealing the image of a rival's tutelary deity is surely connected with medieval Hindu notions that the success of kingship depends on the proper worship of a particular deity (Davis 1997: 51-85; Kulke 1992:131-143). In one medieval account of Hindu resistance to

Muslim conquest it is precisely the theft of an image, the linga at Soma-
natha, that leads the Rajput king Kanhadade to mobilize his army and rise
up against the invaders. It is worth noting that King Kanhadade in the
fifteenth-century Gujarati ballad that celebrates his exploits derives much
of his strength in battle from the worship of his tutelary deity, the goddess
Asapuridevi.

The belief that the sanction of a deity was required for kingship is so
strong that we even see non-Hindu kings receive divine sanction from
Hindu royal goddesses in historical writings in medieval India. Jinaraja,
in his extension of Kalhana's history of Kashmir, in verse 139 asserts that
the Muslim conqueror of Kashmir was vouchsafed a vision of Gauri, who
told him in a dream that his descendants would rule Kashmir. The Jain
ministers Vastupala and Tejahpala are appointed by the Hindu King
Viradhavala on the basis of instructions that the king receives from the
royal goddess, a former Hindu princess who had died an untimely death
and become the royal protectress (*Prabandhakosa* 1935:101).

A sub-genre of *puranic* texts appeared in late medieval times that might
be considered somewhere between a *purana* and an historical chronicle.
Such texts described the close relationship between a royal house and a
tutelary deity which was cared for by an hereditary line of priests. The *Ekalingamahatmya* is a good example of this type of text. It describes the house
of Mewar and the line of priests at the temple of Ekalingaji.[6]

Medieval Jain story literature offers further corroborating evidence for
the hypothesis that royal clan goddesses or deities were of major importance in medieval Hindu India. Jain stories make frequent reference to
royal clan goddesses, most of them Saiva and bloodthirsty, and hotly
condemned by Jain monks. In the *Yasodharacarita* we hear how the King
Yasodhara damns himself to numerous terrible reincarnations by agreeing
to worship the royal goddess after he has told his mother that he has had
a dream that foretold the destruction of the kingdom (Hardy 1990: 118-
139).

Given the consistent emphasis in all manner of religious and historical
texts that correct worship insured the material security of the kingdom, the
Muslim invasions must have presented a major challenge both to religious
groups and to secular leaders. The tendency even in many of the texts of
the period is not to deny at all the connection between religion and secular
welfare, but to point carefully to the lack of proper worship as the direct
cause for political reversals of fortune. The *Ekalingamahatmya*, for example,
does not hesitate to attribute the Muslim conquest to the failure of the king
and his subjects to respect the Ekalinga. Just as plague or famine or
drought had once been described as the result of unrighteous behavior on
the part of the king and his subjects, so now is conquest regarded as the

result of failure to worship the correct god in the correct way. Indeed, one scholar has noted a similar reaction to contemporary political and economic problems in India. The priests of the Minaksi temple in Madurai are said to blame current problems on the improper performance of the temple rituals (Fuller 1992: 69-70).

But to regard political defeat and threats to worship as the direct result of improper worship was not the only reaction to challenges to political stability in medieval India, and particularly to the challenge that came from the Muslims. In this paper I would like to discuss a few Jain stories told of unusual images and what happens to them under pressure from Muslim attacks. My argument will be that the Jains in these accounts choose to withdraw from the problems associated with the strong belief in medieval India that had linked proper worship with the security and welfare of the state. In these stories an image may indeed act in such a way that portends political disaster as the images in the *Visnudharmotttara Purana* do; the Mahavira image of Kanyanayana, for example, sweats before a major Muslim conquest.[7] But Jains do not pretend in these stories to be able to protect the kingdom with their rituals, and images flee rather than fight. Where they do battle those who would destroy them, the result is not the repulsion of an invading army and the restoration of earlier political rule. In these accounts, true to history, existing kingdoms crumble and cities are destroyed. But the images with their unusual activities do manage to secure the safety of the Jain community: the Sultan grants freedom of worship for the Jain community alone. I will try to understand the stories I have chosen by suggesting that in the late medieval period Jains retreated from the pan-Indian rhetoric which linked proper worship with the security of the state as a whole and shifted their focus from that larger community to the smaller community of the Jain faithful. Instead of the model of a stable political entity ritually secured by the close connection of a king with a group of monks or by the protection accorded the king by his tutelary divinity and its priests, these texts offer the vision of a peripatetic Jain community capable of rescuing its own but no longer concerned with and indeed no longer capable of maintaining the integrity of the state.

Before I begin with translations of two Jain accounts of unusual images and political turmoil, I need, I think, to say a few words about how these stories understand images and "image miracles." It will be immediately clear from the translations that it is somewhat of a misnomer to say that these stories are talking about "miraculous images." In some cases, these accounts do not separate the image and the god it represents; in other cases images are protected by superintending deities and it is these deities who make the images move or strike their destroyers with plague.

There is an interesting text of monastic rules, one very important to the Svetambara community in medieval times, that makes very clear one Jain understanding of images and how they may move themselves or perform other unusual feats. The *Nisitha Sutra,* chap. 16, vv. 5100ff., warns against a monk's staying in the same room with an image. The text notes that there are two types of images, those in which a deity is present and those in which no deity resides. The images in which a deity resides can cause particular problems for a monk or nun, in that the deity might try to test the monk or nun or tempt them. Indeed medieval story collections include many accounts of monks who were tested in this way by deities residing in images, usually *vyantaras* or minor deities, and of how the monk conquered the deity and emerged victorious.[8]

The world of these Jain stories at times also shares much with Hindu accounts of images and pilgrimage sites. Many of the "miracles" told of images concern their discovery and the revelation of a buried image occurs in these stories in much the same way as it does in Hindu accounts: for example, a cow drops milk on a hill, flowers do not wilt on a hill. In the language of these stories, while it is clear that we are talking about the discovery of a specific image of a *tirthankara,* the stories speak more simply of the discovery of the "God." The fact that an image is found simply means that the god whose image is discovered is now known to all to be present at that specific location. The strange happenings at the temple or in its vicinity are not at all the result of miracles that an "image" performs, but are simply a manifestation of the power of god, whose presence there is assured by the image.

## Politics and Images: Two Jain Stories

I begin with an account of the Parsvanatha at Phalavarddhi from the *Vividhatirthakalpa,* Jinaprabhasuri's late fourteenth-century collection of various stories associated with Jain holy sites. It is worth noting that Jinaprabhasuri is also the author of the *Vidhimargaprapa* that I cited earlier, in which he says that proper installation of an image insures the prosperity of the realm. The following story clearly belies that claim: the realm is overrun by the Muslims, but the Jains and their images are spared.[9]

> Having worshiped the Jina Parsvanatha who is installed in the glorious temple at Phalavaddhi, I now tell the account of that very Parsvanatha, which destroys the pride of the Age of Wickedness.
> There is a village called Phalavaddhi, which is so beautiful with its many different temples of the Jinas, Mahavira, and the others. This village

is near the city of Medattaya, in the country of Savalakkha. And in that village there stands a temple to the goddess Phalavaddhi, its spire reaching high into the heavens. Although that village was once rich and prosperous, in time it came to be virtually abandoned. Nonetheless a small number of merchants settled there from elsewhere. Among them was a man named Dhandhala, who was like a pearl in the lineage of the Glorious Srimala clan; he was foremost amongst the righteous and a pious Jain layman. There was another man there of like virtue; his name was Sivamkara, and he was like the moon that shone in the sky of the Uvaesavala clan.

Now both of these men had many cows. It so happened that one of Dhandhala's cows ceased to give milk, even though someone tried to milk her day after day. And so Dhandala asked the fellow who herded the cattle, " Say, do you or does someone else milk this cow when you take her out to pasture, and is that why she never gives any milk for us?" The cowherd swore that he was innocent of any crime. And the cowherd watched the cow carefully and he saw one day how she let down her milk from all four of her udders, right on top of a tall hillock, under a tree. He saw that she did this every day and he showed Dhandhala what was happening. Dhandhala thought to himself, "There must be some kind of god here, maybe a yaksa or something, under the ground." He went home and that night as he slept peacefully he had a dream in which some man told him, "The Blessed Lord Parsvanatha is under the hillock, inside a temple buried underground. Take him out from there and worship him."

As soon as morning dawned and he woke up, Dhandhala told his dream to Sivamkara. Both of them, filled with wonder, began to dig up the hillock with spades, after first offering worship to the various spirits who might impede their work. They brought out the Blessed Lord Parsvanatha, over whom a snake spread its seven coils, and the temple. And they both worshiped him with great ceremony every day. And as they worshiped the Lord of the World in this way, one day the superintending deities granted them yet another dream, informing them, "You must build a temple right here."

Both of them felt great joy in their hearts and they began to have a temple built according to their means. They hired architects and workmen, each to be employed at the appropriate task. But no sooner had they finished the first pavilion, when the work had to stop, for they were not wealthy men and they did not have sufficient funds. Both of those pious devotees became agitated at this turn of events. But then at night the superintending deities once more told them in a dream, "Every day at the crack of dawn, even before the crows begin to cry, you must go to the temple and you will find hundreds of coins placed before the God. Use that money to build the temple."

They saw then exactly what the dream had told them they would see, and they took that money and began to complete the task of building. When five pavilions had been completed, and even a subsidiary pavilion, all to the great wonder and delight of every one in the world, indeed when the temple was almost entirely completed, their sons began to think to themselves, "Where are they getting all of this money that allows them to just keep on building and building?" And so one day, at the crack of dawn, they concealed themselves behind a pillar and watched in secret. But that day the gods did not fill the area in front of Parsvanatha with coins. And the reason for this is that when the superintending deities know that a Muslim king is going to conquer the kingdom, even though they are worshiped, they do not give people wealth. The building stopped at that point. In the year 1181 of the Vikrama era, the monk Dharmaghosa, who was famous for his victory over the Digambasa Jain monk Gunacanda, and who had succeeded the monk Stiabhaddasari, the ornament of the monastic lineage known as the Rayagaccha in the presence of the assembled Jain community, monks, nuns, and lay men and women, consecrated the temple to Parsvanatha.

Later, Sultan Sahabadin shattered the main image. When the Wicked Age shows its might, all the minor deities become absorbed in their own silly games and they lose their concentration; the superintending deities, whose task it is to guard the images in a temple, falter in their responsibilities. When the superintending deities took ahold of themselves and became watchful again, the Muslim king and his people were wondrously struck with plagues such as blindness and vomiting blood. And that was why the Sultan issued an order to this effect: "No one shall destroy this temple." But because the superintending deities would not allow any other image of the Lord there, the Jain community did not install another image. That Lord, though his body has been damaged, still performs many great wonders. Every year on the occasion of Posabahuladasami, when the birth of Parsvanatha is commemorated, lay men and women converge on the temple from all the four quarters of the world and celebrate a great and magnificent festival, bathing the image, singing, dancing, playing music, adorning the image with flower garlands, and erecting flags. They honor and strengthen the cause of the Jain faith by performing various rituals, such as honoring the monks and nuns with proper gifts. They destroy the effects of the Wicked Age and they greatly increase the store of merit in the world. And in this temple the superintending deities, Dharanendra, Padmavati, and Ksetrapala, all ward off any harm that might come to the Jain community and they grant the wishes of those who worship there. And the fortunate souls who are destined some day for release and who spend the night in this temple in meditation see a man walking through the temple with a lamp in his hands; its flame never flickers. To see this Parsvanatha, which is a holy object, is to gain the merit of making a pilgrimage to the Parsvanathas at many a holy site, including Kalikunda, Kukkudesara, Siripavvaya, Sankhesara, Serisaya, Mahura, Banarasi, Ahicchatta, Thambhanya, Ajjahara, Pavaranayara, Devapattan, Karahedaya, Nagaddaha, Siripura,

Samini, Carupa, Dinpuri, Ujjeni, Suddhadanti, Harikankhi, and Limbodaya. This is what the elders of the Faith say.

May those worthy souls who hear even this brief account of the Parsvanatha at Phalavarddhi gain great fortune.

And so Jinaprabhasuri has given this account of the Parsvanatha of Phalavarddhi, having taken some of the traditional lore that he heard from the elders.

This brief account of the Parsvanatha at Phalavarddhi makes clear that the Jain images and their superintending gods survive the Muslim onslaught although they are not unscathed: the Parsvanatha is wounded, but it keeps its powers intact. Through its superintending gods it can still ward off harm for the faithful and grant their wishes. Once the Sultan has been chastised by the superintending deities and has given the order to his soldiers to do the Jain temple no further harm, Jinaprabhasuri makes no further mention of any political events and he shifts the focus of his story entirely to the Jain community. We learn that the community still cele-brates a major pilgrimage to Phalavarddhi, on the occasion of the com-memoration of Parsvanatha's birthday; we learn that despite Muslim depredations the holy site and its image have retained a position of prime importance for the Jains. Jinaprabhasuri even says that through the pilgrimage and all of the splendid ceremonies that are carried out annually at Phalavarddhi, the Jain faith has been made to prosper. One could almost turn the verse in the *Vidhimargaprapa* around and substitute "Jain community" for "king and his kingdom" every time those words occur there.

I believe that this short account of Phalavarddhi is consistent with many of the other stories that Jinaprabhasuri tells in the *Vividhatirthakalpa.* It represents a retrenchment of the pan-Indian notion of correct worship as the ritual means to secure the kingdom, and proposes in its stead the ideal of correct worship as the means for the Jain community to protect themselves and their own religious freedom. Other accounts in this text of special Jain images that are damaged, stolen, or destroyed by the Muslims similarly reflect this very inward-looking mood of the Jain community at this point in its history. Jinaprabhasuri's account of Kanyanayana and its Mahavira image, which I mentioned earlier, is actually an autobiographical statement. In that account Jinaprabhasuri manages to impress the Muslim Sultan and win his respect. He then is able to convince the Sultan to return to the Jain community an important image of Mahavira that an invading Muslim army had once captured and taken to Delhi. The account then continues with a veritable catalogue of the important orders the Sultan issued granting religious privileges to the Jain community. Its focus never goes beyond this simple goal of maintaining for the Jains the right to continue practicing their religion.

The second story I translated concerns a much earlier period in history, although it still deals with foreign invaders. It is about the sack of the city of Vallabhi, King Siladitya's capital. The story of the sack of Vallabhi is told in a number of sources, usually tacked on to the biography of the Jain monk Mallavadin.[10] In a somewhat complicated sequence of events we hear how a merchant Ranka becomes exceedingly angry at King Siladitya. Ranka himself is a thief; he has stolen a magic elixir that a wandering mendicant had entrusted to his keeping, and with it he has become very rich. His daughter and the princess become friends and the princess begins to covet some of Ranka's daughter's jewels. When Ranka refuses to give them to the princess, the king is furious and simply takes them anyway. In retaliation Ranka bribes the Huns on Siladitya's borders and they come and sack Vallabhi. All accounts agree that the Jain community for the most part is able to flee the conflagration; they also agree that the Jain images make it to safety, flying through the air to settle in less troubled places. The King Siladitya is killed, as are most of the invading troops.

There is an interesting and diverse medieval collection of biographies and stories that has been published under the title of the *Puratanaprabandhasamgraha* (1936:82-83). What is particularly striking about this version of the story is that the text makes a clear attempt to connect the sack of the city with unrighteousness, but at the same time it distances the Jains from any role in the sins that have led to the fall of city. It also brings the account "up-to-date" by identifying the invaders, Huns, or *yavanas*, with contemporary Muslim invaders, stating for example, that it was the army camp of the Patasahi, the Sultan, that was on the move. In this brief story the conflict becomes one that takes place between Hindus and Muslims, with the Jains playing a very minor role indeed. In the *Puratanaprabandhasamgraha* we will see that it is Hindus who sin and thus usher in their own destruction; it is a Hindu king, Siladitya, ultimately responsible for the righteousness of his kingdom and its subjects, who is left to die, and it is those sinful Hindu subjects who perish. The Jain community escapes and even the Jain images manage to escape. There could be no clearer statement of how the fate of the Jains was separate from the fate of the other subjects in the kingdom. In addition, this account gives a poignant description of how the Jains, even when they tried to intervene at the request of the king, could not secure the safety of the kingdom. The fate of the Jains is totally separate from the fate of other groups in the same city, and the Jains cannot muster any of their rituals or magic formulas to serve the interests of the state. Below is a translation of the sack of Vallabhi according to the *Puratanaprabandhasamgraha*.

Now as the Sultan moved his camp, one Muslim demigod approached the city of Vallabhi. There was no way it could get in. After a few days it noticed one of the ramparts was unoccupied and settled down there. Soon after that, some poor Brahmin sent his wife out to get some ghee from the milk of a cow so that he might perform his daily agnihotra. She was despondent and became possessed by that demigod, and she brought her husband the urine of a donkey instead of ghee. He used it for his oblation. In the morning when he looked at the fire he saw gold there. And he continued to sacrifice in this way day after day. But his wife told her friend, gradually the news got out, and everywhere in the city people began to make their oblations with donkey urine. In this way the city became godless, and the Muslim demigods spread out over the whole city. Then the Muslim army arrived on the scene.

The Glorious Devacandrasuri was asleep one night in Vallabhi, and he saw before him some goddess, a twelve-year old girl. He asked her, "Who are you, lovely one? Tell me, you who are like a goddess, why do you weep?" "O Blessed One, I see the destruction of the city of Vallabhi, and this will be the sign: the water that your monks will get in their bowls when they go for alms will turn into blood. The monks should go and stay at that place where they see the blood turn back into water." Having found out who that girl was, the Jain monk told the Jain community and the king what she had said. Hearing the news, some of the Jain community left the city.

The king said, " Blessed One! You must remedy the situation with your own demigods!" And so the monk sent two demigods. The Muslim demigods grabbed them and beat them up. They kept them prisoner for three days. The monk too was incapacitated.[11] After the three days the Sultan moved his army and the demigods were released. They told the monk everything that had happened to them. The monk left the city. The king remained. On the full moon day of the month of Asvini, at the time of the chariot festival, the Glorious Mahavira went to Sirimalapura; Rsabhanatha went to Kasadraha; the Glorious Parsvanatha went to Harija; and the Lord of Vallabhi went to Satrunjaya. After that all of the Muslims were thrown into battle and defeated by Ranka.

This brief account makes use of a number of concepts that are familiar in medieval Indian religion. We see that a ritual impurity allows the bad demon to enter the city in the first place, reminiscent of the way in which Kali enters King Nala in the famous *Mahabharata* story or Old Age enters King Yayati in the *Padmapurana, Bhumikhanda*, chap. 77. The city goddess also weeps when the city is to be destroyed, and a ritual vessel bleeds, something that, as we have seen above, was said to have happened in Nepal royal chronicles, signaling danger to the realm. But despite these similarities and the use of familiar concepts, I know of no statement in medieval literature that is as frank an admission of incapability as this one, in which we hear how Jain deities simply could not defeat Muslim demigods, and how a Jain monk when asked by a king could not save his kingdom. This is a very different story from other medieval accounts of monks and kings; Siddhasena, for example, can make whole armies for a king whose kingdom is threatened just by using some magic mustard seeds. Here the Jains can do no more than follow their holy images into exile, leaving politics and kings for others to control.

## Conclusions

In this short paper I have used two brief accounts from medieval Jain story collections to show how the pan-Indian belief that correct religious practice would secure the safety of the king and his subjects becomes scaled down to a more limited relationship between the deity and the community of the faithful. The process, I believe, can also be documented in the language of medieval Jain inscriptions and hymns. Where once inscriptions prayed for the welfare of all living beings, now they pray for the welfare of the Jain kingdom.[12]

There is a lengthy inscription in a temple to Srisuparsvanatha in Jaisalmer, dated 1712 A.D. (v.s. 1869). The inscription describes the consecration of a temple erected under the rule of a Vaisnava king. In all its complexity and innuendo the inscription is a remarkable, though somewhat obscure, statement of the vagaries of religious patronage for medieval Jains. While the king ultimately experiences a religious conversion during the dedication ceremonies, the author of the inscription, Nagavijaya, who was also one of the two monks who performed the ceremonies, ends his inscription with a lengthy petition to all the gods that basically ignores the king and his rule. What Nagavijaya asks of the gods is instructive in the context of our discussion. In a series of verses he asks the various deities for their protection of the samgha, that is, the religious community, and not the king or his state. He then asks for the protection of the family that has donated the money for the temple building, and then finally, as if in an afterthought, and very much in a reversal of traditional priorities, he asks for the welfare of all people (Nahar vol.III 1929: 46-51.)

There are other late medieval inscriptions that show the Jain concern with the exclusive welfare of their community. An inscription of 1606 A.D. (Samvat 1663) found in the cemetery at Jaisalmer records the setting up of a pair of footprints at the stupa of a monk. The prayers in the inscription are directed towards the samgha, the Jain community of the faithful, as the author of the inscription declares, "May these footprints last for a long time, as long as the sun and moon shall shine, and may the glorious samgha prosper" (Nahar 1929:128-130). Similarly the inscription in the Adinatha temple at Jaisalmer asks a benediction for those who follow the Jain way (Nahar 1929:137-138).

In addition, the texts on monastic behavior, cited earlier in this paper, could also be used to strengthen my hypothesis that the medieval Jain community was concerned above all with safeguarding its monks and nuns and securing freedom to worship. The commentaries to these monastic texts repeatedly stress gains made for the sake of the *kula* or *gana*, the specific groups to which a monk belonged. It is this same narrowing of perspective that I have sought to find in the stories translated here.

I suspect that the Jains as a minority group, often unable to secure total royal patronage and mass popular conversions, were better prepared to make this accommodation to reality--substituting a concern for the welfare of their own community for an earlier concern for the welfare of the state--than were other religious groups in medieval India. This readiness, in turn might well help account for the success of individual Jain monks like Jinaprabhasuri and Hiravijayasuri at royal courts in late medieval times. These monks would have no longer aimed to convert kings to their own religious beliefs as had Hemacandra or Siddhasena before them; instead they were enormously popular ambassadors who succeeded in winning for their own group important privileges and the promise that they might continue to worship unmolested.

## Notes

1. There is considerable literature on the close relationship between the king/royal power and image and temple worship or religion in general in medieval India. See for example Appadurai 1978; Inden 1978; Inden 1981; Kennedy 1976; Kulke 1978; Shankar 1984; and the various works by Burton Stein. Richard Davis has recently written several papers on the capture of images in medieval India, in which he stresses the ritual function of royal images; to capture the image of a rival king's main god or goddess was in effect to capture the power of the rival king, so closely were kingly function and royal image associated. See Davis 1994:161-179.

The importance of images of the king's clan goddess as the embodiment of the king's power must surely have its parallel in the images that are transmitted in the various sectarian groups of medieval India. Examples are the "svarupas" of Krsna amongst the Vallabhas and the Hayagriva image Ramanuja is said to have received from Sarasvati in Kashmir that is said to be still worshiped in the Sri Brahmatantra Parakala Mutt. On this image see Desikachmarya 1949: 4-5.

Much has also been written by scholars of Sri Lanka on the issue of Buddhism as a state religion and the concept of nationhood expressed in the Buddhist chronicles. A representative sample of articles appeared in Smith 1978; see also Lingat 1989. My own opinion is that the scholarship to date has invariably placed too great an emphasis on the uniqueness of the Sri Lankan case and the role there of Buddhism as a state religion. I think that we need to review the evidence for medieval India itself so that we may be in a better position to judge Sri Lankan treatment of these issues.

There has been insufficient attention paid to Jain parallels to the material in the Sri Lankan Buddhist chronicles, for example, which suggest a pan-Indian context for many of the specific incidents and the general ideas in the Sri Lankan chronicles. As a single example I cite the early career of King Dutthagamani. The King Duttha-gamani begins his career as a self-imposed exile, angered at his father's refusal to fight his enemies. Greenwald 1978 stressed the un-Buddhist nature of the king's anger and determination to fight. One might also have stressed the totally con-ventional nature of this break with his father and manifestation of his own future greatness. It is not so much that King Dutthagamani is acting in an anti-Buddhist manner, but that he is acting in a totally prescribed way for an Indian king. The Jain case makes this clearer. There is an exact parallel to the early career of Duttha-gamani in the Jain account of the Gujarati King Ama, which forms part of the biography of the Jain monk Bappabhattisuri in the fourteenth century *Prabandha-kosa*. Like the young prince Dutthagamani, the future King Ama is disgusted with his father who refuses to allow the young boy to fight the father's enemies, and the prince leaves in anger and begins his own period of self-imposed exile. I have translated the biography of Bappabhattisuri (Granoff 1994b).

Jain parallels also exist to the association of the capital city with the monastic community that authors single out for special note in the Sri Lankan chronicles. The Sri Lankan chronicles describe the sacred territory of the Buddhist community as including the capital, something that modern scholars adduce as proof of their intention to make of Buddhism a state religion. They ignore, however, what we may learn of the very founding of the dynasty of the Capotkatas in Gujarat, in which the first act of the king after ritually demarcating his capital city was to invite a Jain monk and offer him the kingdom. The king then builds Jain temples, one of which is adjacent to the palace. The account in the *Prabandhacintamani* of Meru-tunga then concludes by saying that the kingdom was thus established with the protection of Jain mantras and was therefore invincible to its enemies (Tawney 1901: 18-19).

The reconsideration of the Sri Lankan chronicles in the light of such Jain parallels is not without serious implications for our understanding of medieval India on a number of issues; Bechert in his article in Smith 1978 argues forcefully that history writing did not exist in continental India and that it was only this sense of national/religious mission that we see in Sri Lanka that prompted the reworking of earlier monastic chronicles into the true "history" writing of the *Mahavamsa* there. If we can document the same ideology in these mediaeval Jain accounts of kings and monks, we must either revise our notion of history, and allow that the Jains also wrote history, or search for other factors to account for why they did not write "history." While it is not my intention in this short paper to review the scholarship on the concept of a "state religion" in medieval India, I will try to show that there was a strong pan-Indian tendency to regard all religion--as state religion, if by that we mean that a given practice of a specific religion was said to insure the safety of the kingdom, and, conversely, it was maintained that political and material disasters were occasioned by any failure to follow the dictates of that religion.

2. This does not correspond to anything in that chapter in the edition of Pandita Hrishikeshashastri, Varanasi: Chaukhamba Press, 1975.

3. The hymn is put in the mouth of the mother of Neminatha, and tradition has attributed it to Santisuri of the eleventh century, although this attribution is by no means without question. See the comments of the editor of the *Sripanca-pratikramanasutra* 1925: 337, which also contains the hymn.

4. See n. 1 for some comments on this account.

5. On Siddhasena see Granoff 1989b: 329-384 and Granoff 1990a: 261-304. On Kumarapala see Bühler 1936.

6. I have discussed this text in an article on responses to Muslim iconoclasm in India (Granoff 1991b). In many ways the present paper continues the investigation that I began in that earlier article.

7. For a translation of this acccount from the Jain *Vividhatirthakalpa* see Granoff and Shinohara 1992.

8. See for example the biography of Arya Khapatacarya that I have translated (Granoff 1990b: 153-156) and my article on this biography, Granoff 1989a: 67-99. See also Granoff and Shinohara 1992: 75-80.

9. A summary of this story was published in Granoff 1995: 72-74.

10. See Granoff 1989a: 67-99 for a discussion of the biography and Granoff 1990b: 166-172 for translations of two versions of Mallavadin's biography. A translation of the sack of Vallabhi may be found in Tawney 1901: 172-175.

11. *Userir jata*: this is completely obscure and I am guessing at the meaning.

12. A convenient example of an inscription that prays for the welfare of all living beings may be found in Vijayamurti 1952: 20.

# 7

# Changing Roles for Miraculous Images in Medieval Chinese Buddhism: A Study of the Miracle Image Section in Daoxuan's "Collected Records"

*Koichi Shinohara*

## Introduction

*The question and the nature of sources*

In this paper I would like to discuss how the tradition of miraculous image stories developed in medieval China, paying attention to the roles or functions of these images and image stories.[1] I shall focus my attention on a collection of 50 miraculous image stories that constitute the middle part of the miracle story collection "Collected Records of Buddhist Records in China" (*Ji shenzhou sanbao gantong lu*, JSSGL) compiled in 664 by Daoxuan (596-667)(Taisho.2106: 52.404-435).[2] At least in the eyes of Daoxuan and his collaborator Daoshi (?-668?), this collection must have contained the best known examples of medieval Chinese Buddhist stories about miraculous images. Of course Daoxuan's collection is by no means comprehensive. Although one may argue that the collection of 50 or so stories gathered here by Daoxuan and Daoshi later became the normative collection of miracle stories, these stories may not adequately describe the roles or functions of miraculous images in Chinese Buddhism up to the time Daoxuan and Daoshi assembled their collections. Accordingly, the findings of this exploratory examination need to be interpreted in light of this basic limitation. What we hope to offer here is a set of hypotheses; our suggestions need to be reexamined in the context of a larger and more comprehensive study based on a wider range of sources.[3]

The procedure of my analysis is to move from a careful study of "stories" about miraculous images to "history", speculation about the historical circumstances that surrounded the images themselves or, more specifically, the "historical" circumstances that led to the evolution of these "stories." At least for the purpose of the present study, the "reality" of miraculous images is that of the stories about them that circulated in society. What is attempted here is a speculative history of such miraculous image stories, treated as a tradition, in medieval Chinese Buddhism.

Daoxuan drew from a variety of sources in compiling his comprehensive miracle story collection; for many of the stories it is possible to identify the sources upon which Daoxuan's version has been based and hypothetically to reconstruct the stages through which at least certain parts of the collection were put together (Shinohara 1990, 1991a, 1991c). Even in the case of their miraculous image collections, for which Daoxuan and Daoshi left fewer clues as to the immediate sources of their stories, it is often possible to trace the evolution of the stories by collecting parallel versions in existing sources.

It is, however, important to keep in mind that only two miraculous image stories (nos. 3, 7 in the Appendix below) can be traced further back than the "Biographies of Eminent Monks" (Gaoseng zhuan, GSZ; Taisho.2059: 50.322-424), compiled around 531, while the incidents reported in these stories (e.g., nos. 2, 3, 5, 7, 11, 13, 29, 29a) often bear much earlier dates. GSZ stories, or biographies, were based on earlier sources, though we can seldom identify the specific sources that Huijiao used, except for those biographies that Huijiao took from the "Collected Notes on The Translation of Buddhist Scriptures" (Chu sanzang ji ji. Taisho.2145:55.1-114) or the "Biographies of Famous Monks" (Mingseng zhuan, MSZ; 513), and in the case of the MSZ only if the biography happens to be among those preserved in the Japanese summary of this work (Meisodensho, Xu zangjing:134, 1-35; Shinohara 1988: 129-130). We assume that the miraculous image stories in GSZ biographies often had long histories behind them, and that some of these stories might well have appeared around the time of the reported events, though others were undoubtedly "invented" much later. Unfortunately, the evolution of the stories during the often long period between the occurrence of the miraculous events and the compilation of the GSZ generally remains obscure.

Image miracle stories appear in a variety of sources that were compiled during the period between the GSZ (531) and the JSSGL (664). In addition to reproducing GSZ stories about miraculous images, these sources introduced (1) new details for GSZ stories, describing events that occurred earlier than the compilation of the GSZ, (2) new stories about the miraculous images mentioned in the GSZ, reporting miraculous events that are said to have occurred after its compilation, (3) miracle stories about other images, describing events that are said to have occurred before the compilation of the GSZ but not reported there, and (4) miracle stories about other images, describing events that are said to have occurred after the compilation of the GSZ and consequently not mentioned in the GSZ. By comparing these diverse types of image miracle stories carefully, I hope to develop a variety of very broad hypotheses regarding the evolution of image miracle stories in medieval China. If it is possible to determine that a certain type of image miracle stories was popular in a given period or a location, we might then be able to speculate about the role or function of miraculous images and miraculous image stories in that chronological and geographical context.

*Evolution of image miracle stories in medieval Chinese Buddhism: An overview*

Possibly the earliest and certainly the most elaborate stories of image miracles developed in medieval China around a group of miraculously discovered images; these images were believed to have been among those king Asoka had produced centuries earlier in India (Shinohara 1992: 201-218). These stories about Asoka images probably evolved in China as an offshoot of the better known stories about Asoka *stupa*s or relics.[4] The story that king Asoka constructed 84,000 *stupa*s appears to have been introduced to China through the *Asokavadana*, first translated by An Faqin in 306 and then by Sanghabhadra in 512.[5] Earlier stories about Asoka images report that the images were discovered in the fourth century, sometime after the appearance of An Faqin's translation. It is also significant that Asoka images are generally said to have been discovered in the South (Shinohara 1988: 178-180).

In previous studies I attempted to trace how earlier records of Asoka image stories were incorporated into GSZ biographies; some other stories about miraculous images that were later believed to have also been Asoka images are found in other GSZ biographies, where they are not explicitly identified as Asoka images.[6] By the time the GSZ collection was completed around 531, a variety of stories about miraculous images had developed in Chinese Buddhism. Huijiao appears to have been keenly interested in them; many of the biographies in the "meritorious deeds" section in his collection center around stories about miraculous images of diverse kinds.

In later collections of image miracle stories Asoka image stories are given a prominent place. Stories about Asoka images dominate the beginning section of the large collection of image miracle stories that is preserved in parallel versions in Daoxuan's JSSGL (fascicle 2)(664) and Daoshi's "Jade Forest in the Garden of Buddhist Teachings" (*Fayuan zhulin,* FYZL, Taisho.2121: 53, 269-1030; 668 according to its preface). A T'ien-t'ai Buddhist universal history, "Comprehensive Annals of the Buddhas and Patriarchs" (*Fozu tongji,* FZTJ, Taisho.2035: 49, 127-476) compiled by Zhipan between 1258 and 1269 contains a short section on miraculous images (461c-462a), and this section begins with a series of stories about Asoka images.[7]

As more stories about image miracles appeared over a long period of time, the circle of miraculous Asoka images expanded. Furthermore, new miracle stories evolved around widely recognized Asoka images. Whereas earlier stories about these images centered around their discovery, new stories centered around other themes, such as predicting the fortunes of ruling dynasties.

Although Asoka image stories occupy a prominent place in collections of miraculous image stories in medieval China, it is also significant that, as the scope of these collections expanded, the origin of the majority of the images came to be described differently from those of the Asoka images. Miracle image stories appear to have developed in more than one context in medieval China, though all of these stories probably evolved under influences from India and Central Asia. I am particularly interested in the fact that many of these stories appear to have developed in the North. As we noted above, Asoka image stories appear to have developed in Southern China. I am also interested in the possibility that some of the ideas about miraculous images that first developed in the context of Northern images may have shaped the development of later stories about Asoka images.

The FZTJ passage on miraculous images continues the list into the miraculous images that were said to have been discovered in the Song period (960-1279)(49.462a). Nevertheless, I suspect that these stories became less popular after Daoxuan and Daoshi. The "meritorious deeds" section of the GSZ, compiled around 531, is devoted to the biographies of monks known for such activities as temple building and image production. This section in the GSZ and the corresponding section in its successor "Further Biographies of Eminent Monks" (*Xu Gaoseng zhuan,* XGSZ; Taisho.2060:50.425-708), first completed by Daoxuan in 645 but expanded later with additional material he prepared before his death in 667, place considerable emphasis on stories of miraculous images; some of the biographies in these collections report multiple stories about these images (Huida and Huili biographies in the GSZ and the Sengming biography in the XGSZ). In the "Song Biographies of Eminent Monks" (*Song gaoseng zhuan,* SGSZ; Taisho.2061.50.709-900), presented to the throne in 988, the size of the "meritorious deeds" section is expanded from one to three fascicles. Some stories about miraculous images similar to those found in the two earlier collections are also found in the first of these three fascicles, yet these stories occupy a much less prominent place in this expanded treatment of monks known for "meritorious deeds" from later periods.

Asoka images are distinguished by their origin that connects them to a famous and powerful secular ruler. It would be natural that the stories that developed around them in China relate them to rulers and other prominent secular figures. In such cases an Asoka image might have served as an important point around which secular rulers related to the monastic community; miracles as manifestations of the holy might have held the secular power and the monastic community together. Did other types of miraculous image stories in medieval China also highlight the close relationship between miraculous images and the ruler? A careful study of these stories might provide us with glimpses of the complex and changing patterns of this relationship.

Since around Asoka images, as typical examples of miraculous images in medieval China, there developed elaborate stories about the origin of the images, I will begin my discussion by examining the stories about the origins of miraculous images in the JSSGL. This discussion will enable us to situate the Asoka image stores as a genre within the larger context of the stories about miraculous images in medieval China; whereas Asoka image stories became increasingly stereotyped, other stories show a greater degree of diversity. Since my hypothesis is that the function of miraculous images appears to have changed over time, in discussion of other types of stories I will treat stories from the earlier periods, mostly from the Eastern Jin (265-419) and subsequent periods when China was divided between Northern and Southern dynasties, separately from those from later periods, when China was again ruled under one central power, first by the Sui (581-617) dynasty and then by the Tang (618-907). In examining earlier image stories I will pay attention to stories about the loyal patronage of miraculous images, particularly those of images predicting dynastic fortunes. I will also pay attention to the differences between Northern and Southern stories. The examination of stories from the unified period suggests that the role and function of miraculous images underwent significant changes in this new political environment.

## Origin stories

### Asoka images

Since Asoka images were believed to have been produced by king Asoka in India in the distant past, typical stories about these images begin with accounts of their miraculous discovery. My hypothesis is that images actually existed at one time in temples mentioned in these stories and that stories about them first developed around these existing images. The stories of their miraculous discovery must have served the purpose of authenticating their extraordinary status. This would imply that in each case the discovery story was the original core of the Asoka image story.

In a brief survey of Asoka image stories that I completed recently (Shinohara 1992: 201-218), I examined the Asoka image stories in the JSSGL and suggested that there were four well-known and widely accepted examples of Asoka image stories; these stories center around the two stone images at the Tongxuansi temple in Wu commandary, assigned to the Western Jin period (265-316)(story no. 3);[8] the image discovered by Gao Li under the Eastern Jin (317-419), later housed at the Changgansi temple (no. 5);[9] the image obtained by Tanyi at the Changshasi temple in Jinzhou (Eastern Jin, no. 7)[10] and the Manjusri image at the Donglinsi temple on Mt Lu, which had originally been discovered by Tao Kan (Eastern Jin, no. 13).[11]

In the version of these stories found in the JSSGL, the origin of these images is in each case traced back to the ocean or a river that pours into the ocean: the Tongxuansi image is found near the bay in Wu commandary (no. 3); Gao Li's image on a beach in Danyang (no. 2); Tanyi's image appears to have boarded a boat that changed its cargo in Guangzhou and then came up river to Jingzhou (no. 7); and Tao Kan's image appeared in the ocean near Jianyu (no. 13). In three of these cases the JSSGL story connecting the image to the ocean or the river is based directly on an earlier version found in the GSZ. In the case of the Changshasi image (no. 7), the JSSGL seems to have added a new anecdote that connects the origin of the image to the ocean; this connection does not appear in the earlier versions of this story in the MSZ and the GSZ. Over time Asoka image stories appear to have become stereotyped and details of existing stories adjusted to fit into this general pattern.[12]

In three out of the four cases a secular figure is mentioned prominently in the story of the discovery of the Asoka image: Zhu Ying in the case of the two stone images at the Tongxuansi temple (no. 3); Gao Li in the case of the golden image at the Changgansi temple (no. 5); Tao Kan in the case of the Donglinsi image in Mt. Lu (no. 13). The case of the image at the Changshasi temple (no. 7) appears to be an exception; the prominent name mentioned is that of monk Tanyi.[13] Again in three cases the specific name of a monk or a nun is given in the story of the discovery: Boni in the story of the Tongxuansi images (no. 3); Sengzhen in the story of Tao Kan's image at the Donglinsi on Mt. Lu (no. 13); and Tanyi in the story of Changshasi image (no. 7). The story of Gao Li's image (no. 5) is an exception to this general pattern.

In the story of Gao Li's image at the Changgansi temple (no. 5) it is explicitly stated that the discovery of this image's base and its halo on two later occasions was reported to the court (GSZ, 409c7,15; JSSGL, 414b4,13).

It is also said explicitly in the JSSGL version of the story that the discovery of the two stone images in Wu commandary (no. 3) was reported to the court (414a7).[14] In this case, however, Daoxuan, or his source, appears to have inserted the statement; this statement is absent in the original GSZ version (409c). The stories about the images associated with monk Tanyi (no. 7) and warrior Tao Kan (no. 13) do not mention that the discovery of the image was reported to the court. As we shall examine in further detail below, however, Tanyi's image at the Changshasi appears later to have developed a close relationship with the court. The JSSGL passages on Gao Li's image in the Changgansi (no. 5) and Tanyi's image in the Changshasi (no. 7) contain a series of stories about the relationship between the images and succeeding rulers and other prominent secular figures. These stories are curiously absent in the case of the passages on the two stone images at the Tongxuansi (no. 3) and Tao Kan's image that was later moved to the Donglinsi at Mt. Lu by Huiyuan (no. 13).

These details suggest that the typical examples of Asoka image stories evolved around a complex and changing pattern of relationships between secular power and the Buddhist community. Originally, these stories might have developed without a close relationship to the court. It is local secular figures and monks who play central roles in these discovery stories. Tao Kan must have known Sengzhen at the Hanqisi in Wuchang, to whom he sent the image he discovered in Guangzhou; he appears to have had an earlier connection to Wuchang. Zhu Ying took the nun Boni of the Dongyunsi temple when he went out to welcome the stone images. The secular figure who played the central role in the discovery of the image turned to a monk or a nun, and the image was placed in a local temple.[15]

In all four cases the image is said to have indicated its choice of the community or the temple in which it was to be housed. The two stone images that appeared in a bay at the Wu Commandary refused to come ashore when a local medium or Daoists called for it; only when Zhuying, Boni of the Dongyunsi temple, and a few other Buddhists came to the shore did the images float in quietly (no. 3). When the carriage carrying Gao Li's image came to the street corner in front of the Changgansi temple, the ox pulling it refused to go further, and when the driver let the ox go as it wished it went directly to the Changgansi temple (no. 5). The Changshasi image appeared in response to Tanyi's ardent prayer; according to the earlier MSZ (7Ba14-17) and GSZ (356a4-7) accounts, when the image appeared in the Northern suburb of Jingzhou, 100 monks of the Bomasi temple first attempted and failed to bring the image to their temple; when three disciples of Tanyi arrived the image became light and they could move it easily to the Changshasi temple (no. 7). When Tao Kan attempted to move the image he had earlier discovered and placed at the Hanqisi to a new location in Jingzhou, the image became heavy and the boat on which the image was placed sank; when Huiyuan prayed for it after a new temple, Donglinsi, was built for him at Mt. Lu, the image moved to him miraculously (no. 13). Furthermore, in two cases (stories nos. 7 and 13) the temple is explicitly said to have been recently built. Asoka images appear to have been closely associated with specific temples and served to enhance the prestige of these temples. Each of these temples must have enjoyed the patronage of local political leaders, and it was perhaps this relationship that was reflected in the references to local figures and monks (nuns) of local temples that appear in typical Asoka image stories.

In the two cases of the Changgansi and Changshasi images the JSSGL devotes a long passage chronicling a close relationship between the image and prominent rulers of succeeding dynasties (stories nos. 5 and 7). The images, which were believed to have been originally produced by the pro-Buddhist king Asoka, appear to have attracted the attention of the rulers and thus to have become "royal images" of some kind. The nature of the stories about these images then changed rather noticeably. We will discuss this issue in greater detail below as we turn to later stories associated with these images.

## Other miraculous images

The majority of the 50 miracle image stories collected in the JSSGL note the origin of the images concerned rather carefully. The table of contents in the Taisho edition of the JSSGL identifies the stories in terms of the ruling dynasties; in most cases they are the dynasties under which the discovery or production of the image is said to have taken place.[16] Of the 50 stories included in Daoxuan's collection, the first 27 stories are attributed to dynasties earlier than the Liang (502-557), under which Huijiao produced the GSZ.[17]

In addition to the widely recognized Asoka image stories discussed above, there are 18 cases in which the origin of the image is described in the form of miraculous discovery.[18] In another 18 cases the circumstances under which the image was produced are described explicitly and often in considerable detail.[19] A third category consists of two types: sometimes, the origin of the image is explicitly said to be unknown;[20] in other cases the stories reproduced does not say anything about the origin of the image.[21]

In contrast to Asoka image stories, where we can detect a distinct tendency toward sterotypification, these other origin stories show a greater degree of diversity. Let me review the range of this diversity briefly.

It is striking that the majority of these stories fail to mention the specific Buddhas and Bodhisattvas that the images represent. While two of the four typical Asoka image stories discussed above mention explicitly what the images represented,[22] only 10 of the remaining 46 stories identify the image in terms of what they represented.[23] With the exception of story no. 31, even in stories that identify the image in terms of the Buddha or Bodhisattva represented, this identification does not play a significant role in the plot of the story.[24] The miraculous qualities described in the story are attributed primarily to the image itself rather than to the Buddha or the Bodhisattva it represents. Perhaps this is why the stories are more concerned with properties that belong to the image itself than with the Buddha or Bodhisattva supposedly represented, focusing their attention on questions such as who made the image (e.g., king Asoka), how the image was discovered, and when and where miracles occurred.

By far the largest majority of the images described in these stories are explicitly said to have been "golden" or "metal" (*jin*) images.[25] But some are stone images,[26] and in one case the image might have consisted of a piece of translucent stone (no. 38 [Sui]) or of iron ore (nos. 34 [Nothern Zhou]);[27] some of these images appear to have been carved on rock cliffs or large pieces of rock.[28] In four cases the image is said to have been wooden;[29] in three cases the story centers around a painting;[30] in three cases the story does not make the material of the image clear.[31] Some stories center around footprints of the Buddha (nos. 42, 43, 44 [Tang]) and one story concerns a set of letters carved on stone (no. 42). These findings may be compared to the earlier observation that three of the four typical examples of Asoka images discussed above are said to have been golden, or metal, images and in only one case (story no. 3 about the two images at Wu commandary) are the images said to have been stone images.

Of the 50 stories collected here the first 35 stories are attributed to dynasties earlier than Sui (581-617). Senglang's image at Mt. Tai, attributed to the Western Jin dynasty (265-316; no. 4),[32] and the image Dao'an produced in Xiangyang (no. 6) as well as the image of Gautama as a prince in a reflective pose (no. 12), both attributed to the Eastern Jin (317-419), were all closely affiliated with Northern dynasties. In addition, seven other stories within this group of 35 earlier stories are listed as stories of Northern dynasties. Of these seven, two stories (nos. 14 and 31) name the Northern Wei (386-534); two stories (nos. 15 and 16) the Northern Liang (412-439); three stories (nos. 33, 34, and 35) give the Northern Zhou (557-581).[33] Four of these Northern stories (nos. 4, 12, 14, and 34) contain accounts of miraculous discovery; five (nos. 6, 15, 16, 31, and 33) mention the circumstances of production of the images, and one (no. 35) states explicitly that the origin of the image is unknown.

It is notable that five of the seven images attributed to Northern dynasties (nos. 14, 15, 16, 33, 34) are explicitly said to have been stone or rock images; in one case the image is said to have been a golden (or metal) image (no. 31, 420a20), and in another it is said to have been an old wooden image (nos. 35, 420c22-23).

In a few cases the images are said in this collection to have been Asoka images, though they are not so identified in the earlier versions that are found in the GSZ (nos. 2, 29b, and possibly 34). In other cases, of images not said to have been of Asokan origin, there are considerable similarities between the story in question and the typical Asoka image stories discussed above. For example, the miraculous image discovered by a daughter of Zhou Ji (no. 8 [Eastern Jin]) is said to have come floating on water, emitting golden light; Sun Yanceng's wife Wang Huicheng discovered a shining golden image and a base, which bore an inscription stating that the image was produced by Faxin and Sengxing of the Waguansi temple in the sixth year of the Jianwu period (confused date)(no. 20 [Song]). Daoxuan claims that he saw with his own eyes the image that had been discovered at the bank of the Li river in Yongzhou, bearing an inscription dating its origin to the twentieth (or the first) year of the the Jianyuan period of [Former] Qin (384 or 365)(no. 47 [Tang]).

But images are also discovered around the palace (nos. 2 [Southern Wu], 11 [Eastern Jin]), in a temple (no. 19 [Song]), in fields (no. 18, 21 [Song]), and in mountains (nos. 34 [Northern Zhou], 39 [Sui], 40 [Tang]) or given by a Brahman to a layman in a forest (no. 11 [Eastern Jin]).[34]

In one case (no. 14 [Yuan Wei]), the appearance of a rock image in Liangzhou in Northwestern China was predicted by Liu Sahe. The story of the rock image in Qinzhou, again in the North in present Shanxi province (no. 48 [Tang]), bears some resemblance to this story about Liu Sahe's image: the image suddenly sent forth light and illumined the forest and valley.

Sometimes the images are said to have been sent or brought from distant imaginary kingdoms or kingdoms in India or Central Asia (nos. 8 [Eastern Jin], 28 [Liang], 37, 38 [Sui]). It may be possible to see some remote connection between these stories and the idea of Asoka images. In the story of the image given by a Brahman to Wu Cangying (no. 12), the Western origin of the image is indicated indirectly by the story about the famous pilgrim Faxian (339?-420?) and the statement that the image was given to Wu Cangying by a Brahman.

In the majority of cases the location of the image is carefully noted. Exceptions include story no. 8 (Eastern Jin, where it is explicitly stated that the image had been lost, though its halo still exists in the Zhang family, 416c12); the series of stories nos. 18, 19 [?], 20, 21 (all of which are said to record events that occurred during the Yuanjia period of the Song, or 424-453, and may well have been taken from the same source); and no. 37 (which speaks of "the present temple" without giving its name, 421b1). Images were usually placed in temples; in some cases they are said to be located in villages (nos. 40, 47 [Tang]); the rock images described in nos. 14 [Yuan Wei] and 48 [Tang] were not moved, though a temple building was erected later at the sight of Liu Sahe's image.

In the majority of cases the name of a layperson who played the central role in the discovery of the image is mentioned.[35] In two cases the central layperson is a woman (no. 8 [Eastern Jin], 20 [Song]). In four cases the name of a monk or a nun is given as the central figure in the discovery of the image.[36]

Early Asoka image stories probably influenced the evolution of some of the other miraculous image stories in medieval China. This influence might have focused attention on the question of the origin of miraculous images and stimulated the appearance of a variety of miracle discovery stories.[37]

It is also likely, moreover, that a variety of other influences shaped many of the miraculous image stories in medieval China. This review of the origin stories suggests that the stories about miraculous images carved on a rock or a cliff may have originated in the North, as contrasted with the Southern origin of the Asåoka image stories. Later medieval Chinese traditions of miraculous image stories might have evolved as these originally disparate traditions were brought together into a coherent whole.

### Stories about miracles not associated with the origin of the images: stories of royal images

Asoka images were clearly identified as a distinctive group and distinguished from the large number of other miraculous images that appear in existing sources; as a way of authenticating this special status, the stories about the Asoka images describe their miraculous origin in considerable detail. Over the years a distinct pattern of Asoka image discovery stories appears to have developed that included a variety of idiosyncratic details.[38]

Later sources such as the JSSGL, however, also frequently report miraculous events that are said to have occurred later in the temples where the images were housed. These stories indicate that larger traditions of miracle stories developed around Asoka images. The nature of these later miracles appears to have been less closely determined by the identity of these images as Asoka images than was the case with the discovery stories. There is a greater diversity among these later stories, though certain *topoi* are found frequently, such as the image miraculously escaping fire and other calamities, protecting the community around it from invading troops, or predicting dynastic fortunes. I believe that these later stories reflect the roles that these images played in the Buddhist community over extended periods of time.

As we noted above, later sections of the Changgansi (no. 5) and Changshasi (no. 7) image stories in the JSSGL contain similar stories about the images' miraculous power to predict the future. These stories are strikingly absent in the two other cases of the Wu commandary (no. 3) and Mt. Lu (no. 13) images. Gao Li's image housed in the Changgansi and, even more notably, Tanyi's image in Changshasi appear to have developed close relationships with succeeding dynasties in the area and become their "royal images"; their close relationship to the rulers of these dynasties is reflected in the stories of later miracles that these images were said to have performed. Such a relationship appears to have been absent in the case of the other two Asoka images.

This relationship was not confined to the cases of Asoka images; similar miracle stories are told about images whose origins were believed to have had no relationship to king Asoka.[39] I have summarized elsewhere in some detail the series of miracle stories describing the interaction between the Changgansi and Changshasi images and the rulers of the succeeding dynasties in their respective regions (Shinohara 1988: 160-163 and 1992: 154-179). In this paper I would like to examine the nature of these stories a little more closely by placing them in the larger context of related stories that are told of other miraculous images collected in the JSSGL.[40]

*Emperor Wu\* of the Liang dynasty*

The famous pro-Buddhist emperor Wu\* of the Liang dynasty (r. 502-549) figures prominently in many of the image miracle stories in the JSSGL. I begin my exploration of the relationship between miraculous images and ruling dynasties by focusing on such passages.

Emperor Wu\* is not the earliest ruler in these miracle stories who showed interest in these images. The discovery story of the Changgansi image (no. 5), best known in the version found in the Huida biography of the GSZ, mentions explicitly that the discovery of the image and its accessories was reported to the court. Emperor Jianwen (371-372) of the ruling Eastern Jin dynasty is mentioned in this context (JSSGL: 414b13; GSZ: 409c6). The Changshasi image (no. 7) is said to have shed tears toward the end of the Taishi period of the Song dynasty (465-472), foretelling the demise of emperor Ming (r. 465-472). Northern Liang ruler Juqu Mengsun, who held power from 401 to 433, is mentioned in stories nos. 15 and 16. But emperor Wu\* is the first and most noticeable ruler who is mentioned in a large number of miracles stories in the JSSGL (nos. 5, 6, 7, 28, 29, 30, 32, 38); in addition he plays a central role in many of these stories (nos. 7, 28, 29).[41]

The discovery story of the Changgansi temple (no. 5) is followed by a long series of later stories: the section begins with a story about the monk Huisui, who obtained the temple's permission to make copies of the image by causing it miraculously to shine and turn toward the west, but the substance of this section consists of passages chronicling the interaction between the image and succeeding rulers. The first emperor who is mentioned in this long section is the emperor Wu* of the Liang dynasty, who is said to have added deities and bodhisattvas around the halo of the image.

Emperor Wu* also appears in the long section describing the miracles of the Changshasi image (no. 7). In the second year of the Yongyuan period of Qi dynasty (500), the image moved outside of the hall and appeared to want to go down the stairs, surprised the two monks who saw it, and then returned to the hall. This appears to have been taken as a sign predicting the rise of emperor Wu* to the throne. The central event in this account of the relationship between the image and emperor Wu* is the arrival of the image in the capital city Jinling in the year 532. Details of the image's visit are recorded: the emperor went eighteen miles outside of the city to welcome it; after a great feast the image was brought to the Tongtaisi temple, where the hall was specially decorated for the image. When emperor Wu* came to the Tongtaisi several years later, the image shone, illuminating the scenery around it for a long time during the night. When the Tongtaisi temple burnt down, the hall that housed the image escaped damage. In 548 the image sweated greatly; in the 11th month of that year Hou Jing's rebellion occurred. After the rebels had been pacified, a monk at the Changshasi brought the image back to the temple. The Changshasi image appears to have become closely associated with the Liang dynasty and its ruling Xiao family from this point on; it had become a "royal image" of some kind. The relationship is focused around the idea of an image that predicts the fortunes of ruling dynasties, an important theme in miraculous image stories in medieval China.[42]

Emperor Wu* plays a prominent role in several stories about the non-Aśokan miracle images collected in the JSSGL. Story no. 28 begins by reporting that emperor Wu* dreamt of a sandalwood image entering his kingdom on the eighth day of the first month of the first year of the Tianjian period (502). Consequently an annoucement was made calling for volunteers to go on an expedition looking for the image.

The story about this image, which is said to have been placed at the Zhihuansi (Jetavana) temple, mentions two sources: the "Records of Buddha's travels in India"(*Fo you tianzhu ji*) and the two-fascicle version of "King Udayana scripture" (*Youtian wang jing*).[43] The Buddha went up to the heaven of 33 gods and preached to his mother. King Udayana sent 32 carpenters and sandalwood and requested Mahamaudgalyayana to use his supernatural power to produce an image of the Buddha ("*tu foxiang*", "draw a picture of the Buddha's appearance"?). Mahamaudgalyayana accomplished the mission and returned with the sitting image, five feet in height, which was placed in the Zhihuansi temple and has remained in worship, we learn, up until the time of the story-teller. Emperor Wu* wanted to bring this image to his kingdom.

General He Qian, Xie Wenhua, and 88 others responded to the announcement calling for volunteers. When they arrived and presented the request, the king of Sravasti refused to send away his heavenly image; instead he ordered another image (or picture, "*tu*") to be carved by 32 carpenters. When this image was completed, it sent forth light, fine rain came down, and an extraordinary fragrance pervaded the air. The "King Udayana scripture" is quoted again: "When the original image disappears, the second image will appear and widely and greatly benefit sentient beings." He Qian and others brought this second image across tens of thousands of miles, overcoming great difficulties. A miraculous encounter with a monk and a dream of a deity are mentioned. On the fifth day of the fourth month of the tenth year of the Tianjian period (505) He Qian's group arrived at the capital city of Yangdu. The emperor, accompanied by a large number of officials, traveled 40 miles outside of the capital city and welcomed the image to the Dajidian hall in the palace. A feast was held, monks were ordained, and a large number of criminals were pardoned. Weapons were transformed into lotus flower decorations around *stupas*. The emperor ate only vegetarian meals.

Emperor Wu* passed away in the third year of the Taiqing period (549); the prince of Xiangdong reestablished the dynasty in Jiangling, changing the era name to Chengsheng ("Inheriting the holy"). The new emperor sent for the image in Yangdu and placed and worshiped it in Chengguangdian ("Inheriting the light") hall in the new capital city of his dynasty Jingzhou. In the eighth year of the Later Liang dynasty, the Damingsi temple was built in Jingling to the north of the city. The image was then sent there, where it still existed in Daoxuan's time.

Story no. 38 is about a small transparent stone image, 9 inches tall and 5 inches in diameter, which is said to have been brought by an Indian or Central Asian monk during the Taiqing period (547-550) toward the end of emperor Wu*'s reign. When Hou Jing's rebellion occurred, the image was placed atop the image in the Xilinsi temple in Mt. Lu.

Like the stories about the Changgansi (no. 5) and Changshasi (no. 7) Asoka images, these two stories of miraculous images emphasize the fact that the images in question were brought from the West, i.e., Central Asia or India. This cluster of stories suggests that emperor Wu* was believed to have shown particular interest in miraculous images that arrived from India or Central Asia, and at least in one case played an active role in obtaining one. In another case the emperor played an important role in bringing a miraculous image of Asokan origin to the capital city.

Emperor Wu* is also said to have produced new images and worshiped them. Story no. 29 is about the golden image, eighty feet tall, at the Guangzhaisi temple; the image was made in the beginning of the Tianjian period (502-520) when emperor Wu* donated his residence to be turned into this temple. At the time of casting, [pieces of] copper filling 15 carriages arrived miraculously, and after the image had been completed, it seemed to grow taller without changing its shape. This story also mentions the temple, called Da'aiqingsi, and its large image that emperor Wu* built for his father at Mt. Zhong. A statement to the effect that many of the Buddha images under the Liang dynasty produced miracles is followed by a long passage on the stone image in the Shan district (no. 29b). In this story the image is said to have been completed by monk Sengyou at the request of Prince Jian'an of Liang.

Story no. 30 is about the two images in gold and silver that emperor Wu* produced and placed at the Chongyundian hall. The emperor worshiped these images diligently and ceaselessly for over 50 years; the pattern of ten toes appeared on the spots where his feet touched the stone.[44]

In another story (no. 6) about the famous walking image that is said to have been produced by Dao'an at the Tanqisi temple in Xiangyang on the eighth day of the fourth month of the third year of the Ningkang period (375), the ruler of the Liang dynasty is said to have produced a bronze flower base of a massive size on the eighth day of the fourth month of the third year of the Putong period (522). After this base was decorated properly, they sent it to the site of the image [i.e., Xiangyang in the North?] along the water route. An inscription (composition by Liu Xiaoyi and caligraphy by Xiao Ziyun) was also raised. The ruler who issued the edict must have been emperor Wu*.

These stories suggest that emperor Wu* of the Liang dynasty, or at least emperor Wu* as a character in Buddhist story literature, played an important role in the development of miraculous image stories in China. In an earlier study on the long tradition of the Changgansi Asoka *stupa* stories I suggested that in these stories the image of the Liang emperor Wu*, a pro-Buddhist emperor in early medieval China, came to be overlaid on top of the image of king Asoka, the prototypical pro-Buddhist emperor in India (Shinohara 1988: 129). A similar development appears to have occurred in the case of Asoka images, and in this case the role of emperor Wu* as the Chinese counterpart to king Asoka spilled over into other stories of miraculous images. Emperor Wu* is represented as a ruler who was particularly eager to seek miraculous images that came from India, and who was also capable of producing new miraculous images in China. As I noted earlier, among the earlier accounts of their discovery, the direct relationship between typical Asoka images and the ruler appears only in the case of Gao Li's image in the Changgansi temple. We may thus conclude hypothetically that in the South, where all the earlier Asoka *stupa* and image stories appear to have originated, it was through the figure of Liang emperor Wu*, who came to be associated with some of these and other miraculous images later, that the paradigmatic pattern of relationship of the ruler to Asoka images and other miraculous images became firmly established.

*Other stories about predicting dynastic fortunes*

The idea of a royal image miraculously predicting dynastic fortunes constituted an important theme among image miracle stories in medieval China. Asoka images were not the only miraculous images about which stories about predicting the future of ruling dynasties were told. The JSSGL contains a variety of stories about other images that predicted dynastic fortunes.

As I noted above, Liu Sahe predicted the appearance of the rock image, one eighteen feet tall, in Liangzhou; this story centers around the theme of dynastic fortunes predicted by the image (story no. 14).[45] Liu Sahe predicted that when the image was complete, with all its parts in their appropriate places, there would be peace and prosperity in the world. Eighty seven years later in the first year of the Zhengguang period of the Northern Wei dynasty (520), the torso of the image appeared, but it lacked the head. The head was discovered in the first year of the rule of the Northern Zhou dynasty (557). In the first year of the Baoding period (561) emperor Wu* of this dynasty (r. 560-578), who later persecuted Buddhism, established the Ruixiangsi ("Auspicious image") temple for the image. Just before this emperor Wu* began the persecution in the Jiande period (572-578), the image's head again fell off spontaneously. The emperor made the prince [Xian] of Qi go and personally confirm this miracle.[46] The prince placed the head back on the neck of the image and stationed soldiers to guard it. But by morning the head had again fallen down. Eventually, this occurrence was interpreted as a sign of the approaching end to the dynasty. Monk [Yao] Dao'an (n.d.) wrote an inscription for this image. The persecution of Buddhism under the Northern Zhou rule did not reach this image. When the Sui dynasty came into power and opened the new Kaihuang period, the temple was reestablished. The temple still existed in Daoxuan's time. Many attempted to produce drawings of the image, but the image changed its size [and shape] and no one could capture it in a fixed drawing.[47]

Story no. 16. As we noted above, the rock image, sixty feet in height in a mountain temple, that Juqu Mengsun had produced for his mother, shed tears when he later turned against Buddhism after his son Xingguo was killed in battle. This miracle caused Mengsun to return to supporting Buddhism.

Story no. 25. The Piyeli (Vaisali) temple in Fanyu [in the present Guangdong province] had an old Southern stone image, whose origin was unknown (Soper: 58b-59a). Its shape was unusual and it was so heavy that even seventy or eighty people could not move it. During the Jianyuan period of the [Southern] Qi dynasty (479-482) a fire in the neighboring field reached the temple which stood in the direction of the wind. The ten or so nuns who were at the temple did not know what to do. Three or four among them who could not stand doing nothing tried to raise the image. The image rose easily, weighing less than the stone weight of a scale. After the image was brought out, the building was burned down. Often this image emitted light. When the area was to be invaded by soldiers, the image would suddenly shed tears and sweat would flow all over its body. People in the Lingnan area took these signs of the image as reliable oracles. Later, regional inspector Liu Jun sent the image, accompanied by a memorial, to the capital city. Daoxuan notes that the image was probably in a temple in Jiangzhou (or Jiankang) at the time he wrote this entry.

Story no. 26. Wang Zhongde, regional inspector of Xuzhou under the Song dynasty, produced a large metal image, eighty feet in height, at the Songwangsi ("King of Song") temple in Pengcheng. At times when barbarous soldiers appeared along the Northern border, or when catastrophies befell the monastic community, the image would sweat. The amount of sweat corresponded to the gravity of the difficulties. People in the commandary relied on these signs of the image as oracles. In the beginning of the Jianyuan period of [Southern] Qi (470-482) the image again sweated. In the winter of that year [Northern] Wei soldiers appeared above the Huai river. At that time a private army was organized in several commandaries around Yanzhou, and monks were forced to participate in the war against the Wei army. The Wei army reported this to their government, suggesting that these monks should be executed. At this time the image sweated greatly, and the floor of the image hall was covered with dampness. The prince of Liang, who was serving as the regional inspector of Xuzhou under the Wei, was a pious Buddhist. He came to the temple himself and ordered several people to wipe the image with a cloth. The sweat poured forth ceaselessly even as the image was being wiped. Even when several dozens of people joined in the wiping, the sweat still kept pouring forth. The prince then burned incense and, taking a piece of cloth, said, "The monks are not guilty, and I swear to protect them, so that they will not be harmed. If there is really a miraculous response to this oath, the sweat will cease when I wipe the image." Having said this, the prince wiped the image, and indeed the parts of the image that he touched became dry. The prince presented a detail report of this to the court and the monks were all forgiven by an imperial edict.

Story no. 33. Toward the end of the Northern Qi rule monk Senghu of the Lingshisi ("Miraculous stone") temple in Jinzhou is said to have discovered this image in a valley to the north of the temple (Soper: 115). On the day Jinzhou was to fall to the soldiers of the Northern Zhou dynasty (in the year 576) the image is said to have sweated.[48]

Story no. 35. The origin of the walking image [of the Buddha] at the Huayansi temple in Mt. Xian* in Xiangzhou in the present Hubei province is unknown. This old wooden image, which could have been as tall as fifty feet, was known for the beauty of its head and face. During the persecution of Buddhism under the Northern Zhou someone hid its head. The head was brought out again when the pro-Buddhist Sui dynasty came into power; the image was then decorated as before and called Lushena (Vairocana) Buddha. Just before emperor Wen of Sui died, the nose of the image started running down to its chest; gold leaf began to peel off and the parts that mucus ran over emitted light. When people went to wipe the mucus, they found no mucus; yet from a distance the mucus still appeared to be there. In the fourth month of the twenty-third year of the Zhenguan period (649), the nose again started running over the image's chest. Later emperor Taizong died, and people knew that the running of the mucus was an omen.[49] In the sixth month the nose again started running. Everyone in the region was frightened, not knowing what calamity was to follow. In the seventh month Hanshui river flooded and came inside the city wall. The water became over ten feet deep and many people drowned.[50]

Four out of the above six stories are about images in the North: the torso of the image in story no. 14 appeared in Liangzhou in the first year of the Zhengguan of the Northern Wei dynasty (520), and its head in the first year of the Northern Zhou rule (557); Juqu Mensun of the Northern Liang dynasty in the story no. 15 was in power during 401-433 in nearby Guzang; the image in story no. 33 was produced toward the end of the Northern Qi rule (550-577) in Jinzhou; the wooden image in story no. 35 in Xiangzhou is said to have existed under the Northern Zhou dynasty (557-581) and performed miracles under the Sui (581-617) and Tang (618-907). Story no. 26 is a marginal case; the image was originally produced under a southern dynasty of Song (420-479), but the main story took place when Xuzhou, where the image was located, was under Northen Wei rule. Only in one case the images are unambiguously of Southern origin: the stone image in Fanyu (no. 25). In three cases the story begins with an account of the production of the image (nos. 15, 26, and 33). In two cases the origin of the image is explicitly said to be unknown (nos. 25 and 35). Story no. 14 is an exceptional case: its appearance was predicted by Liu Sahe, a figure who had a close connection with Asoka image stories, but this image in

Liangzhou in the Northwest is not said to have been an Asoka image. It is a large image, eighteen feet tall, carved on a cliff, quite unlike any of the typical Asoka images in the South.

None of the images described in these stories is said to have been an Asoka image; typical attributes of Asoka images, such as their Southern origin and the emphasis on a distinctive discovery story, are generally absent. Nevertheless these images were renowned for their power to predict dynastic fortunes. We have noted earlier that of the four cases of typical Asoka image stories, only two, ie., those of Changgansi and Changshasi stories, grew in later years by accumulating stories about their ability to predict dynastic fortunes. Stories of this kind do not seem to have developed around either of the two stone images at Tongxuansi temple in the Wu commandary (no. 3) or Tao Kan's image at Mt. Lu (no. 13). The power of predicting dynastic fortunes (which constitutes the heart of what I earlier called "royal images") probably was not a part of the original idea of Asoka images. Nevertheless, this idea about the miraculous power of images appears to have been also of Indian origin, and thus we are led to speculate that the idea might have been brought to China through context(s) other than that of Asoka images (Granoff 1992c: 1-19). The fragmentary evidence reviewed above suggests that the idea might have become popular in northren kingdoms during the fifth and sixth centuries.[51] If this was indeed the case, the idea appears to have spread quickly to the South, as the examples of the two Asoka images (in stories nos. 5 and 7) and that of the southern stone image in Fanyu (no. 25) indicate.[52] The examples of the Changgansi and Changshasi images (stories nos. 5 and 7) indicate that when the stories about miraculous images crystallized around the image of Liang emperor Wu*, the capacity to predict dynastic fortunes was probably considered to be one, though not necessarily the only defining characteristic of miraculous images.[53]

## Developments in unified China: Sui and Tang stories

*References to the Sui restoration of Buddhism*

Stories nos. 36-39 are designated by Daoxuan as stories from the Sui period, under a Northern pro-Buddhist dynasty that succeeded in bringing all of China under its rule.[54] Several other stories about image miracles, listed under earlier dynasties in the JSSGL, mention developments around images that are said to have occurred during the Sui period (581-617). Miracles that occurred during this period are reported in three of the four typical Asoka image stories from the South (nos. 5, 7, 13).[55] In stories nos.

4, 12, 14, 33, 34, and 35, references to developments under the Sui dynasty appear in stories about Northern images.[56]

In some cases developments during the Sui period are mentioned immediately after comments on the fortunes of the image during the persecution of Buddhism under the Northern Zhou.[57] Since many images appear to have been destroyed in the North during the persecution of Buddhism under the Northern Zhou dynasty, authors of stories about miraculous images in the North must have been particularly concerned about what happened to these images during this period. The restoration of the worship of these images under the Sui dynasty then would have constituted a natural sequel to these stories. The predominance of Northern images in the group of miraculous images for which Daoxuan included some comments about developments under the Sui may be explained to some extent by this observation.

It is striking that all the images for which Daoxuan notes new developments under the Sui dynasty happen also to be images whose origins were attributed to miraculous discovery (nos. 4, 12, 14, 33, 34, 35 of Northern images and Asoka images from the South, which were also miraculously discovered). Among the newly discovered images stories nos. 37, 38, and 39 center around unusual circumstances of their discovery. The story no. 36 is about an image whose miraculous character first came to be knwon under the Sui. This pattern suggests that in restoring the state support for Buddhism the leaders of the Sui dynasty, or the chroniclers of the fortunes of miraculous images under this dynasty, may have been particularly interested in this distinctive types of images, and not in others, i.e., the images which were explicitly known to have been produced in China.

The theme of predicting dynastic fortunes appears to have become less prominent in the stories about developments under the Sui.[58] I suspect that when the empire was unified by the Sui (581-617) and the Tang (618-907) and the period of rapid changes in dynastic fortunes both in the North and in the South came to an end, the miraculous images slowly lost their effective role as "royal images" that predict dynastic fortunes.[59] The meaning of their miracles and, more broadly, their role in the state and the Buddhist community within it had to be explained differently.

It is somewhat remarkable that miracles in general appear to occur less frequently in the passages describing the relationship between the images and the Sui rulers. Founding emperor Wen plays a role in the story about Gao Li's image that changed its position when this emperor brought it to the Xingshansi temple (no. 5). But it is striking that no miracles are reported in other passages where this emperor is reported to have restored the worship of miraculous images. He reestablished the temple at the site of Liu Sahe's image (no. 14). This emperor also rebuilt the temple where

Jiangming's iron ore image was located and gave it a new name (no. 34). It was under the emperor Wen's rule that monk Mingxian brought out the copy of the painting of miraculous origin; after authentification this copy that Mingxian had received from the Northern Qi monk Daochang was circulated widely, presumably under imperial order (no. 37). Nor are miracles mentioned in the passages describing how emperor Yang, who succeeded Wen, worshiped miraculous images. Emperor Yang worshiped Liu Sahe's rock image and gave a new name to the temple when he traveled there in 609 (no. 14). He also carried the small stone image, originally presented to Liang emperor Wu* by an Indian or Central Asian monk, and placed it in concealment at the Riyansi temple (no. 38). In story no. 4 a new name is said to have been given to Senglang's temple by the Sui court without mentioning the ruling emperor's name. When temples were given new names by the emperor, they must have acquired a new and important status as imperially sanctioned centers of the Buddhist community; and yet none of the passages reporting that a new name was given to a temple housing a miraculous image contains miracle stories.

Miracle stories in the passages describing events that occurred under the Sui rule center around different themes. In stories nos. 7 (about the Changshasi image) and 36 the images are said to have miraculously escaped fire. The fire in the temple was set by the soldiers in the city who shot fire arrows against bandits led by Zhu Can in story no. 7. The image is said to have protected Mt. Lu against bandits in the story about Tao Kan's image (no. 13). The passage in story no. 33 centers around the theme of the image forcing the thief to return its flags and decorative umbrella by appearing in a dream. It is perhaps significant that these miracle stories have little to do with dynastic fortunes; rather they center around the theme of the images' miraculous capacity to protect themselves and the Buddhist community around them.[60] Again it is tempting to read these findings as a sign pointing to the changing role of miraculous images in unified China; they lost their role as in effect "royal images," and became more the concern of the monastic community.

### Tang stories

According to Daoxuan's colophon (435a), he compiled the JSSGL hurriedly on the twentieth day of the sixth month of the first year of the Linde period (664). In my earlier study I suggested that the parallel collection in the thirteenth and fourteenth fascicles of the FYZL may have been based on the JSSGL and that the collection appeared to have been expanded further by Daoshi, the compiler of the FYZL. I was particularly intrigued that the list of more recent stories appears to have been expanded in Daoshi's collection (Shinohara 1991a: 208, 209).[61] Lively interest in miraculous images appears to have existed in the first half century or so under the Tang.[62]

New developments under the Tang are frequently mentioned in stories about images which focus on events that occurred earlier. Daoxuan appears to have used the expression *"jin*\*" (now) to provide this kind of information. Frequently, the comment only confirms that a particular image still existed at the time Daoxuan compiled the collection and sometimes gives the name of the temple where the image is located.[63]

In some cases Daoxuan introduces new stories that developed under the Tang. Emperor Taizong worshiped the iron ore image in Fangzhou, in a manner similar to the conduct of Sui rulers, who also worshipped miraculous images (no. 34).[64] The wooden image in Huayensi prediced the death of this emperor (no. 35).[65] One of the daughters of this emperor, princess of Xianyang, produced copies of the Tongxuansi temple images (no. 3).[66] The translucent stone/image in story no. 38 was brought into the inner quarters of the palace (no. 38).[67] These stories indicate that the ruling family of the Tang dynasty, at least in this early period, showed interest in miraculous images. The Changshasi image is said to have responded to repeated requests for rain (no. 7).[68] During the rule of Southern dynasties the image discovered by Gao Li was often brought to the palace for the same purpose (no. 5; 414c2-4). In the unified world under the Tang this role of the miraculous image might have become more important. No reference is made to the court or government officials in the story about the bronze image at the Xinghuangsi (no. 36)[69] and in the account of Tao Kan's image at Mt. Lu (no. 13);[70] these stories describe how supernatural beings appear to have protected the images.

Although emperor Taizong and others around him are said to have shown some interest in miraculous images, the close relationship between the emperor and miraculous images ("royal images") appears to have declined under the Tang. No stories of images predicting dynastic fortunes appear in the group of newly discovered miraculous images. In some cases Daoxuan's account of the discovery of new images notes that the images in question still existed in the "villages" (nos. 40, 47) or a "mountain temple" (no. 46). At this point Daoxuan might have been reproducing stories about miraculous images that he and his colleagues gathered from local sources; the tradition of miraculous image stories might have dispersed over a wider geographical area by this time, as the close relationship between these images and the court slowly declined.

## Concluding comments

A set of general hypotheses emerges from the exploratory investigation above:

(1) The tradition of Asoka images appears to have developed in the South, where these images served to enhance the prestige of temples, many of which had only been recently established in areas where Buddhist missionaries had arrived relatively recently. One function of the discovery and location stories would then have been to illustrate dramatically the importance of a new temple as the miraculously chosen home of a specially powerful image.

(2) In the South the concern for miraculous images later crystallized around the figure of the emperor Wu* of the Liang dynasty.

(3) The idea of a "royal image" that predicted dynastic fortunes appears to have developed in the North, independent of this Southern tradition of Asoka image stories. This idea also appeared in some of the later stories of Asoka image, some of which evolved into "royal images" in the South.

(4) When the empire was unified under the Sui, and a more stable era was introduced under the Tang, stories about "royal images" appear to have become less popular. Though Sui and early Tang rulers seem to have shown considerable interest in miraculous images (at least in the tradition of miracle stories), the close relationship observed in the earlier period between the central court and locally based traditions of miraculous images may have declined after this point.

In this discussion I have focused on the evolution of the role or function of "royal images" in medieval Chinese Buddhism. As this role became less significant in unified China, new roles or functions for miraculous images may have evolved, though not entirely successfully. One of these new roles in this later period was to perform rain magic at times of drought. My suspicion at this stage of my work is that no single new role as powerful as that assigned the earlier royal images emerged, and that for this reason stories about miraculous images gradually decreased in number and importance. I hope to return to this topic and study later sources to confirm this suggestion.

## Notes

1. The research for this paper was assisted by a grant from the Social Sciences and Humanities Research Council of Canada.

2.The date of compilation is given in Daoxuan's collophon, 435a. This collection is reproduced with some additional material in fascicles 13 and 14 (with further parallels in fascicles 15, and 16) of the Buddhist encyclopedia *Fayuan zhulin*

(Taisho.2122: 53.269-1030), completed in 668 by Daoshi, Daoxuan's collaborator at the Ximingsi temple in the capital city Chang'an (Shinohara 1991b: 207-210).

The material that parallels the miraculous image section of the JSSGL appears in the long miracle story segment of subsection 3, entitled "contemplation of the Buddha" (*guanfo*) of the section on "Paying respect to the Buddha" (*jingfo*) in the *Fayuan zhulin* (fascicles 13 and 14). Subsequent subsections are devoted to materials related to Amitabha (fasc. 15), Maitreya (fasc. 16), and Samatabhadra and Avalokitesvara (fasc. 17). Since these subsections also are accompanied by small miracle story segments, it might be possible to read these collections as additions that Daoshi produced to the earlier collection of miraculous image stories compiled by Daoxuan.

A few of the JSSGL stories appear to have been moved to these later subsections. The JSSGL story no. 12 is found in the FYZL, fasc. 91 (955c); no. 19 in fasc. 16 (407b), no. 37 in fasc. 15 (401ab). Story no. 26 is found in fasc. 14 (388bc) and in fasc. 15 (400bc). Fasc. 17 contains a section on Samantabhadra (408cb-409b) and Avalokitesvara (409b411c), but there is no overlap between the stories in this section and those in the JSSGL.

3. Soper attempted a more comprehensive review, basing himself on Omura Seigai's larger work (Soper 1959: xi-xii).

4. Stories about these *stupas* and images appear side by side in the GSZ biographies of Kang Senghui (Taisho.2059: 50.325a-326b) and Huida (409b-410a) as stories associated with the same temples (Jianchusi and Changgansi temples respectively).

5. The story is told in Taisho.2042: 50.101a-102b and in Taisho.2043: 50.133c-135b respectively. John Strong has translated the Sanskrit original of this story (Strong: 214-221).

6. For example, Sun Hao's image [no. 2] in Kang Senghui's biography; Dai Andao's image [no. 9], Dai Yong's image [no. 36], and Wang Mi's image [no. 11], all of which are found in Huili's biography, 410ab; the great stone image in the Shan District [29b] in Senghu's biography, 412ab.

7. This work also contains a section on setting up images, and some of the stories mentioned in this section also mention miraculous occurrences (Taisho.2035: 49.463ab).

8. These images appeared in the first year of the Jianxing period (313). Though the GSZ passage on these images does not mention their connection to king Asoka, these images are mentioned in the earlier "Records of Supernatural Signs" (*Mingxiang ji*, as preserved in an entry in the FYZL, Taisho.2122: 51.920a18,19) where they are explicitly said to have been Asoka images. In the parallel collections in the JSSGL and theFYZL they are explicitly said to have been Asoka images (52.404b18 and 53.585b1 respectively)(Shinohara 1988: 164).

9. During the Xianhe period (326-335) Gao Li saw unusual light on a beach near the Zhanghouqiao bridge in Danyang; this led to the discovery of the image; pearl fisherman who later discovered the image's halo in Jiaozhou also saw unusual light at the bottom of the ocean.

10. The image appeared in response to the monk Tanyi's impassioned request in the sixth year of the Yonghe period (350), in the northern suburb of Jingzhou.

11. Tao Kan discovered the image when he investigated a report from a fisherman who saw light in the ocean near the coast in Jianyu; Tao Kan then sent the image to Sengzhen at the Hanqisi in Wuchang; later Tao Kan failed to move the image to Jingzhou, but when Huiyuan prayed for it at Mt. Lu, the image appeared spontaneously.

12. In the two cases of Gao Li's image and Tao Kan's image strange light seen on the beach near the ocean is mentioned.

13. "Teng Jun, whose name is given as Teng Han elsewhere, of Jiangling, the Governor Changsha" is said to have originally donated his residence to establish the Changshasi temple, and in response to his request Tanyi was sent there by Tao'an (415b18-19; ref. GSZ, 355c8-9). Although Teng Jun/Han's name does not prominent appear in the account of the discovery of the miraculous image, this secular figure remained in its background.

14. A close relationship with the ruler or a prominant government leader is mentioned explicitly in the stories about Sun Hao's image (no. 2) and the image discovered by Wang Mi (no. 11). These images, however, are not explicitly said to have been Asoka images in the GSZ versions of the stories about them (326a and 410b). In the above mentioned earlier survey of Asoka image stories in China, I suggested that these images acquired the designation either as an Asoka image or possibly a copy of an Asoka image only in later versions of the stories about them (Shinohara 1992: 205-206).

15. It is difficult to determine to what extent these and other details of Asoka image stories were based on history. Even if they happen not have been based directly on historical facts, they would still illustrate common assumptions about the Asoka images at relatively early stages in the evolution of their stories.

16. This would not necessarily mean that the images were in fact discovered or produced at the times mentioned in these stories, or even that the stories about these events appeared around those times. Nevertheless, in compiling the JSSGL, Daoxuan must have collected these stories from sources that existed at his time. Some of Daoxuan's source may well have originated not much later than the dates of the events they reported. Except in cases where there are specific reasons for question them, I have generally followed the chronology offerred in Daoxuan's presentation.

17. I did not include the three stories attributed to the Liang dynasty (nos. 28-30). The image in story no. 14, attributed to the Yuan Wei dynasty which ruled the north in Huijiao's time, is said to have been discovered in 520, 417c12. The events in story no. 31, also attributed to Yuan Wei, occurred later than that of the compilation of the GSZ.

18. Stories nos. 2 [Southern Wu, 222-280], 4 [Western Jin], 8, 11, 12, 14 [Eastern Jin], 18, 19, 20, 21 [Song, 420-479], 28 [Ling, 502-557], 34 [Nothern Zhou, 557-581], 37, 38, 39 [Sui, 581-618], 40, 47, 48 [Tang, 618-907]

19. Stories nos. 1 [Eastern Han, 25-220], 6, 9, 10 [Eastern Jin], 15, 16 [Northern Liang, 397-439], 17, 22, 24 [Song], 26 [Qi, 479-494], 29, 29b, 30 [Liang], 31 [Yuan Wei, 385-556], 32 [Chen, 557-589], 33 [Nothern Zhou], 36 [Sui], 47 [Tang].

20. Stories nos. 25 [Qi], 35 [Northern Zhou], 46 [Tang].

21. Stories nos. 23 [Song], 27 [Qi], 41-45, 49, and 50 [Tang].

22. Stories no. 3 [Western Jin] and 13 [Eastern Jin].

23. They are identified as Sakyamuni (nos. 1 [Eastern Han], 10 [Eastern Jin], 28 [Sui]), Prince Gautama (no. 12 [Eastern Jin]), Amitabha (nos. 6 [Eastern Jin], 50 [Tang]), Manjusri (nos. 17 [Song], 49 [Tang]), or Avalokitesvara (nos. 27 [Qi], 31 [Yuan Wei]). Story no. 22 mentions wall paintings of bodhisattvas (418b27).

24. In story no. 31 the Avalokitesvara image that Sun Jingde worshiped seems to have caused a monk to appear in a dream and teach him to recite a scripture about this Bodhisattva. The scripture promises that the Bodhisattva would then come rescue (ref. Taisho.262 9:56c16-17).

25. Stories nos. 2 [Southern Wu], 4, 5-8, 10, 11, 13 [Eastern Jin], 17-21, 23 [Song], 26, 27 [Qi], 29-30 [Liang], 31 [Yuan Wei], 36 [Sui], 46, 47 [Tang]. Often the size of these images is also carefully noted.

26. Stories nos. 3 [Western Jin], 14 [Yuan Wei], 15, 16 [Northern Liang], 25 [Qi], 33 [Norhern Zhou], 48, and 50 [Tang].

27. The stone image in story no. 40 is said to have been closely related to the image in story 34, but here is no suggestion that, as in the case of the image in story no. 34, it was a rock, or iron ore, that looked like an image but could not have been carved or polished (421b).

28. Stories no. 14 [Yuan Wei], 15, 16 [Northern Liang], 33 [Northern Zhou], 40, 48, and 50 [Tang]. The story no. 49 mentions a vision of a rock image (422c25, 26).

29. Stories nos. 9 [Eastern Jin], 24 [Song], 28 [Liang], and 35 [Northern Zhou].

30. Stories nos. 1 [Eastern Han], 22 [Song], 37 [Sui].

31. Stories nos. 12 [Eastern Jin], 45, 49 [Tang].

32. The image in this story is said to have been sent from seven imaginary kingdoms. Though this may not be a story of discovery, I counted it as one since the image sent from these fictitious kingdoms must have been discovered at some point. Zhu Senglang's biography is found in fasc. 5 of the GSZ, which mentions his temple on Mt. Tai (Taisho: 50.354b8-12).

33. The Northern Liang dynasty was established when the Juqu clan took the city of Guzang from the Southern Liang dynasty in 412. In 421 the Northern Liang conquered the Western Liang, based in Dunhuang, where it had become independent from the Northern Liang in the year 400. The Northern Liang dynasty was conquered by the Northern Wei dynasty in 439. The stories no. 15 and 16 center around rock images that Juqu Mengsun built: in story no. 15 he is said to have carved images on a long line of cliffs 100 miles from the site of the regional government (zhou); story no. 16 is about a rock image, 60 feet tall, that he built for his mother. Juqu Mengsun led the Juqu clan during the period 401-433 and became the founding ruler of the Northern Liang dynasty. A short biographical entry on him is found in the Songshu, fasc. 98 (8.2412).

Story no. 15 does not mention the name of the regional center explicitly, either as Guzang or as Dunhuang; story no. 16 only states that the rock image Mengsun produced for his mother was placed in a mountain temple. Nagahiro Toshio, in his introductory survey of Chinese rock cave temples, tentatively identifies the rock caves "in Liangzhou" that Juqu Mengsun is said to have established as the group of rock caves at the Matisi temple in Zhangyi, particularly the golden stupa cave temple, or the group of rock caves at Mt. Wenshu near Jiuquan (1.14). Soper mentions the identificantion of the site at Mt. Tianti (Soper, 92, note 34).

Story no. 16 ends with a comment, stating that the 280 Buddha images along the 2 mile tall cliff at Mt. Sanwei, 30 miles southeast of Shazhou (418a24, 26). These images appear to refer to the images at the Mogaoku caves at Dunhuang. The comment is introduced by the formulaic expression "*jin*\*" ["now"] that Daoxuan used to comment on the current state of the images described in the stories he collected, and was probably added by Daoxuan when he incorporated this story into his collection. This suggests that Daoxuan believed this image, produced by Mengsun for his mother, to have been among the numerous images at Dunhuang (Soper, 92b).

It is tempting to speculate about the relationship between the stories about rock images and Dunhuang. Dunhuang was under the Northern Liang rule between 421 and 439; sources mention a variety of events for this period indicating that Dunhuang was then a prospering Buddhist center. Nagahiro briefly summarizes the activities during this period in Dunhuang and in the area around it (Nagahiro: 263).

Story no. 16 describes how Mengsun turned against Buddhism when his son Xingguo was killed in a battle; Mengsun returned to Buddhism only when he saw the rock image he had produced for his mother shed tears. According to fasc. 9 of the *Chu sangzang ji ji* (Taisho.2145: 55.64c) Juqu Xingguo joined over 500 lay people in 426 at the capital city [Guzang] of the Northern Liang and requested Tan Mochen, better known as Tan Wuchen or by the reconstructed Sanskrit name Dharmaksema, to translate the lay precepts (*Youposaijie jing*, Taisho.1488: 24.1034-1075).

We might also keep in mind that the Yungang rock caves in Datong were first established in 460 and the rock caves in Longmen date from the Loyang period of the Northern Wei dynasty (494-534); perhaps the extensive carving of rock cave temples in this period is related to the stories of miraculous rock images.

Story no. 37 is classified as a story from the Sui period in the table of contents (Taisho.2106: 52.413b17), though the word Sui is missing from the heading in the main body of the text (421a17). Since monk Mingxian is said to have obtained a copy of the painting in question from dharma master Daochang of the Northern Qi ("*gaoqi*", 421a28), we might assume that the tradition of this painting associated with the legendary vists of Jiaye and Moteng to Luoyang survived in Northern dynasties. Nevertheless, since the calculation here is based on Daoxuan's attribution of miracle stories to specific dynasties, I have not included this story in the number of Northern stories from the period of division.

34. In story no.34, the story suggests in a manner that reminds us of the story of Tanyi's image that the discovered image was in fact an Asoka image 420c16; ref. 415B23-25.

35. Stories nos. 2 [Southern Wu], 8, 11 [Eatern Jin], 19, 20, 21 [Song], 28 [Liang], 34 [Northern Zhou], 37 [?][Sui], 40[Tang].

36. Stories nos. 4 [Western Jin], 14 [Yuan Wei], 19 [Song], 48 [Tang].

37. This influence, however, does not appear to have been confined to these discovered images. In one case, in the appended story in story no. 29 [Liang], an

image is explicitly said to have been an Asoka image in the JSSGL collection in spite of the fact that its origin in China appears to have been widely known (419c17,18).

38. The story of the miraculous image at the Famengsi temple, explicitly said to have been produced by Asoka's fourth daughter, is told in Huicui's biography in Daoxuan's XGSZ (507bc) in a manner that closely parallels the earlier and better-known story of Gao Li's image (Shinohara 1988: 220-221, n. 125)

39. Stories nos. 6, 14, 16, 25 [418c27, 28], 26, 30/32, 33, 35.

40. Other sources, including the Famengsi image in Huicui's biography in the XGSZ mentioned above, will be taken into account in the discussion here.

41. In three of these eight cases the story in the JSSGL have the GSZ antecedent (nos. 5, 7, 29); in four cases the antecendent is in the XGSZ (nops. 6, 30, 32, 38). This pattern may reflect that fact that the GSZ collection was compiled around 531 in the middle of the reign of emperor Wu* (502-549), the XGSZ attempted to collect biographies from periods that followed.

42. Stories of later miracles about Fajun's image at the Famengsi temple in Jizhou, which is said to have been produced by the fourth daughter of Asoka, contain themes that parallel the later stories about the two Asoka images in Chang-gansi (no. 5) and Changshasi (no. 7). The similarity to the Changshasi image stories is particularly notable. Toward the end of the Tianjian period (502-519) the image emitted light that filled the room. Emperor Wu* then was about to bring the image to the capital, but circumstances prevented him from doing so. In the seventh year of the Datong period (541/2) the image sweated; in this year Liu Jingxuan rebelled and burned down the regional city. The entire temple was burned down except for the Buddha hall. In the tenth year of the same period (544) the image again sweated. Thereupon, the Prince of Xiangdong, who was later to reestablish the Liang dynasty at Jiangling, brought the image to Jiangling; when the prince prayed to the image it emitted light. In the twelfth year (546) the image was returned to Jizhou, where it emitted light for three days. In the sixth year of the Tianjia period (565) the ruler of the Chen dynasty which had succeeded the Liang dynasty added further decoration to the image. As in the case of Changshasi image (no. 7), it appears that a particularly close relationship existe between this image and emperor Wu* as well as Prince Yi of Xiangdong, who played a prominent role as a leader of the Liang dynasty in its last years.

43. The Bussho kaisetsu daijiten [vol. 1, p. 221] identifies this title as an alternate title for the Foshuo zuo fo xingxiang jing or "The Buddha's sermon on making Buddha images", in one fascicle that is found in the Taisho collection (Taisho.692: 16.788). The date of the translation is given here as Later Han in accordance with the colophon in the Taisho text (788a13). The title of this text is mentioned in fasc. 4 of the Chu sanzang ji ji, compiled by Sengyou (445-518)(Taisho.2145: 55.22b1). An alternate translation under the title Foshuo zaoli xingxiang fubao jing, also in one fascicle, appears next in the Taisho collection (Taisho.693: 16.788-790).

A more detailed account of the circumstances around the production of this image summarized in Daoxuan's story no. 28 is found in the Foshuo dasheng zaoxing gongde jing, "Mahayana scripture on the merits of image making", in two fascicles, that is found immediately after this second work (Taisho.694: 790-796). The translator of this text is given as Tiyunbanro, who engaged in translation work in

Loyang during the period between 689 and 691, i.e., shortly after Daoxuan's death in 667 (Taisho.2061: 50.719b/ *Hobogirin* index: 241b).

Story no. 1 mentions the painting of the Buddha attributed to king Udayana in connection with the famous story of emperor Ming's dream (413c8).

The story of king Udayana's image is also told in Xuanzang's *Datang xiyuji*, fascicle 5 (*Datang xiyuji xiaozhu*: 468, 469).

Sengyou's work also mentions a text called "*Fo you tianzhu ji*" in the list of texts brought back by Faxian (339?-420?)(12a8). Alexander Soper discussed this reference in his detailed treatment of the Udayana image (Soper: 260b-261b; the essay on the image is found in 259-265; main sources for this summary are discussed in 46-49, 70-71, and 88-89). Early legends about king Udayana's image are also summarized in Takada (Takada: 10-14). A copy of this image that was taken to Japan by Chonen had been discussed earlier by Henderson and Hurvitz. In her comprehensive discussion of Udayana image and image stories Martha L. Carter notes that Chinese stories of the Udayana image proliferated during the later fifth and early sixth centuries (Carter 1990:10).

44. Story no. 32 describes a miracle that occurred later around these same images at the Chongyundian. When emperor Wu* of the Chen dynasty (557-559) died, his elder brother's son Chen Qian, who succeeded him as emperor Shi (r. 559-566), wanted to use the decorations and treasures presented to these two images for the funeral of the deceased emperor. Suddenly a heavy rain came down, thunder was heard, and lightning covered the sky. The images stood high up in the sky guarded by heavenly soldiers. After the storm, people went back to the site of the images and discovered only their stone foundations. Several months later people came from Dongzhou and said on that day he saw the images fly in the sky over the ocean. Sometimes people still see the images when they look across the ocean. The two stories nos. 30 and 32 appears to have originally been one long story. In the collection of miracle stories included in the XGSZ biography of Sengming (693bc) the two stories form one large whole. This long story appears to have been broken up into two independent stories later in the JSSGL and *Fayuan zhulin* collection (389bc, 389c-390a).

45. Liu Sahe's GSZ biography tells stories of his visits to temples in the South where Asoka stupas and images existed, as well as stories about the discovery of the old Asoka *stupas*.

46. According to the XGSZ biography of Huida, upon which the present JSSGL passage appears to have been based, "prime minister (*dazhongzai*) and the prince of Qi" went to confirm the miracle (645a16). Prince Xian, whose biography is found in fasc. 12 of the *Zhoushu* (1.187-200), had been given the title of the Duke of Qi (1.187) and later became the *dazhongzai* (1.189). The passage was summarized incorrectly in my earlier discussion (Shinohara 1988: 173). In the XGSZ biography the date of the event is given as the "beginning" (*chu*) of the Jiande period (572-578); the emperor Wu*'s official persecution of Buddhism began in the third year of the Jiande period (573)(Kamata: 111).

47. This is a tentative translation of an obscure sentence (417c25,26)(Shinohara 1988: 173, 224 [n. 143]). See also the corresponding passage in the XGSZ biography of Huida (645a23, 24).

48. In my earlier summary of the version of this story that is found in Sengming's biography in the XGSZ (693c15-28), I failed to note that a version of this story also appears in the JSSGL (Shinohara 1991b: 212-213). The JSSGL version appears to have been based on the XGSZ passage.

49. Earlier the Changshasi image is said to have shed tears and predicted the death of emperor Ming of the southern Song dynasty (415c11).

50. The story of the two images the emperor Wu* produced at the Chongyun hall, which later flew up in the sky and disappeared (nos. 30 and 32), may be read as one calling attention to the close relationship between the presence of the images and the fortune of the Liang dynasty. This story has been mentioned above, with a summary in footnote 38.

51. Yang Xuanzhi's *Luoyang qielan ji* , composed around 547, describes the temples at the Northern Wei capital in Luoyang during the days of its glory, and contains several passages describing miraculous images. The golden image at the Pingdengsi temple predicted dynastic fortunes by sweating ("shedding tears") in 527, 529, 530 (Taisho.2092: 51.1007c, Wang: 98-99); in 533 the stone image outside the gate of the same temple moved spontaneously, raising its head up and down; later in the fall of the same year the capital city had to be moved to Ye [when the Northery Wei dynasty split into Eastern and Western Wei] (1008c, Wang: 109-110). In 531 the golden image in the Jingningsi temple grew hair, which was taken as an ill omen (1010a, Wang: 123). The copper image owned by Hou Qing of Nanyang appeared to his wife in a dream; the image pointed out that the couple promised two years ago to use the money they obtained by selling a cow to coat the image with gold, but [that they spent the money for other purposes and] had not replaced it; the image was therefore to take their son to make them pay for this; after the son died the image shone in golden light (1016a; Wang: 189-190). In 529 the lacquered image that Meng Zhonghui produced at [Yuan] Jinghao's residence walked around in the hall; the image suddenly disappeared in 534; in the fall of that year the capital was moved to Ye (1018a, Wang: 208). The long record of Songyun's travel to the West mentions the golden image at Hanmo which always faced east. It flew back to its original location when the king of Khotan worshiped it and took it away (1018c, Wang: 219). Songyun also mentions the pratyeka Buddha's shoe that has not rotted in Khotan (1019a, Wang: 222), and the miraculous Buddha's shadow in Quboluolong cave at Najie, which appeared on the wall from a distance, but could not be seen when one moved closer to the wall (1021c-1022a, Wang: 244). These passages point to the popularity of miraculous image stories under the Northern Wei rule. I am struck by the fact that none of these stories about miraculous images was reproduced in Daoxuan's collection.

52. My suggestion here is only tentative. Another possibility is that the Northern stories about the miraculous images which predicted dynastic fortunes might have been modeled after the prediction stories attributed to the Asoka images at the Changgansi and Changshasi temples (stories nos. 5 and 7) or others similar to them that first appeared in the South. In the Changshasi image passage, the first instance of such a prediction is mentioned in connection with the death of emperor Ming of the Song dynasty (r. 465-472). Though this date may well have been projected backward at some later date when the miracle story evolved, it is earlier

than many of the dates mentioned in the stories about Northern images (the stories [nos. 15 and 16] about the Northern Liang ruler Juqu Mengsun constitute exceptions). Yet another possibility is that the idea, which appears to have been of Indian origin, reached China through multiple routes.

Suwa Gijun pointed out that the historical records that describe emperor Wen of the Northern Qi dynasty (r. 550-559) appear to have been modeled after the accounts of emperor Wu* of the Liang dynasty in the South. He suggests that contemporary aristocratic circles in the Northern Qi dynasty looked up to Liang emperor Wu* as their ideal rather than to the rulers of the preceding Northern Wei dynasty (Suwa: 244). The activities of Liang emperor Wu* appear to have been widely known in the North.

53. The story about predicting dynastic fortunes does not appear in other examples of miraculous image stories associated with the Liang emperor Wu*.

54. Two of the images described in these stories appear to have been of Southern origin: story no. 36 about the large bronze image(s) in the Southern capital city Jiangzhou (or Jiankang) and the image in story no. 38 said to have been originally said presented to Liang emperor Wu* by an Indian or Central Asian monk.

55. Story no. 5. The Changgansi image is said to have predicted the end of the Chen dynasty; the founding emperor of the Sui dynasty heard about this and brought the image to the inner quarters of his palace. The emperor ordered a sitting version of the image made and sent the two images to the Daxingshansi temple. The images were placed in the temple facing north, but were found facing south the following morning. Monks turned the images around again facing north, but again in the morning they were facing south.

Stories about the demise of a dynasty were probably circulated after the new dynasty had come into power; such a story then would have served the purpose of legitimizing the new dynasty. In this case, however, the story appears to make a nuanced point. As I suggested earlier, this story needs to be read in the light of the old tradition according to which it was the ruler who sat facing south (Shinohara 1988: 162; Soper, 12). Thus, the story appears to suggest that it is the image, and not the victorious Sui emperor, who is the ultimate ruler.

Story no. 7 During the twelfth year of the Daye period (616/7) the miraculous image of the Changshasi image sweated. Bandit Zhu Can camped in the temple and shot arrows toward the city wall; soldiers guarding the city shot fire arrows back at the temple and set fire to the temple. But the image secretly moved during the night into the city and stood outside the gate of the Baoguangsi, thus escaping the fire (Shinohara 1992: 165).

Story no. 13. Toward the end of the Sui rule, bandits appeared in the area and monks left the temple. The image persuaded an old monk to stay in the temple. Followers of bandit Dong Daochong came to the temple and tried to execute the old monk, but the sword pierced the executioner's heart. Bandits fled to Huiyuan's tomb, where thunder and lightning killed nine of them. Consequently, though the nearby city of Jiangzhou was looted, the bandits did not dare to go onto Mt. Lu (Shinohara 1992: 187).

56. Story no. 4. During the Sui period, Senglang's temple at Mt. Tai, where the miraculous image sent from seven imaginary kingdoms is said to have been located, was reestablished as Shentong daochang ("Practice Hall of Supernatural Occurrences"). This temple is mentioned in three biographies in Daoxuan's XGSZ: in Fazan's biography (506c29-507a2); in Tanqian's biography (573b18); and in Fa'an's biography (652a6,7). The image in in this temple, presented by imaginary kingdoms, may be counted as one of the miraculously discovered images.

Story no. 12. The image that had been given to Wu Cangying by a Brahman had been hidden by monks during time when Buddhism was persecuted under the Northern Zhou dynasty. It was brought out during the Sui period.

Story no. 14. The Ruixiangsi temple in Liangzhou, where the rock image whose appearance had been predicted by Liu Sahe was reestablished in the same form as before during the Kaihuang period; in the fifth year of the Daye period (609) emperor Yang traveled westward and worshiped the image, changing the name of the temple to Gantong daochang ("Practice Hall of Miraculous Occurrences") that reminds one of a similar name used for Senglang's temple.

Earlier, this image predicted the demise of the Northern Zhou dynasty. At the beginning of the Jiande period (572-578) shortly before emperor Wu* of the Northern Zhou dynasty began the persecution of Buddhism, the image's head fell off, and this event was taken as the sign for the imminent persecution and the end of the Northern dynasty.

Story no. 33. In the fifteenth year of the Kaiyuan period (595) someone stole the flags and the decorative umbrella over the huge rock image, eighty feet tall, that monk Senghu of the Lingshisi ("Miraculous stone") temple in Jinzhou had carved on the miraculous stone he discovered in a valley north of the temple. Then the thief dreamed of the image entering his room; he became frightened and returned the objects.

As I noted above, this image is said to have been carved by Senghu on a miraculous rock that he discovered in a valley to the north of the temple. Since it appears to have been the rock, rather than Senghu's work on it, that was believed to have been the cause of miracles, I classify this story as one about an image whose origin is attributed to miraculous discovery.

Story no. 34. The image, which appears to have been a piece of iron ore, was discovered by Jiangming in a mountain in Mingzhou in the third year of the Jiande period of the Northern Zhou dynasty (574). This image had been placed in the Daxiangsi ("Great Image") temple, taking the name from the new period name Daxiang (579-581)(The era name Daxiang is here written as "great image", though elsewhere it is written with a slightly different character for *xiang*, as "great sign"). When the Sui dynasty began supporting Buddhism, the temple was rebuilt and the name of the temple was changed to Xianjisi. People went back to the place where the image was originally discovered, and learned that neither large rocks nor metal ore existed in that deserted location. Thus it was concluded that the image must have been brought there by the miraculous power of king Asoka.

Story no. 35. At the beginning of the Sui rule, people brought out the head of the walking image at the Huayensi of Mt. Xian in Xiangzhou, which they had hidden during the persecution of Buddhism under the Northern Zhou. The image was redecorated and named Vairocana Buddha. Just before emperor Wen of Sui died, the nose of this image started running.

57. The image is said to have been hidden by monks in story no. 12, while the image in story no, 14 is said not to have been affected by the persecuion. The head of the image in story no. 35 was hidden. In two cases the central event in the story is said to have occurred under the rule of the Northern Zhou: (1) the image in story no. 33 was discovered toward the end of the rule of the Northern Qi dynasty; when Northern Zhou armies conquered the city of Jinzhou, they set fire to temples and *stupa*s and the image was also burned, but its colour did not change and only two fingers were damaged; (2) the location of an image discovered while the rule of Northen Zhou dynasty was persecuting Buddhism is said to have been named as Daxiangsi temple in story no. 34.

58. A few stories of this nature, regarding the demise of the Southern and Northern dynasties that the Sui conquored, do appear: the Changgansi image predicted the fall of the Chen dynasty (no. 5) and Liu Sahe's rock image the imminent persecution of Buddhism, which it escaped, and the end of the Northern dynasty (no. 14). By describing how images predicted the demise of the Chen and Northern Zhou dynasties, these stories legitimized the Sui conquest. Only one such story about the demise of the Sui appears toward the end of the entry on the Changsha image (no. 7, 416b). This appears to indicate that the interest in "royal images" that predict dynastic fortunes declined gradually.

59. It is of course natural that no stories predict the end of the Tang dynasty that occurred over 200 years after Daoxuan compiled this collection. It might be of some significance that none of the post-Tang stories about miracle images in the short sections on images in the FTTJ (461c-462a; 463ab) tell a story of predicting dynastic fortunes.

60. The large rock image carved by Senghu (story no. 28) is also said to have escaped a fire unharmed, except for some damage to two fingers. The image later appeared to a pious person in a dream, and complained about the pain in his fingers; thereupon the man repaired the damage to the image's fingers. These events are said to have occurred under the rule of the Northern Zhou.

61. With the exception of the Sakyamuni's image that Faqing of the Ningquansi temple produced, and that is attributed to the Sui period, all the new stories are listed as stories under the Tang.

62. Stories nos. 40-50 in the JSSGL are attributed to the Tang period. In this series of stories Daoxuan collected stories about images that were said to have been discovered during the Tang period, and the stories generally center around the circumstances of their discovery.

In two cases Daoxuan states explicitly that he visited the site of the image (stories nos. 47 and 48; 422b17 and c5)(Daoxuan also mentions that he also saw the translucent image/stone at the Riyensi temple, where he resided for a time, see story no. 38). Story no. 48 states that the discovery of the image was reported to the court; the emperor sent monk Xuanxiu of the Dazi'ensi temple to confirm the discovery, and the emperor ordered a drawing made of the miraculous image (422c4). Monk Huiji of story no. 49 was sent by the ruler to repair the temples and stupas at Mt. Wutai; the story about the Manjusri image must have been reported to the court. Story no. 50 states that a drawing of the rock image was submitted to the court. With the possible exception of story no. 48, where the person involved is a monk, the emperor or a figure closely connected with the court plays a role in these stories. In other cases, i.e., stories nos. 40, 46, and 47, no mention is made of any connection with the court. Story no. 45 is a story of a rain miracle, which refers to a regional inspector (*cishi*) without mentioning any specific name.

Three stories listed here (nos. 41, 43, and 44) are about Buddha's footprints, and another (no. 42) appears to have been about a stone on which letters were carved (*shibiaowen*).

63. These comments are found in stories no. 4 (414a25), no. 5 (414c16), no. 6 (415b7), no. 7 (416b), no. 9 (416c22), no. 12 (417b3), no. 13 (417c2), no. 14 (417c25), no. 16 (418a24), no. 25 (418c29), no. 28 (419c5), no. 33 (420c4), no. 34 (420c20), no. 35 (421a3), no. 37 (421b2), no. 40 (421c11), no. 44 (422a24), no. 45 (422b4), and no. 46 (422b14). The comment toward the end of the story no. 31 uses the expression "*jin*\*" in referring to the popular name of the Avalokitesvara in Daoxuan's time (420b3).

64. The temple of the iron ore image discovered by Jiangming was named Xiangjisi by the founding emperor of the Sui, and the Tang rulers did not change its name. Toward the end of the Zhenguan period (627-649) a Daoist temple was built to the west of this temple; the Daoist temple (*gong*) was named Yuhua (Jade flower). But the image was still kept in the original location, which stood in a garden 30 miles to the east of the Daoist temple. Emperor Taizong once went to worship the image, and finding the image too plain, made donations to decorate it. During the Yonghui period (650-656) [of the succeeding emperor Gaozong] the Daoist temple was changed into a Buddhist temple, though with the same name, Yuhua. The location currently belongs to Fangzhou. In the dusk of evenings the image frequently emits light. Both monks and laymen who see the light invariably marvel at it (Soper: 121).

65. I summarized above the story of the image at the Huayansi temple in Xiangzhou that had a runny nose in the fourth month of the twenty-third year of the Zhenguang period, predicting the death of emperor Taizong, and again in the sixth month, predicting a flood in the following month. The image is said to have been still in the temple, and many who wished to have children prayed to it (Soper: 116a).

66. The JSSGL passage on the two stone images at the Tongxuansi temple in the Wu commandary ends with a note that begins with the expression "*jin*\*:" (414a12): "the princess of Xianyang, the sister of the reigning emperor (*chang gongzhu*)" in the capital city heard about the miracles and sent someone to the Tongxuansi to draw diagrams of the images. When the princess began the project of reproducing copies of the images, miracles are said to have occurred.

I have not been able to identify the "princess of Xianyang". Since the comment at the end of the entry of the Tongxuansi images appears after the interlinear note giving the source of the passage on these images, and the comment is absent in the corresponding passage in the *Fayuan zhulin* (383c16), I am inclined to believe that this last comment was added by Daoxuan himself at the time Daoxuan compiled the JSSGL in the first year of the Linde period. The expression "*jin*\*" (now) at the beginning of this comment (414a12) indicates that the following event occurred under the rule of the Tang dynasty. The emperor at that time was Gaozong; the list of the 21 daughters of Gaozong's father emperor Taizong in the *Xintangshu*, fasc. 83, does not mention "princes of Xianyang" (Zhonghua shuju edition, vol.12, pp. 3645-3649. The princess of Dongyang is said to have been appointed as *da changgongzhu* (p. 3646); other names that might have become corrupted would include those of "princes of Chengyang (pp. 3647-48) and "princess of Jinyang" (pp. 3648-3649).

67. At the end of this story about the translucent stone image originally brought from India or Central Asia under the rule of emperor Wu* Daoxuan describes how he himself originally had not believed in the miracle of this image. This image appears to have been a piece of translucent stone, and when Daoxuan purified himself and observed the stone, a silver *stupa* and then a silver image appeared. People, whether monks or laymen, saw different things in the stone. If a person prayed to the stone and asked what creature he was in his previous births and where he will go in the future, the stone manifested the appropriate forms. Thus, the stone served as a mirror that showed the workings of karma. In the seventh month of the sixth year of the Zhenguan period (632) the image/stone was taken into the inner quarters of the palace and offerings were made to it.

68. In 621 when soldiers of the Tang came near the city, Monk Fatong of the Changshasi circumambulated the miraculous image in this temple and the image emitted light. During the Tang the image responded to requests for rain in years of drought; the example of the miracle in the sixth year of the Zhenguan period (632), in which Wu Wa, Duke Yinguo and the area commander-in-chief plays the central role in praying for rain, is mentioned (Soper: 27b-28a).

69. The large bronze image that survived the fire at the Xinghuangsi temple in Jiangzhou had been moved to the Bomasi temple by Daoxuan's time. In the second year of the Yonghui period (651), a thief wanted to cut a piece of metal off the image. He sawed a window grille and tried to crawl through the space, when someone grabbed his arm, and he could not free himself from the grill. In the morning monks questioned him. The thief said that "a man inside the hall, wearing white clothes, had grabbed his arm and he could not get away."

70. During the Wude period (618-627) wind blew and made the pavilion in which Tao Kan's image was housed lean northward; when monks prayed to the mountain deity, another wind blew in the opposite direction and made the pavilion stand again at the correct angle (Soper: 32a).

# Appendix

## Image Stories included in Daoxuan's Collection
(Headings based on the table of contents in 413ab)

1. The painting of Sakyamuni in Luoyang (produced by king Udayana, which matches the dream of Emperor Ming)(Eastern Han)
*Parallels:*
   FYZL, fasc. 13 (Taisho.2121: 53.383b); also, fasc. 12 (379bc).
*Secondary sources:*
   Soper: 1b-2a (translation).

2. The gold image dug out from the ground in Jianye (Sun Hao's image)(Southern Wu)
*Parallels:*
   FYZL, fasc. 13 (53.383b)
   GSZ, fasc. 1 (Taisho.2059: 50.325c-326a)
   *Shijia fanzhi,* fasc. 2 (Taisho.2088: 51.971b7-13)
   *Guang hongming ji,* fasc. 15 (Taisho.2103: 52.202a)
*Secondary sources:*
   Soper: 6b-7a; Zurcher: 278; Shinohara 1992: 201-202.

3. The stone images that came floating on Jiang river near the Wu commandary (of former Buddhas Kasyapa and Viparsya made by king Asoka, were later placed in the Tongxuansi temple) (Western Jin).
*Parallels:*
   FYZL, fasc. 13 (53.383bc); also, fasc. 12 (379c-380a) and fasc. 86 (920a19, quoted from the *Mingxiang ji*).
   *Hongming ji,* fasc. 11 (Taisho.2102: 52.71c)
   *Mingxiang ji* (quoted in the FYZL, fasc. 86 (919b-920b)
   GSZ, fasc. 13 (50.409c)
   *Guoqing bolu,* fasc. 3, document 64 (Taisho.1934: 46.809b)
   *Bianzhenglun,* fasc. 3 (Taisho.2110: 52.505a29-b2)
   XGSZ, fasc. 14 (Taisho.2060: 50. 535b10-18)
   *Shijia fanzhi,* fasc. 2 (51.971b13-20)
   *Guang hongming ji,* fasc. 15 (52.202b)
   FZTJ, fasc. 36 (Taisho.2035: 49.339b7-11), fasc. 53 (461c10-12)
   An inscription by a Liang prince who later became emperor Jianwen (r. 549-551) is reproduced in *Tushu jicheng,* fasc. 497, 14B.
*Secondary sources:*
   Soper: 12b-13a; Shinohara 1988: 163-164/ 1992: 203.

4. The golden images sent from seven kingdoms at Mt. Tai (Western Jin)
*Parallels:*
   FYZL, fasc. 13 (53.383c)

*Secondary sources:*
   Soper: 86ab, 94a

5. The golden image discovered at a beach at Yangdu (Gao Li's image later placed at the Changgansi temple) (Eastern Jin)
*Parallels:*
   FYZL, fasc. 13 (53.383c349b)
   GSZ, fasc. 13 (50.409bc)
   XGSZ (Taisho.2060: 50.693a28-b21)
   *Bianzhenglun,* fasc. 3 (52.505a17-28, also 530b16-20)
   XGSZ, fasc. 14 (Taisho.2060: 50. 535b10-18)
   *Shijia fanzhi,* fasc. 2 (51.972a3-26)
   *Guang hongming ji,* fasc. 15 (52.202b, also 181b10,11)
   FZTJ, fasc. 36 (Taisho.2035: 49.339c12-17), fascicle 53 (461c15,16)
*Other stories about the image:*
   *Daoxuan lu¨ shi gantong lu,* 524 (Taisho.2107: 52.439b9-22); *Luxiang gantong zhuan* (Taisho.1898: 45.879a16-29); *FYZL,* fasc. 14 (397a13-27)
*Secondary sources:*
   Soper: 8b-12b (partial translation, 11a-12b); Zurcher: 279, note 179; Shinohara 1988: 160-163/ 1992: 202.

6. The golden image that travelled around mountains in Xiangyang (produced by Dao'an)(Eastern Jin)
*Parallels:*
   FYZL, fasc. 13 (384b-385a)
   *Guang hongming ji,* fasc. 15 (198bc, 202bc)
   XGSZ, fasc. 29 (692c5-12, 693a9-28)
   *Shijia fangzhi,* fasc. 2 (971b22-c15)
*References to the image:*
   *Bianzhenglun,* fasc. 6 (530b24); *Guang hongming ji,* fasc. 13 (181b13)
*Secondary sources:*
   Soper: 15a-18b (partial translation, 16a-18a); Zurcher, 188, n. 46.

7. The golden image that came down from afar at Jinzhou (Tanyi's Asoka image that was later placed at the Changshasi temple)(Eastern Jin)
*Parallels:*
   FYZL, fasc. 13 (385a-386a)
   *Guang hongming ji,* 15 (202b)
   *Mingseng zhuan* (quoted in the *Meisoden sho* [*Zokuzokyo,* 134.7Ba])
   GSZ, fasc. 5 (355c-356a)
   XGSZ, fasc. 29 (692c12-22)
   *Shijia fangzhi,* fasc. 2 (971c16-972a27)
   FZTJ, 36 (341b), fasc. 53 (461c)
*Other stories about the image:*
   *Daoxuan lu¨¨ shi gantong lu,* 524 (52.439b9-22); *Luxiang gantong zhuan* (45.879a16-29); *FYZL,* fasc. 14 (397a13-27)

XGSZ, fasc. 14 (537b29-c1), fasc. 16 (556b)
FYZL, 14 (392c16-393a8)
*Hongzan fahua zhuan*, fasc. 6 (26bc)
*References to the image*:
   *Guang hongming ji*, fasc. 13 (181b15)
   *Bianzhenglun* 6 (530b25)
*Secondary sources*:
   Soper: 22a-29a (translation, 23a-28a); Zurcher: 279; Shinohara 1992: 154-202.

8.The golden image discovered in water at Wuxing (Eatern Jin)
*Parallels*:
   FYZL, fasc. 13 (386b)
*Summary:*
   A daughter of Zhou Ji, Governor of Wuxing welcomed the miraculous image
   that came floating on water, emitting golden light. Later, the image appeared
   to her in a dream, complaining of pain in the left knee. When she examined,
   she found a hole on the left knee of the image, which she repaired with gold.
   The daughter later married, and the image followed her. When she died of
   illness, people saw her go up in the sky. Later generations of the family neglected the image, and it disappeared. Only the halo of the image is still said to
   exist in the family.

9. The wooden image in Kuaiji that caused an incense miracle (Eastern Jin)
*Parallels:*
   FYZL, fasc. 13 (386b)
*Secondary sources*:
   Soper: 19a-22a 9. The wooden image in Kuaiji (Eastern Jin)

10. The golden image in Wu commandary (produced by Huihu)(Eastern Jin)
*Parallels:*
   FYZL, fasc. 13 (386b)
*Secondary sources*:
   Soper: 18b, 42b

11. The golden image dug out at the Dongye gate (Wang Mi's image)(Eastern Jin)
*Parallels:*
   FYZL, fasc. 13 (386bc)
   GSZ, fasc. 13 (410b)
   *Bianzhenglun* 3 (505a4-6)
   FZTJ, fasc. 53 (461c)
*Secondary sources*:
   Soper: 37a38a; Shinohara 1992: 202

12. The image of prince Gautama in the meditating posture at Xuzhou (Eastern Jin)
*Parallels:*
   FYZL, 91 (955c)

XGSZ, fasc. 29 (692a27-b20)
*Other stories about the image:*
JSSGL, fasc. 1 (52.410a1-21)
*Secondary sources:*
Soper: 29a-30b

13. The golden image of Manjusri image at Mt. Lu (discovered by Tao Kan discovered and later moved by Huiyuan to the his new temple Donglinsi at Mt. Lu) (Eastern Jin)
*Parallels:*
FYZL, fasc. 13 (386c-387a)
*Guang hongming ji*, 15 (203a)
GSZ, fasc. 6 (358c3-15)
*Bianzhenglun* 3 (505a)
*Beishanlu* (589a18-21)
*Lushan ji*, fasc. 1 (1028a25-b14); fasc. 3 (1039b3-5)
FZTJ, fasc. 26 (261b27-c8), fasc. 36 (339b24-c3; 341b5-7), fasc. 53 (421c12-14)
*Fozu lidai tongzai*, fasc. 7 (525b12-18)
*Other stories about the image:*
XGSZ, fasc. 19 (586a); fasc. 29 (698c-699a)
*Secondary sources:*
Soper: 30b-32b; Zurcher: 243-244, 279; Shinohara 1992: 180-200; 202-203

14. The rock image that appeared when a mountain broke up in Liangzhou (Huida's image)(Yuan Wei)
*Parallels:*
FYZL, fasc. 13 (387a)
*Guang hongming ji*, 15 (202a)
XGSZ, fasc. 25 (644c-645a)
*Shijia fangzhi*, fasc. 2 (972a28-b18)
*Other stories about the image:*
*Daoxuan lushi gantong lu*, 524 (52.37b13-c5); *Luxiang gantong zhuan* (45.876c5-27); FYZL, fasc. 14 (395b26-c19)
*Secondary sources:*
Soper: 112a-113a (XGSZ version); Shinohara 1988: 171-181.

15. The image carved on a rock cliff by the prince of Henan (Northern Liang)
*Parallels:*
FYZL, fasc. 13 (387ab)
*Guang hongming ji*, 15 (202b)
*Secondary sources:*
Soper: 90b-93b (especially, 92a-92b)

16. The rock image, sixty feet tall, produced by Juqu (Northern Liang)
*Parallels:*
FYZL, fasc. 13 (387b)

*Secondary sources:*
  Soper: 90b-93b (especially, 91b-92a,92b)

17. The golden image of Majusri in the capital city (Song)
*Secondary sources:*
  Soper: 57a

18. The copper image dug out from the ground in Dongyang (Song)
*Parallels:*
  FYZL, fasc. 14 (388a)
*Summary:*
  In the twelfth year of the Yuanjia period, under the Song (435) Liu Yuanzhi,
  who cultivated potatoes, burned the field. One are of grass strangely did not
  burn, and when he dug the ground there, he discovered a sitting image.

19. The golden image that was discovered in Jiangling by the light in a tree (Song)
*Parallels:*
  FYZL, fasc. 16 (407b)
*Summary:*
  In the fourteenth year of the Yuanjia period (437) the nun Huiyu first lived at
  a temple in Chang'an and saw red and white light. Later a golden Matreya
  image was discovered at the place of light. Later, she moved to Jiangling and
  again saw light on a tree to the east of the Lingmusi temple. A golden sitting
  image was discovered.

20. The golden image discovered by the light on a beach (Song)
*Parallels:*
  FYZL, fasc. 14 (388a)
*Secondary sources:*
  Soper: 85b-86a

21. The golden image discovered in a marsh at Shangming near Jiangling (Song)
*Parallels:*
  FYZL, fasc. 14 (388a)
*Secondary sources:*
  Soper: 52b

22. The wall paintings in Jingzhou (Song)
*Parallels:*
  FYZL, fasc. 14 (388a)

23. The small golden image in Jiangling to which Sengding's sister made the vow
(Song)
*Parallels:*
  FYZL, fasc. 14 (388ab)

*Secondary sources:*
Soper: 58a

24. The sandal wood image in Xiangzhou, for which the halo was made from a paulownia shield (Song)
*Parallels:*
FYZL, fasc. 14 (388b)
*Secondary sources:*
Soper: 55

25. The stone image in Fanyu that became light in a fire (Qi)
*Parallels:*
FYZL, fasc. 14 (388b)
*Secondary sources:*
Soper: 58b-59a

26. The metal image in Pengcheng that sweated as a sign (Qi)
*Parallels:*
FYZL, fasc. 14 (388bc); fasc. 15 (400bc)
GSZ, fasc. 13 (412bc)
*Secondary sources:*
Soper: 38a-39b.

27. The golden Avalokitesvara image in Yangdu (Qi)
*Parallels:*
FYZL, fasc. 14 (388c)
*Secondary source:*
Soper, 53a.

28. The sandalwood image of king Udayana in Jingzhou (Liang)
*Parallels:*
FYZL, fasc. 14 (389a)
*Guang hongming ji,* 15 (202ab)
GSZ, fasc. 11 (50.402c19--list of images)
*Shijia fangzhi,* fasc. 2 (972b29-c5)
*Secondary sources:*
Soper 70-72; see also 46-49, 88-89, and 259-265; Shinohara 1993; Carter 1990.

29. The golden image at the Guangzhaisi temple in Yangdu (Liang), with the story of the stone image in Shan appended.
*Parallels:*
FYZL, fasc. 14 (389ab)
*Guang hongming ji,* 15 (203a)
GSZ, fasc. 11 (50.402c19--list of images)
*Shijia fangzhi,* fasc. 2 (972b29-c5)

*Secondary sources*:
    Soper: 66a-68b

29a. The stone image in Shan district
*Parallels*:
    *Fayuah zhulih*, fasc. 14 (389b)
    GSZ, fasc. 13 (50.412ab)
    XGSZ, fasc. 29 (693c15-28)
*Secondary sources*:
    Shinohara 1991b: 210-216.

30. The life-size image of gold and silver produced by emperor Wu* (Liang)
*Parallels*:
    FYZL, fasc. 14 (389bc)
    XGSZ, fasc. 29 (693b21-c3)
    Related to story no. 32 below.
*Secondary sources:*
    Soper: 64a-65b (*FYZL* version)

31. The golden Avalokitesvara image of Prince Gao (probably referring to Gao Huan, 596-547) in Dingzhou (Yuanwei)
*Parallels*:
    FYZL, fasc. 14 (389c); fasc. 17 (411bc)
    *Guang hongming ji*, 15 (203a)
    XGSZ, fasc. 29 (693c22-693a9)
    *Shijia fangzhi*, fasc. 2 (972b18-28)
    *Datang neidian lu*, fasc. 10 (Taisho.2149: 55.339a)
*Secondary sources*:
    Soper: 114; Makita: 272-289; Shinohara 1991c: 95-99

32. The image in the Chongyundian hall that flew into the ocean (Chen)
*Parallels:*
    FYZL, fasc. 14 (389c-90a)
    *Guang hongming ji*, 15 (203a)
    XGSZ, fasc. 29 (693c3-15)
    *Shijia fangzhi*, fasc. 2 (972c6-15)
    Related to story no. 30 above.
*Secondary sources:*
    Soper: 64a-65b (*FYZL* version)

33. The stone image in Lingshisi temple in Jinzhou ([Northern] Zhou)
*Parallels:*
    FYZL, fasc. 14 (390a); fasc. 16 (407b-408a: "based on the *Liang Gaoseng zhuan*
        biography"!)
    XGSZ, fasc. 29 (693c15-27)

*Secondary sources:*
  Soper: 115ab

34. The stone image of iron ore from Beishan in Yizhou ([Northern] Zhou)
*Parallels:*
  FYZL, fasc. 14 (390ab)
  *Guang hongming ji,* 15 (202c)
  XGSZ, fasc. 29 (692a)
*Other stories about the image*
  (reading *feishan,* 52.439b15 as *beishan,* as in 45.879a32 and 52.41314)
  *Daoxuan lüshi gantong lu,* 524 (52.439b9-22); *Luxiang gantong zhuan* (45.879a16-
    29); *FYZL,* fasc. 14 (397a13-27)
*Secondary sources:*
  Soper: 120b-121b

35. The walking image at the Huayansi at Mt. Xian in Xiangzhou ([Northern] Zhou)
*Parallels:*
  FYZL, fasc. 14 (390b)
  *Guang hongming ji,* 15 (203a)
*Secondary sources:*
  Soper: 115b-116a

36. The image at the Xianghuangsi temple in Jiangzhou which moved in fire (Sui)
*Parallels:*
  FYZL, fasc. 14 (390b)
  *Guang hongming ji,* 15 (203b)
*Secondary sources:*
  Soper: 43a
*Summary:*
  During the Kaihuang period of the Sui dynasty (581-600) the Buddha hall of
  the Xinghuangsi temple in Jiangzhou was burned down. A large bronze image
  [of the Buddha], sixty feet tall, and two bodhisattva images, both sixty feet tall,
  were in the hall. When the fire reached the hall, people saw the image(s)
  suddenly rise and take a step. The building collapsed, but the image remained
  whole; though flames touched the image(s), the gold color did not change.
*Note:*
  The *Guoqing bolu* contains a letter from monastic leaders of Jiangzhou, which
  is dated the eighth day of the second month of the twelfth year of the Kaihuang
  period. Jiangzhou, or Jiankang, was the capital of the recently conquered Chen
  dynasty (557-589), and in this letter monks report that officials of the new Sui
  dynasty are destroying many temples in the city and plead to Zhiyi for help.
  In the *Guoqing bolu,* this letter (document 32) is followed by Zhiyi's appeal to
  Prince Jin, who was in charge of the area (document 33) and the prince's reply
  promising support (document 34). The Buddha hall of the Xinghuangsi temple
  might have been burned down as a part of the Sui campaign to subjugate the
  Buddhist community in the area. See Tsukamoto Zenryu 1975: 154-156.

37. Mingxian's fifty bodhisattva images (Sui)
*Parallels:*
    FYZL, fasc. 15 (401ab)
*Summary:*
    The painting of the Amitabha Buddha and 50 bodhisattvas is said to have been
    originally given by this Buddha to bodhisattva Wutong in India. After em-
    peror Ming had the famous dream and Kasyapa Matanga arrived in Loyang,
    Matanga's sister brought this painting to China. This long-forgotten painting
    is said to have been rediscovered under emperor Wen. Monk Mingxian ob-
    tained a copy from monk Daochang for the Northern Qi, and after its authen-
    ticity was confirmed, copies of the painting were sent everywhere in the
    empire.

38. The miraculous stone image at the Riyansi temple in the capital city (Sui)
*Parallels:*
    FYZL, fasc. 14 (390c)
    *Guang hongming ji*, 15 (202c)
    XGSZ, fasc. 29 (692b20-c5)
*Summary:*
    In the tenth year of the Kaihuang period (590) future emperor Yang was based
    in Yangzhou; he learned about the stone image which had been brought there
    by Indian or Central Asian monks during the Taiqing period (547-550) under
    the rule of the Liang emperor Wu*. He sent Wang Yanshou to search for it, and
    after Wang had found the image the future emperor carried it around in a
    black lacquered box as he travelled everywhere and in the end sent it to the
    Riyansi temple in the capital city Chang'an under order to have the image
    sealed so that outsiders would not be able to see it. The Riyansi temple had
    been founded by emperor Yang himself.

39. The four-faced image at the Shahesi temple in Xingzhou (Sui)
*Parallels:*
    FYZL, fasc. 14 (390c-391a)
    *Guang hongming ji*, 15 (203bc)
*Summary:*
    The four-faced Buddha in the Shahesi district temple in Xingzhou was dis-
    covered on a mountain during the rule of the founding emperor of the Sui
    dynasty. A man went onto the mountain and saw a monk guarding this
    copper image, over 3 feet tall, and when he requested that the monk give him
    the image the monk obliged him and then disappeared. Monks in many places
    who heard about the image tried to bring it down from the mountain, but
    could not lift it. When some monks of the Shahesi temple pulled the image, it
    followed their hand and came to the temple. Later, someone discovered near
    the temple a pile of gold which had the mark of a crow on it and an inscription;
    the inscription read "for the purpose of coating the four-faced image." The
    image was coated with gold; marks of a crow appeared all over the image. The
    image later disappeared suddenly. In the small river at the side of the temple

shining spots appeared at several places; people then scooped the image up [at the spot indicated by these lights in the river]. The last ruler of the Sui (Prince Tong, who reigned as emperor Tong during 617-618?) heard about the image and sent metal workers to make a copy of it, but in the end they were unsuccessful. After over two hundred days they produced a copy, but later they discovered flaws in it and gave up the project.

40. The stone image in Fanzhou that was discovered in a mountain (Tang)
*Parallels:*
FYZL, fasc. 14 (391a)
*Guang hongming ji,* 15 (203b)
*Summary:*
The stone image that He Bian and He Ji, who lived to the southwest of Ziwu river near Fangzhou, discovered on a mountain at a spot where deer gathered is said to have been among the 40 images that were hidden at the time of the Buddha Kasyapa. The image is said to have looked like the iron ore image to the east of the Yuhua, unambiguously referring to the image discovered by Jiangming described in some detail in story no. 34. It is also said that two of these 40 images had appeared by Daoxuan's time; others are still hidden on mountains. These comments appear to imply that by the time story no. 40 was written, the idea had developed around the Fanzhou region that both the image located in a temple to the east of the Yuhua temple, originally discovered by Jiangming on a mountain, and the image that He Bian and He Ji discovered on a mountain were among 40 images that were thought to have been hidden at the time of Kasyapa Buddha. As we noted earlier, the iron ore image in story no. 34 is said to have been brought there by the supernatural power of king Asoka. The explanation of the origin of these images appears to have changed.

41. The Buddha's footprints in Jianzhou which emitted supernatural light (Tang)
*Parallels:*
FYZL, fasc. 14 (392a); 36 (568a)
*Guang hongming ji,* 15 (203b)
*Other stories about the image:*
*Daoxuan lushi gantong lu,* 52.438b; *Luxiang gantong lu* (878b)
*Summary:*
This story centers around two miracles: supernatural lanterns appeared in the sky around the footprints of the Buddha on the mountain; then in the tenth year of the Zhenguan period (636/7) monk Fazang was picked up by an armoured deity and thrown to a spot seven miles outside of the temple.

42. The Buddhist stone inscription that was found in a mountain in Liangzhou (Tang)
*Parallels:*
FYZL, fasc. 14 (391ab)

43. The Buddha's footprints at the Xiangsisi in Yuzhou (Tang)
*Parallels:*
    FYZL, fasc. 14 (391b)
    *Guang hongming ji,* 15 (203a)
*Note:*
    This story mentions the miraculous lotus flower in the temple.

44. The Buddha's footprints at the Lingkansi temple in Xunzhou (Tang)
*Parallels:*
    FYZL, fasc. 14 (391b)
    *Guang hongming ji,* 15 (203b)
*Summary:*
    This story reproduces a legend of the elders: during the Jin dynasty (265-419)
    a monk found the footprints of the Buddha and encountered a mountain deity;
    later during the Song period (420-479) two monks, who recited the Lotus scrip-
    ture, went back and saw a deity; when they conferred precepts on the deity
    and his family members; the monks rediscovered the footprints of the Buddha
    nearby.

45. The walking image that moved from Fuzhou to Tanzhou (Tang)
*Parallels:*
    FYZL, fasc. 14 (392ab)
    *Guang hongming ji,* 15 (203b)
*Summary:*
    In the fourth year of the Xianqing period (659) there was a drought and the
    regional inspector of Fuzhou, surnamed Zu, prayed for rain to no effect. A
    man saw an image walking on a mountain to the east of Fuzhou. No one knew
    where it had come from. A man from Tanzhou reported that it was the image
    that had disappeared from a temple there. When people examined the route
    from there, two footprints, each two feet long, were discovered at locations five
    miles apart from each other. In order to do something about the long-lasting
    drought, the regional inspector immediately went to the image to pray, and
    officials and private citizens from everywhere in the region brought incense
    and flowers, walking the distance of over 20 miles. They described their plight
    in tears and earnestly worshiped the image. When three people lifted the
    image, the image rose easily, and they returned it to the original temple. As
    they travelled the route, clouds covered the sky and at night it poured rain.
    The image is presently located in Fuzhou.

46. The golden image that was discovered inside a rock at Lantian in Yongzhou
(Tang)
*Parallels:*
    FYZL, fasc. 14 (392b)
*Summary:*
    A story of a golden image, discovered in [first year of?] the Yonghui period
    (650) by a monk at the temple in Mt. Wuzhen in Yongzhou, is followed by

another about one image of the Buddha and two images of bodhisattvas that appeared in the same year at the top of a pillar in the Guangmingsi temple in Yizhou. Even after people shaved the images off, they reappeared. The images are said to have been originally placed in the Jiulong Buddha hall, but to have been moved by Zhang Xu to the Guangmingsi, where they still existed at the time Daoxuan wrote the passage.

47. The golden image that appeared in Li river at Exian District in Yongzhou (Tang)
*Parallels:*
    FYZL, fasc. 14 (392b)
*Secondary sources:*
    Soper: 87b-88a
*Summary:*
    The story of the discovery of a golden image in a turbulence in the Li river. Daoxuan saw the image with his own eyes and copied the inscription on its base, describing the circumstances of its production on the eighth day of the fourth month of the twentieth year of the Jianyuan period of [Former] Qin dynasty (384). We noted above the similarity of this discovery story to earlier discovery stories of Asoka images.

48. The image in Qinzhou that illumined forests and valleys (Tang)
*Parallels:*
    FYZL, fasc. 14 (392bc)
*Summary:*
    In the second month of the third year of the Longsu period (663), the central figure among the three stone images in an ancient cave in Qinzhou emitted light. This was reported to the court, and the emperor sent monk Xuanxiu of the Dazi'ensi temple in the capital city. When he arrived the light flew up and blazed like fire. At that time white clouds reached the cave and covered the light. When the clouds lifted, the light reappeared. The emperor ordered a drawing of this light prepared. The light is said to have continued until the present time, though Daoxuan, who went there in the third year of the Zhenguan period (629), could not see it.

49. The image at Mt. Wutai in Daizhou that was surrounded by miraculous sounds (Tang)
*Parallels:*
    FYZL, fasc. 14 (393ab)
*Summary:*
    In the first year of the Longsu period (661) Huize, a monk at the Huichangsi temple, was ordered by the emperor to go to Mt. Wutai and repair temples and *stupa*s. Between the Taihuaquan pond and a small spring attached to it at the top of the central peak were two *stupa*s. There was also an image of Manjusri there. In the second year of the Longsu period (662), Huize was again ordered to go to Mt. Wutai to repair the temple buildings. As he went to the central peak with over 20 people, he saw a stone image move its hands and body.

When he came to the place of the image, all he saw was a square stone. He repaired the two *stupa*s and the Manjusri image. When he was resting near the *stupa*s, he suddenly heard the repeated sound of bells, and a strange fragrance pervaded the area. When he went to the western peak he saw a monk riding a horse come up from the east. Huize and others with him waited, and when no one came he went down to welcome the monk. The monk had turned into a stump. The [Manjusri?] image sometimes appeared miraculously and then disappeared; the sound of the bell accompanied by the strange fragrance was heard frequently.

50. The image that appeared spontaneously when a mountain collapsed near the pass to the land of Liao (Tang).
*Summary*:

   During the Longsu period (661-664) Xie Rengui, army counselor of Liaodong, was sent on a mission and reached the place where a Sui ruler had fought with Liao people. He then saw a [rock?] image on a mountain at a quiet place where no one travelled. Local elders said that the image had appeared earlier. Xie had a drawing of the image made and sent it to the court.

# 8

# Dynastic Politics and Miraculous Images: The Example of Zhuli of the Changlesi Temple in Yangzhou

*Koichi Shinohara*

The *Xu gaoseng zhuan* biography of Zhuli centers around a remarkable story of this monk performing self-immolation in front of the image hall that contained two famous images. Yet Daoxuan (596-667), who compiled this biographical collection, placed this biography in the section on "merit-making" (*xingfu*), and not in the section on self-immolation (*yishen*).[1] Daoxuan gathered a variety of materials about miraculous images in the "merit-making" section (e.g., biographies of Sengming, Huida, Daoji, and Huiyun). Daoxuan thus appears to have seen Zhuli's life as one that centered around a relationship to miraculous images

In this paper I hope to clarify the special relationship between famous images and self-immolation in Zhuli's life. A reconstruction of the historical circumstances surrounding this event will be followed by a brief comparison of Zhuli's self-immolation with the many examples collected in the self-immolation section of Daoxuan's collection. I will also attempt to interpret the significance of Zhuli's refusal to let his images be moved by reviewing some well-known stories of miraculous images that occasionally would not move. This investigation of Zhuli's life will throw some light on the complex role of miraculous images in dynastic politics in medieval China.

## The outline of the biography

Let me begin my exploration with a brief summary of Zhuli's biography:

1) The introductory paragraph begins in a conventional manner, noting that his secular surname was Chu and that his family originally was from Yangdi in Henan, but escaping political disturbances there had moved to Qiantang in Wu Commandary. This brief comment may have been intended to call the reader's attention to Zhuli's northern background.[2] Zhuli left the householder's life at the age of eight, and his good reputation as a monk was widespread among monks and lay people.

2) Emperor Xuan of the Chen dynasty (r. 568-582), who is designated here as Zhongzong, had built the Taihuangsi temple in the eastern part of the city. In the second year of the Zhide period (584-5) Zhuli was appointed as the administrative head (*sizhu*) of this temple. This would have taken place under the reign of the last emperor of Chen, Chen Shubao ("Houzhu"), who reigned 582-589.

3) When the Chen dynasty was conquered by the Sui (581-617) in 589 and the monks were dispersed, Zhuli embarked on a journey in search of a good place to settle down. He travelled to Jiangdu and decided to stay at the Changlesi temple there.

4) The main body of the biography is devoted to the description of Zhuli's activities at the Changlesi temple. This section may be divided into three parts.

a) Zhuli prospered under the Sui, receiving generous support, particularly from its second ruler emperor Yang.

In 593 Zhuli built a beautiful five story stupa there.

In 597 "Emperor Yang" (who at that time was known as prince of Jin, the area commander-in-chief based in Jiangdu) returned to the region and, recognizing Zhuli's work in repairing the temple buildings at the Changlesi, placed him in charge there. Zhuli moved two images to his temple. One was King Udayana's image, which had been obtained by Emperor Wu* of the Liang dynasty. This image, which was known for its numerous miracles, had been housed in Danyang at the Longguangsi temple, which had been burned down.[3] The second was the image of Dingguang (Lamp Lighter Buddha) discovered by Wang Mi.

With the support of the entire congregation ("four divisions"), both nobles and common people, Zhuli built a special tall building, with a wing on each side, to house these images. This building was completed before the end of the year.

In 608 monks' residences were built on all four sides surrounding the hall for the images; there were also subsidiary buildings outside of the main gate, a kitchen, and storage houses. Zhuli visited the capital for a second time, where he was treated generously, and returned to Jiangdu. Kind words from the court followed.

In 614, at his own expense, Zhuli carved copies of the miraculous images, along with two bodhisattva images from fragrant sandal wood, and placed them in the image hall.

b) The second part of this Changlesi section of the biography describes the difficulties that Zhuli encountered when the Sui dynasty collapsed in 618. Refugees of monks, nuns, and lay people, as well as rotting corpses, filled the city streets. Vowing to protect the temple buildings, Zhuli remained in the temple, which had become deserted. With "a rabbit as his companion" Zhuli struggled to maintain the building in good repair. The Tang dynasty was then established, and declared its pro-Buddhist policy widely. Former monks and other supporters returned to the temple. The city had been burned down but the temple building remained intact.

c) The third part consists of the description of the circumstances of Zhuli's self-immolation.

In 623 Fu Gongyou rebelled in the region "south of the Jiang river." Shortly before he openly rebelled, Fu Gongyou (perhaps in his capacity as an official of the Tang, i.e., vice-director of the branch department of the state affairs, Huainan Circuit) "moved and scattered"(*sasong*) one hundred Buddhist and Daoist temples across the Jiang river to the region "south of the river" (*Jiangnan*). Zhuli sent letters repeatedly, requesting that this policy be reversed; he vowed that, if the request were denied, he would perform self-immolation in front of the image hall in order to remain at the site of the present temple buildings forever.[4] Fu Gongyou declared himself to be the emperor of a new dynasty; his ambition was to overthrow the present rule. He disregarded Zhuli's letters completely.

Zhuli told his disciples that he would now perform self-immolation in front of the Buddhas; he could not bear to see the images cross the Jiang river. Predicting that after his death the images would definitely cross the river southward, he offered his robes and other personal belongings to the images. A description of Zhuli's self-immolation follows: having bathed in fragrant water, he sat facing west with his legs crossed and lit the firewood he had ordered his disciples to pile up. It was on the eighth day of the tenth month and Zhuli was 80 years old.

After Zhuli's death the images were moved southward, but the temple buildings escaped destruction by fire. The "treasures of dharma" (scriptures?) and the congregation of monks were restored to their previous state of prosperity. Disciple Huian and Zhize took seriously their debt to the deceased master and raised an inscription inside the temple precinct. Yu Shinan (558-638), Companion of the Crown Prince, composed the text of the inscription.[5] Daoxuan, who included this biography in his collection, comments that he heard that the images were returned to the hall from which they had been taken.

## Historical background

I begin thinking about this biography by asking the question: why did Zhuli care about the images so much that he was willing to perform self-immolation to protest the order to have them moved across the Jiang river? In order to answer this question we will also have to explore the meaning of the rebel leader Fu Gongyou's policy of moving and scattering Buddhist and Daoist temples to the region south of the river. I explore the question from several related points of view.

The complex relationship between the Buddhist community in South China, which had been generously supported by the Chen court, and the new Sui dynasty which conquered the Chen in 589 has been discussed in considerable detail by Tsukamoto Zenryu (Tsukamoto: 147-190). In 590, shortly after the conquest of the Chen; a massive rebellion against the new Sui rule spread in south China. Though the rebellion was put down without great difficulties, the appointment of Prince Guang of Jin, a strong figure in the Sui court who had played the central role in the conquest of Chen, as the area commander-in-chief in Jiangdu in the same year, was a direct consequence of this rebellion (Ref., *Tongjian*, fascicle 177 [12.5529-30; 5532]). This site of the Area Command had been generally known as Guangling; under the Sui, it was also known as Yangzhou, though it is at some distance accross the river Jiang to the north of the old Yangzhou under the Southern dynasties.[6] The Sui government appears to have manipulated place names in the South very carefully: the name Jiankang that had been used by preceding Southern dynasties was eliminated; the name Yangzhou, which referred to the region around the capital city Jiankang under Southern dynasties, was used by the Sui to refer to the region around the new Area Command situated outside of the domain of the Chen dynasty.

Some members of the local monastic community in the South appear to have been involved in the rebellion, and new policies were introduced to strengthen the government's control over this community. Tsukamoto refers to a passage in the biography of Huijue (554-606) which mentions a new regulation promulgated by the Sui court allowing only two temples in each Region (516b5-9); one important achievement of this monk was to have this regulation rescinded (516b4-8; Tsukamoko, p. 153). The *Guoqing bolu* contains letters between monks in Jiankang, renamed Jiangzhou by the

Sui, Zhiyi, and Prince Guang; these monks complained about the destruction of vacated temples and requested Zhiyi's assistance in putting an end to this practice (Ikeda, pp. 288-295).

This development is particularly noteworthy since the Sui court generally adopted a pro-Buddhist stance and generously supported Buddhist communities all over the empire. A variety of initiatives were taken to support the Buddhist cause in the South as well. Shortly after arriving at his new post in Jiangdu, Prince Guang received the Bodhisattva precepts from Zhiyi; a close relationship between the prince and Zhiyi developed, which extended beyond Zhiyi's death in 598 into the support of the Tiantai community Zhiyi left behind. Tsukamoto also describes how at Jiangdu Prince Guang gathered a wide range of Buddhist writings and established a canonical collection in his residence (pp. 174-178). Prince Guang's effort to gather eminent monks from South China in the newly established Riyansi temple in Jiangdu is also described in some detail (pp. 180-184). In this latter context Tsukamoto notes that some monks appear to have refused to respond to Prince Guang's invitation; such an invitation appears to have carried with it an element of coercion, which exposes its purpose partly in controlling and domesticating the conquered people (p. 184).

In this context, Tsukamoto also briefly mentions Zhuli's activities at the Changlesi temple (p. 178). The *Xu gaoseng zhuan* biography summarized above indicates that after the Chen dynasty fell, Zhuli went to Jiangdu, the seat of Sui power in the South, and we may safely assume that his remarkable activities at Changlesi were supported by the Sui leaders, particularly Prince Guang, who later became the second emperor Yang. I am inclined to believe that it was this close connection with the Sui power that enabled Zhuli to have the two famous miraculous images brought across the Jiang river from the Longguangsi in the old southern capital Jiankang to his temple Changlesi in Jiangdu. Sui rulers based in Jiangdu may have been particularly interested in having famous images which had close relationships with a variety of southern dynasties brought to a temple under its control.

Martha L. Carter recently reviewed the wide range of evidence concerning the history of this image.[7] Carter suggests that the Udayana image legend was concocted in China between 385 and 420 around the image that had been brought first to Chang'an before 400 and then was moved to the Longguangsi in Jiankang in 417 (Carter 1990: 10, 15). The image that Zhuli is said to have "recovered from the ruins of the Lung-kuang-ssu (Longguangsi) after it was burned down by Sui troops in 588-89" might well have been a copy of this image (Carter: 16; also 10).

Around the fifth and early sixth centuries many Chinese stories about the Udayana image appeared. Carter mentions in this connection the story of the image at the Damingsi temple, told in Daoxuan's miracle story collection (story no. 28 in the *Ji shenzhou sanbao gantong lu*, Taisho.2106: 52.419bc) (Carter: 10). In this story the image is closely associated with the famous pro-Buddhist emperor Wu* of the Liang dynasty. When this image arrived from India on the fifth day of the fourth month of the tenth year of Tianjian (511), Emperor Wu* welcomed it by going 40 miles outside of Yangzhou; here this place name probably refers to the capital city Jiankang. Daoxuan states that the image was ultimately housed in the Damingsi temple, which was built in 562 in the Northern suburb of the capital city Jingzhou (or Jiangling).[8] The author of the *Xu gaoseng zhuan* biography of Zhili appears to have been familiar with this story, since he describes the Udayana image that Zhili moved to the Changlesi temple as the one that was obtained by Emperor Wu* of the Liang dynasty (695a17).

The story of the image discovered by Wang Mi (360-407) under the Eastern Jin dynasty (317-419) is also found in Daoxuan's collection (no. 11, Taisho: 52.417a), where it is said that the founder of the Song dynasty (Liu Yu, r. 420-422), who had not originally believed in Buddhism, began to respect the religion after obtaining this image (a9,10). In this entry, based on the early passage describing this image in Huili's biography in the *Gaoseng zhuan* (410b5-9), the image is said to have first been placed at the Waguansi and later moved to Longguangsi.[9] If King Udayana's image was located at the Longguangsi temple, as Zhuli's biography notes explicitly, the two images attributed respectively to King Udanayna and Wang Mi would both have been housed in this same temple in Jiankang, and were only later moved by Zhuli to the Changlesi temple.[10] Names of eminent southerners figure prominently in the stories about these images, indicating that they could easily have served as important symbols of the southern dynasties and the Buddhist community supported by them.

If Zhuli's activities at Jiangdu were supported generously by the Sui, the long paragraph describing Zhuli's difficulties when the Sui dynasty fell may convey a rather specific message; since he and his temple were known to have prospered under the Sui, their situation was particularly difficult as their patron had been defeated.

The biography of Fu Gongyou is found in the two dynastic histories of the Tang.[11] These biographies note that Fu Gongyou had an old friend called Zuo Youxian, with whom he cultivated a heterodox Daoist teaching of avoiding grains, and Zuo Youxian played a crucial role in the rebellion. Having rebelled, Fu Gongyou called his dynasty Song and chose the old Chen capital as his own.

It is not clear what the expression "moving and scattering (*sasong*) one hundred Buddhist and Daoist temples to the region south of the Jiang river" means. As Tsukamoto noted, many of the temples in the land formerly under Chen rule appear to have been destroyed when the widespread rebellion in 590 was put down. I wonder if Fu Gongyou's initiative to have temples brought back and scattered in this same region ("south of the Jiang river") roughly thirty years later had something to do with this background. Fu Gongyou appears to have attempted to restore the tradition of the southern dynasties. His insistence on having the images that Zhuli had brought to Jiangdu returned to Jiankang might have been a part of this larger ambition.

According to his biography Zhuli told his disciples that he "could not bear to see the images crossing the Jiang river" (b14). Since the Jiang river marked the northern border of the Chen dynasty, Zhuli appears here to be refusing to return the miraculous images to the general area (or more specifically to the former capital city of Jiankang) from which they had been brought to him earlier. Fu Gongyou's close friendship with Zuo Youxian, who appears to have been a follower of a Daoist teaching, might also indicate that Fu had been interested in religious matters for special personal reasons.

### Zhiyi (539-598) and Zhuli on miraculous images: points of contact

Zhuli (544-623) was a younger and a less prominent contemporary of Zhiyi under the Chen and Sui dynasties. Both these monks were first supported by the Chen court, and when this dynasty fell, again became favored monks of the new Sui dynasty. Here I am particularly interested in possible connections between the circumstances of Zhiyi's death and Zhuli's activities in Jiangdu.

As I discussed in greater detail in an earlier study, Zhiyi deliberately chose the location of the large Maitreya image in Shicheng as the place of his death (Shinohara 1991b: 203-207). On the twenty-first day of the eleventh month of the seventeenth year of the Kaihuang period (very early in the solar year 598), Zhiyi made a vow in front of this image "to bring together and repair the two images of Vipasyin and Kasyapa in the Wu Commandary, to repair the damaged temple of the Asoka stupa in Mao District, and to redecorate with gold leaf the stone Maitreya image, 10 *zhang* tall, in Shan" (Ikeda: 359.1, 2).[12] The Maitreya image at Shan is the image in front of which Zhiyi was making this vow. The story of the two miraculous stone images in the Wu Commandary is found in a variety of sources, including the *Gaoseng zhuan* biography of Huida (Taisho.2059: 50.409c18-28).[13] Although in this biography the images are not explicitly said to have been Asoka images, they are designated as such in other sources.[14] According to Huida's biography, Huida stayed for three years at the Tongxuansi temple where these images were placed and then went to Kuaiji where he discovered a stupa in Mao, "also made by king Asoka" (410a1; Shinohara 1988: 164-167). The third item in Zhiyi's vow refers to this stupa.

The *Xu gaoseng zhuan* biography of Zhuli states explicitly that he was placed in charge of the temple by Prince Guang of Jin, who had returned to Jiangdu in "the 17th year of the Kaihuang period" (695a15,16). This lunar year, which began in January, 597 and ended in February, 598, was also the year of Zhiyi's death. Guanding's biography of Zhiyi, "*Sui tiantai zhizhe dashi biezhuan,*" states that in the tenth month of the seventeenth year of the Kaihuang period (597), Prince Guang returned to his post in Jiangdu. Around the time he returned from the northern capital region to Jiangdu in the South, Prince Guang made the arrangements to bring Zhiyi back from Mt. Tiantai to Jiangdu. The *Guoqing bolu*, document 62, is a letter from prince Guang to Zhiyi, dated the twenty-second day of the ninth month; this appears to have been the letter that the prince's emissary Gao Xiaoxin took with him when he went to Mt. Tiantai to bring Zhiyi back to Jiangdu (Ikeda: 357). The prince was also aware that Zhiyi was not well at that time. Another letter mentions the medicine that the prince was sending to Zhiyi (Ikeda: 358, 359); the medicine which Zhiyi is said to have refused to take in the corresponding passage in the *Biezhuan* probably had been sent to him by the prince (196a14-17).[15] On the twenty-fourth day of the eleventh month, that is, three days after he made the vow in front of the Maitreya image, Zhiyi passed away. Zhiyi left a testamental letter for the prince, and in his response to this letter (*Guoqing bolu*, document 66; Ikeda: 379-389) the prince promises to decorate the miraculous stupa in Mao, the stone images in Wu, and the Maitreya image in Shan District (Ikeda: 380.42, 43).

This sequence of events around Zhiyi's death suggests that there may have been some important connection between Zhiyi's death and Zhuli's success in obtaining the famous images attributed to King Udayana and Wang Mi. The poor conditions of the three famous miraculous images and stupa mentioned in Zhiyi's vow may have been caused, at least in part, by the suppression of the indigenous Buddhist leadership and the widespread destruction of temples that resulted from the rebellion of 590. Zhiyi had appealed to Prince Guang earlier on behalf of the leading monks in Jiankang/Jiangzhou to have the destruction of temples stopped; shortly before his death Zhiyi might again have requested the prince to repair important cultic centers in the South which had been damaged or neglected. This hypothesis would make it easier to understand why Zhiyi raised as the central concern in his last vow the issue of repairing the stone images in the Wu Commandary and the Asoka stupa in the Mao District. The prince might then have responded properly to Zhiyi's request by directing his attention not only to the images and the stupa mentioned in Zhiyi's vow, but also to other famous images that had been similarly neglected since the fall of the Chen. Prince Guang, who was intent on turning Jiang-du into a major Buddhist center, may thus have expanded the scope of his promise to Zhiyi to repair the two images and a stupa into a larger project that included transferring some well-known images from Jiankang to Jiangdu.[16]

The second part of my hypothesis, more central to the exploration here, is that in carrying out this larger project, Prince Guang may have turned to Zhuli, and possibly to many others, to rectify this situation of the wide-spread neglect of miraculous images and/or to take advantage of it to bring other well-known images under his direct control in temples at Jiangdu.[17] Obtaining two such images and building an image hall, other buildings surrounding the hall, and carving copies of these images along with two Bodhisattva images that were also placed in the image hall, constituted the main part of Zhuli's accomplishments. The biography of Zhuli summarized above states clearly that Zhuli accomplished these feats after Prince Guang returned to Jiangdu in "the seventeenth year of the Kaihuang period (597)" and placed Zhuli in charge of the Changlesi temple. Since Prince Guang became the Crown Prince in 600 and rose to the throne in 604, the emperor who treated Zhuli kindly at the court when he went up to the capital in 608 was in fact Emperor Yang, formerly known as Prince Guang.[18] His support for Zhuli in Jiangdu continued beyond the prince's return to the capital city of Chang'an in the North.[19]

In this hypothetical reconstruction Zhuli emerges as a figure who addressed one of the important concerns that preoccupied Zhiyi before his death and dealt with it in his own way, with the support of Zhiyi's patron prince Guang of Jin, whose own political fortunes rose meteorically after Zhiyi's death. Both Zhiyi and Zhuli received generous support from this powerful figure of the Sui dynasty. Since these two monks had received generous support from the conquered Chen court, their relationship with the new dynasty may have been a delicate matter. While responding to Prince Guang's offer of generous support, Zhiyi also appears to have been careful to maintain a certain distance from him; Zhiyi's refusal to stay in Jiangdu indefinitely (*Guoqing bolu*, document 29, Ikeda: 282,283; *Biezhuan*, Taisho.2050: 50.195a21) and his choice of Mt. Tiantai in the South as the location of his community might have been motivated by this concern.

Zhuli, in contrast, appears to have sided with prince Guang whole-heartedly. Paradoxically, after Zhiyi's death the fortunes of the Tiantai community became closely tied to the fortunes of the Sui dynasty, and this close relationship is said to explain the decline of this school under the subsequent Tang dynasty (Weinstein: 290-291). Zhuli, who identified himself with the Sui more wholeheartedly, appears to have succeeded in securing continuing support from the Tang as well.

But this continuing imperial support under the Tang might have been secured to a large extent by Zhuli's self-immolation. Zhuli had obtained the two famous southern images with the help of the Sui ruler, Prince Guang, who later became the second emperor of the Sui. Because of this close association with the Sui, Zhuli's position under the new Tang dynasty (618-907) was probably somewhat precarious. Then Fu Gongyou rebelled against the Tang in 623; Fu appears to have attempted to establish a new southern dynasty. The return of the images across the river Jiang might have been a part of the larger symbolic and religious gesture declaring this intention. Zhuli's refusal to return the images might have had a larger meaning; he was declaring his allegiance to Northern powers by taking this stance. Zhuli vowed to perform self-immolation to dramatize his un-willingness to return the images; at this point Zhuli's primary concern might have been to keep the images in his temple. By the time Fu's open disregard of Zhuli's vow compelled him to carry out the threat of self-immolation, Zhuli knew that the images would cross the Jiang river after his death anyway, and he said as much to his disciples. Thus the meaning of his self-immolation appears to have changed by this time: rather than a way of keeping the images in his temple, Zhuli was very publicly declaring his opposition to the southern rebel Fu Gongyou by this act, and by implication he was emphatically affirming his allegiance to the ruling, Northern, dynasty of Tang. The fact that an eminent statesman Yu Shinan, who was close to Emperor Taizong (r. 626-649), wrote Zhuli's inscription probably indicates that this message of Zhuli's self-immolation was registered by the Tang court. Moreover, this demonstration of his loyalty appears also to have served Zhuli's original purpose in the long run. The biography ends by noting that by the time Daoxuan compiled his bio-graphical collection in the middle of the seventh century the images had been returned to Zhuli's image hall.[20]

If we disregard the fact that Zhuli had performed self-immolation, while Zhiyi died a natural death, the story of Zhuli's death contains some interesting parallels to that of Zhiyi's death 25 years earlier. Before he died Zhiyi made a vow in front of a well-known image, which included an indirect plea to his patron prince Guang, and left the text of this vow with his final letter to the prince. Zhuli also made a vow, requesting the local ruler Fu Gongyou to have the images he had gathered exempted from the order to be moved across the Jiang river. Fu Gongyou was not a patron of Zhuli, but quite possibly a figure whom Zhuli knew to be hostile to him. But Zhuli must have also known that Zhiyi's vow followed by his death had had a powerful impact on Prince Guang, who carried out the deceased monk's requests with great enthusiasm. I speculate that Zhuli, who I suspect benefited directly from Zhiyi's legacy in this matter, might have symbolically recapitulated Zhiyi's earlier feat with his self-immolation. Having wagered his own life against the permission to let the images remain in his temple, and having lost, Zhuli saw no other option but to live out the consequences of his vow. But he might also have thought of his own death in front of the two famous images as something similar to that of Zhiyi.

## Other stories of self-immolation

As I noted earlier Daoxuan placed Zhuli's biography in the "merit-making" section of his biographical collection. This may mean that Daoxuan saw Zhuli's self-immolation as rather different from other known examples of this act, and saw the primary significance of his life in his relationship with the images he guarded in his temple. What made Zhuli's self-immolation different from other examples must have been its rather obvious motive. Zhuli's self-immolation was a part of his vehement protest again Fu Gongyou's policy that involved moving the two miraculous images Zhuli had brought to his temple; without this specific political context Zhuli would not have performed this act. Such political goals are seldom mentioned in stories of self-immolation; in most cases self-immmolation is presented as a feat of intrinsic religious value.

Biographies in the self-immolation section of the *Gaoseng zhuan* and the *Xu gaoseng zhuan* collections mention a variety of motives that led their subjects to perform this act. References to the Medicine King chapter of the Lotus Sutra are found frequently, indicating that often monks were inspired to perform self-immolation by the story of Bodhisattva Sarva-sattvapriyadarsana (Fayu, Taisho: 50.404c13; Huishao, 404c28; Sengyu, 405a11,18; Huiyi, 405b24; Huitong, 683c20,22, the two nuns in Jingzhou, 684a3). Monks in the *Xu gaoseng zhuan* biographies who are said to have burned their fingers and arms must also have been inspired by the same example in the Lotus Sutra (Faning, 678b7-10; Sengya, 768c21, 679a1-6 [note the reference to the Mahayana Sutra, a13]; Dazhi, 682b22).[21] Sometimes the teaching of rebirth in Pure Land led people to commit religious suicide: Faguang, who was a practitioner of Pure Land scriptures, performed this deed to be reborn there (405c21); a person who was instructed by Shandao about rebirth in the Pure Land threw himself off a willow tree and died (684a15-19). In some earlier stories monks are said to have offered their bodies to feed hungry animals or people (Tancheng, 404a24, Fajin, 404b8-120). Other stories about offering one's own body to others include the story of Sengfu, who offered his inner organs to redeem a child from a thief (404b28-c7), and that of Puyuan, who gouged his eyes out and then cut his head off to offer to "an evil man" who asked for them (680c5-7).

In a few cases the relationship with secular rulers is highlighted in the story of monk's self-immolation. In a year of famine, Fajing cut off pieces of flesh from his body to feed the starved; this conduct which led to his death also forced Anzhou, the leader of the Northern Liang state, to send a large quantity of grains and open his storage houses to feed the people (404b14-16).[22] Though he appears to have had no specific political agenda, Huiyi's self-immolation was performed in full public view, with Emperor Xiaowu of the Song dynasty (r. 453-464) and members of his court in attendance. Dazhi is said to have gone to the Eastern Capital (Luoyang) and presented a memorial, seeking permission to set fire to one arm at Mt. Song "in order to repay the generosity of the state." The burning of the arm, which led to his death, was performed with the court's permission (682bc).

Zhiming, or Zheng Ting, was a well-known political figure under the Sui, who continued to serve under the short-lived dynasty called Zheng, established by Wang Shichong briefly in Luoyang.[23] According to the *Xu gaoseng zhuan* biography, Zheng Ting had requested permission from Wang Shichong to renounce the householder's life, but the permission was not given. He read Mahayana scriptures in the evenings, and when he got to the Lotus Sutra, he made the decision to renounce the householder's life, against the will of the ruler. After he and his wife shaved each other's head, Zheng Ting said to his wife, "My wish (or vow) is fulfilled." He then appeared at the palace wearing monk's robes and holding a staff, declaring that he had already renounced the householder's life. Wang Shichong was angered and order him to be executed. Zheng Ting was delighted, saying, "My wish is again fulfilled." When he was taken to the execution ground along the Luo River, Zheng Ting requested to be executed immediately, saying that otherwise he might be forgiven, against his wishes, and so he would not permit the monks and laymen gathered there to postpone the execution until the evening. After he was executed, the order to release him arrived, a little too late. In this story the idea of disobeying the order of a secular ruler and seeking death in connection with this act are given positive religious significance, though unlike Zhuli's story, the religious goal in question is Zhiming's personal salvation, rather than a matter of keeping specific images in his temple.

Sengqing is said to have performed self-immolation in front of an image of Vimalakirti (405c6), and at age 70 Faning lit his finger on fire in front of the Buddha image (678b7). In both these cases, however, there is no suggestion that self-immolation in front of a Buddha image was carried out to send messages to secular rulers.[24]

This review of the self-immolation stories suggests that in spite of occasional parallels regarding the monk's conflict with secular power, Zhuli's story of self-immolation, particularly if it is read in the manner proposed here, is distinct at least from the majority of the stories in the "self-immolation" sections of the two relevant biographical collections.

### The moving of Asoka images

As I noted earlier in my study of Asoka images, stories about such images in China often mention that they expressed their wishes to go to specific temples (Shinohara 1992: 216-217). To list several better known examples, the ox pulling the cart carrying the image discovered by Gao Li stopped at the corner of the road leading to the Changgansi temple, refusing to obey the command of the man in charge; when allowed to follow its own wish, the animal went straight to this temple (Taisho.2059: 50.409c3-5). When leaders of the local medium cult and followers of Huang Lao's teaching went out to welcome the two stone images that came into the bay in Wu Commandary, the weather turned violently stormy; when pious Buddhists paid their respects and chanted songs, the weather turned quiet, and the images accepted their welcome (409c20-26). When an Asoka image appeared in the northern suburb of Jingzhou, presumably in response to the fervent request of Tanyi of the Changshasi temple, monks from the Baimasi first went out to take the image to their own temple, but the image would not move. Tanyi sent three of his disciples, and the image became light and flew up, allowing them to bring it to the Changshasi temple (356a3-7). The image which the famous general Tao Kan is said to have found in Guangzhou and sent to the Hanqisi in Wuchang is another example. When Tao Kan attempted to move the image to another location, the image became very heavy and the boat that carried it sank. Later, when his temple at Mt. Lu, called Donglinsi, was completed, Huiyuan (324-416) prayed sincerely requesting the image to come to the new temple; the image became light and floated [over to Huiyuan's temple] (358c3-17).

It is perhaps significant that both the story of Tanyi's image and that of the image associated with Tao Kan and Huiyuan, located in Mt. Lu and in Jingzhou outside of the immediate southern capital region, mention that the temples to which the image agreed to move had recently been established. The story of Tanyi's image suggests strongly that the rivalry between the Baimasi and the newly established Changshasi lies behind the story. In the earlier above-mentioned study I focused on the ambivalent attitude toward Tao Kan in the *Gaoseng zhuan* story, and speculated that the story might have evolved in two stages: first, as a story about a famous local military hero in Wuchan and the image he brought from Guangzhou to a local temple called Hanqisi; second, as a story describing how this image was moved to Mt. Lu, when the famous monk Huiyuan established his temple there (Shinohara 1992: 185-189). At least in the case of these two stories the story of an Asoka image miraculously indicating the temple to which it wished to be taken appears to have developed in the context of complex temple politics, which in turn must have been shaped by larger changes in the secular world.

Stories about miraculous images, many of which were said to have been produced by King Asoka and brought to China, often attempt to trace the routes the images were believed to have traveled to reach China and then the temples and palace buildings in which they were housed in China. In many cases the moving of miraculous images from one location to another was not a particularly sensitive matter. But sometimes it must have been a highly sensitive matter, both religiously and politically, and I am inclined to believe that some of the stories about images miraculously indicating the temple to which they were to be taken may have developed to legitimize controversial transfers.

If we follow the reading of Zhuli's biography proposed above, the transfer of the two famous images first to Changlesi in Jiangdu and then back across the Jiang River, probably to the former southern capital Jiankang, appears to have been a highly controversial matter. But the active agent in this story is not the images but the monk who guarded them; a story of a monk's self-immolation takes the place of stories of images performing miraculous feats. Nevertheless, I am intrigued to note that here again a story of an extraordinary event is presented in connection with the account of the transfer of famous images. I also wonder whether this shift in the nature of the extraordinary event might indicate that the cult of miraculous images had declined significantly by early Tang. [In an earlier study on the function of miraculous images I noted that miraculous images often predicted dynastic fortunes, and that these images appear to have lost one important function after the unification of China (Shinohara 1992: 64, 65).]

# Notes

The research for this paper was assisted by a grant from the Social Sciences and Humanities Council of Canada.

1. On self-immolation sections in the three standard biographical collections, see Jan Yün-hua: 243-268.

2. N. 3 in Taisho.2060: 50.695 indicates that the three variant editions from the Sung, Yuan, and Ming periods read this last line as "For this reason [Zhuli] renounced the householder's life there." This reading, by providing the reason why Zhuli underwent this ceremony in Qiantang in the South, appears to emphasize his Northern background.

3. The name Danyang is here used to refer to the old southern capital of Jiankang. In the *Zizhi ton gjian*, fasc. 190 (13. 5971), the city that rebel Fu Gongyou chose as his capital is specified as Danyang; the same sentence then proceeds to state that Fu repaired the old palace building of Chen and resided there. The palace building of the Chen dynasty must have been located in its capital city Jiankang.

4. The original passage (695b11) may also be read to mean "to keep the temples [at the present site]". Assuming that the sentences here reproduce (or are meant to reproduce) the content of a letter Zhuli sent to Fu, I have chosen the interpretation presented here for the following reason: in such a letter Zhuli is more likely to have addressed the secular leader with utmost respect, thus maintaining the surface appearance that he is seeking only the permission to perform the ritual suicide to fulfil his personal wish to remain in his own familiar temple; to tie the question of self-immolation directly to that of keeping the temple at the present site would have given the impression of openly challenging secular authorities.

5. Yu Shinan's biographies are found in the *Jiu tangshu*, fasc. 72 (8.2565-2571) and the *Xin tangshu*, fascicle 102 (13.3969-3973). Tsukamoto suggested that the *Xu gaoseng zhuan* biography was based on this inscription by Yu Shinan (Tsukamoto: 189, n. 23).

6. The *Tongjian* passages state that Prince Jin was appointed as the "Area Commander-in-chief of Yangzhou, based in Jiangdu." After Princes Guang of Jin and Jun of Qin led the forces and conquered the Chen dynasty, their father, the founding emperor of Sui, first appointed Prince Jun in that position, and appointed the more forceful Prince Guang as the Area Commander-in-chief of Bingzhou. In describing the earlier appointment of Prince Jun as the Area Commander-in-chief of Yangzhou, the *Tongjian* notes that he was appointed in that position "based in Guangling" (12.5518). The Area Commander-in-chief was based in Guangling, located to the north of the Jiang river. The location was renamed as Yangzhou by the Sui government when the Area Command was established there in the 589; the Commandary was also known as Jiangdu, the Jiangdu palace was found within it (*Suishu*, fasc. 31 [3.873.2, 4]). Liuhe, where Prince Guang's army was based during the campaign again the Chen (*Tongjian*: 12.5497.14, 5504.7) was placed under the control of this Commandery (*Suishu*, fasc. 31 [3.873.13-874.1]). The two names Yangzhou and Jiangdu are both used in referring to the base of Prince Guang's Command in the *Guoqing bolu* (Yangzhou: 26, 47, 81, 83, 86, 93; Jiangdu in documents nos. 43, 47, 65, 76, 85, 89). Yangzhou was a name that had been used earlier

to refer to a location near the Southern capital Jiankang; this location was called Danyang by the Sui government (*Suishu*, fasc. 31 [3.876.12]). It is important to keep in mind that the same place name was used to refer to a different location under the Sui.

7. Earlier discussions of this famous image includes one by Alexander Soper (Soper: 259-265; also, 46b-49a, 70b-72b and 88a-89b; the *Ji shenzhou sanbao gantong lu* passage is translated in 70b-71b). Early legends about King Udayana's image are summarized also in Takada, pp. 10-14. Henderson and Hurvitz discussed the Seiryuji image, which was a copy of this image brought to Japan by Chonen (1956). The story of this image is also told in Xuanzang's *Datang xiyuji*, fasc. 5 (*Datang xiyuji xiaozhu*: 468,469).

8. Daoxuan thus preserved contradictory sources about the location of the Udayana image: it is said to have been located at the Damingsi temple in Jingzhou in a miracle story collection; in the *Xu gaoseng zhuan* biography of Zhuli, also compiled by Daoxuan, it is said to have been housed at the Longguangsi temple in Jiankang.

Daoxuan was apparently aware that there was more than one Udayana image in China. In the spring of the second year of Qianfeng period (667), only several months before his death on the third day of the tenth month of the same year, deities visited Daoxuan and answered a variety of questions. The record of this conversation, preserved in variant versions as *Daoxuan lüshi gantong lu* (Taisho.2107: 52,435-42), *Lüxiang gantong lu* (Taisho.1898: 45.874-882), and in the *Fayuan zhulin*, fasc. 14, contains an exchange about the sandalwood image at the Damingsi temple. After noting that the tradition describes the image at the Damingsi temple (in Jingzhou) as the original copy of the Udayana image, which was brought to China during the Liang dynasty, Daoxuan pointed out that Udayana's image also existed in the capital city (Chang'an) at that time. Which was the original copy? The god then explained to Daoxuan that the copy which existed in the Daxingshansi temple in the capital city was produced in 589 when emperor Wen of Sui sent Liu Guyan to the Damingsi temple to welcome the image to the new temple in the capital city. Liu Guyan, who was originally from the Jingzhou area, produced a new copy of the image, which also proved to produce miracles, and left the original at the Damingsi temple. Therefore, the Damingsi image is the original Chinese copy of the Udayana image (52.438b1-17; 45.877b23-c11; 53.396b19-6; Soper, 71b,72a).

After telling this story Daoxuan comments that the miraculous image refused to move to the North (52.438b13; 45.877c7; 53.c2, Soper, 72a [I read this passage differently from Soper: "*gufo*," or "old Buddha," simply refers to the original copy of the image]). Daoxuan may have been aware of the earlier controversy about moving this image when he made this comment.

The way in which Daoxuan presented this piece of information, as a special and personal revelation from god, leads me to believe that this story about the origin of the Daxianshansi image was not attested in existing historical sources. Nevertheless, this story calls attention to the fact that more than one Udayana image existed in China during Daoxuan's lifetime, and Daoxuan was aware and somewhat puzzled by this fact.

Yet another story about the origin of the Udayana image is found as the deity's answer to another question ("the miraculous image at the Longguangsi in the area south of the Jiang River," *Daoxuan lüshi gantonglu*, 52.437c, *Lüxiang gantong lu*, 45.876c-877a, *Fayuan zhulin*, 53.395c-396a (Soper, 47ab). In this passage, the deity explicitly rejects the view that the image had been brought by Kumarajiva.

The *Ji shenzhou sanbao gantonglu* passage on the Udayana image is discussed in further detail in my other contribution to the present volume, "Changing Roles of Miraculous Images in Medieval Chinese Buddhism: A Study of the Miracle Image Section in Daoxuan's *Ji shenzhou sanbao gantonglu*."

9. According to the *Gaoseng zhuan*, the image was first presented to the founding emperor of the Song, who welcomed it to the court. It was during the Jingping period (423-424) that the image was moved to the Waguangsi (410b8,9). I commented briefly on the stories about this image in the discussion of Asoka image stories appended to my study of the biography of Zhiyi (Shinohara 1992: 208, 215, and 216).

10. Zhuli's biography states explicitly that the Longguangsi temple was in Danyang, which, as I noted earlier, meant Jiankang. The list of the the three monks from major temples in Jiankang/Jiangzhou who appealed to Zhiyi regarding the desctruction of vacated temples includes a monk called Faling of the Longguangsi temple (Ikeda: 288). This suggests that the Longguangsi was a major temple in Jiankang at that time.

11. *Jiu tangshu*, fasc. 56 (7.2269-70); and *Xin tangshu*, fasc. 87 (12.3724-25); see also *Zizhi tongjian*, fasc. 190 (13.5970-776).

12. The expression "bring together" (*juhe*, Ikeda:359.1) used in connection with the two stone images in Wu Commandary suggests that these two images which, according to the *Gaoseng zhuan* account, had been housed at the Tongxuansi temple, had by then been separated from each other and placed in two different locations.

13. I discussed these stories in my earlier articles (Shinohara 1988: 163-167; Shinohara 1992: 209, 212, 216, 218).

14. The context of the passage on these images in the *Gaoseng zhuan* probably also indicates that the compiler of collection Huijiao also considered them to have been Asoka images. The main part of this biography is devoted to stories of Asoka stupas and images.

15. The prince's letter, document 63, is not dated but placed between the letter of the twenty-second day of the ninth month and the above mentioned text of Zhiyi's vow dated the twenty-first day of the eleventh month. Since the documents in the *Guoqing bolu* are arranged chronologically this letter was probably written between the two dates and received along with the medicine shortly before Zhiyi's death.

16. Tsukamoto calls attention to a passage in Daoxuan's *Ji shenzhou sanbao gantong lu*, where Prince Guang, later Emperor Yang, is said to have sought widely for superior figures and gathered a wide range of written records (Tsukamoto: 175; the passage in Daoxuan's work is found in 421b7-9). This statement is then followed by the story of the stone image, whose existence was first learned from a work characterized as "miscellaneous records" (421b9). The prince carried the image with him wherever he went, and eventually placed it in the Riyansi which

he later established in Chang'an (not the first Riyansi mentioned earlier that the prince had established as a major Buddhist center in Jiangdu). This story indicates that Prince Guang was interested in gathering miraculous images around him during his posting in Jiangdu.

17. Tsukamoto notes that in his vow regarding the establishment of the Baotai tripitaka collection Prince Guang states that many of the "miraculous images and venerable scriptures" (lingxiang cunjing) suffered damage and neglect as the consequence of the pacification of Chen and subsequent rebellion (Tsukamoto: 177; and Taisho.2103: 52.257b). Repairing of miraculous images appears to have been an important concern of Prince Guang.

18. The visit might have taken place a few years later than this, but not later than 614.

19. As noted earlier, the Xu gaoseng zhuan biography records that in 616, during the reign of Emperor Yang, this monk produced in Luoyang a copy of the sandal-wood image which had been brought to China by Kumarajiva (633c23,24). Soper identified this image as the Udayana image, which was housed at the Longguangsi temple. Carter is skeptical about the tradition that the Udayana image was brought to China by Kumarajiva (Carter: 14).

Huicheng's biography also notes that this monk, who had been a prominent monk at the court of the southern dynasty Chen, responded to Prince Guang's call and moved to the Riyansi temple in Jiangdu, and there he was called a "family monk," jiaseng (633b5). After Prince Guang rose to the throne, Huicheng followed him to Luoyang (633c12). These facts suggest that the Udayana image may have had a particularly prominent status within the circle of monks who collaborated closely with Prince Guang.

20. Daoxuan's own preface to the biographical collection mentions that he had collected biographies from the period that began with the establishment of the Liang dynasty and ended in 645 (Taisho.2060: 50.425b22, 23). But the existing version of this collection contains biographies that Daoxuan appears to have continued to collect after this date until the end of his life in 667.

21. The story of burning arms is also found in the Medicine King chapter of the Lotus Sutra, Taisho.262: 9.53c and 54a.

22. Anzhou's rule is described in the Songshu, fasc. 98 (8.2417-2418).

23. See Zizhi tongjian, fasc. 187 (13.5851-5853); Zheng Ting's appointment as censor-in-chief is mentioned in 13.5852.13.

24. The story of Tanyou in the Hongzan fahua zhuan (Taisho.2067: 51.26bc) combines the two themes of performing self-immolation in front of a famous image, in this case that of the Asoka image at the Changshasi temple, and that of imitating the self-immolation in the Medicine King chapter of the Lotus Sutra.

# 9

# The Replication of Miraculous Icons: The Zenkoji Amida and The Seiryoji Shaka

*Donald F. McCallum*

## Introduction

This paper considers two miraculous icons, the Zenkoji Amida Triad and the Seiryoji Shaka, which became central to important cults in Japan. The former, a small gilt-bronze sculpture, is regarded as a "Living Buddha"; the latter, a life-size wood sculpture, is considered to be an exact portrait of the historic Buddha, executed directly in his presence. Extraordinary claims are made for these icons, claims which resulted in the extensive development of their cults, particularly during the Kamakura period (1185-1333). Both traditions have central temples which are the primary focus of religious activities, and which produce numerous replications of the main image. These replications and their broader significance will be the primary concern of the present study. But first a brief description of the original icons and the legends of the two traditions is necessary.[1]

### The Zenkoji Triad[2]

It is extremely difficult to try to describe the "original" Zenkoji Amida Triad, for this icon is now a totally secret image (*hibutsu*), locked within its shrine at Zenkoji in Nagano City, Japan.[3] This image is never shown even to the faithful, and at the important *kaicho* ("curtain opening") ceremony held there once every seven years it is the Maedachi Honzon (the "Image that stands in front") which is revealed to the worshipers.[4] For this reason, our only access to its appearance is through textual sources and the numerous replications; consequently, the following is a generalized and idealized description based on this material (see Figures 11-18). The earliest text states that the central image, a standing figure of Amida, is supposed to be one *shaku*, five *sun* (approximately 45 cm) tall; the two standing attendant Bodhisattvas, Kannon and Seishi, are each one *shaku* (approximately 30 cm) tall. Zenkoji triads were usually made of gilt bronze, although occasionally other materials were employed. Amida wears a standard monastic robe, with the drapery folds sweeping across the front of the body in the style typical of Buddha images of the Asuka (ca. 590-ca. 650) and Hakuho (ca. 650-710) periods. His hands are held in the *semui* and *yogan* mudra.

The flanking Kannon and Seishi figures are readily identifiable as Zenkoji-related Bodhisattvas by their characteristic hand positions: the arms are held up, in front of the chest, with the palms together. In one version, perhaps the original, the palms are represented as grasping a jewel; in another frequently-seen version the palms are flush, presumably a misunderstanding of the jewel-grasping position. Although the costume and jewelry of the flanking figures are typical of Japanese Bodhisattvas, most examples have unusual hexagonal or octagonal crowns of a type otherwise not seen on Bodhisattvas. Consequently, one can generally recognize a Zenkoji-style Bodhisattva on the basis of its hand position and crown form.

All three figures stand on tall pedestals, which are often mortar-shaped, and the group is backed by a large, boat-shaped mandorla. Pictorial evidence indicates that the three pedestals and the mandorla were supported by a base element (see Figures 11-16), but extant sculptural copies lack this feature. In most replications the mandorla is lost, and frequently the pedestals are also missing.[5]

As mentioned earlier, the original Zenkoji Amida Triad is enshrined at a great temple in what is today Nagano City, Nagano Prefecture, located in the mountainous central region of Honshu. The temple is usually referred to as "Shinano Zenkoji," utilizing the pre-modern province name. When exactly Shinano Zenkoji, or a forerunner, was established is unclear, although it certainly was a flourishing religious center by the later Heian period (11th-12th centuries). Then, in the Kamakura period, Shinano Zenkoji experienced explosive growth, becoming one of the key cult sites outside of the capital regions. What factors may have contributed to this growth?

Legendary accounts, appearing in complete form in the various versions of *Zenkoji engi* (Legends of Zenkoji), include a miraculous story explaining how the triad was created in ancient India at the very time that Shaka, the historical Buddha, was on this earth. A wealthy man, Gakki-choja, had everything he desired, with the exception of a child; then, when he was old, a daughter, called Nyoze-hime, was born to his wife. Gakki was delighted, and indulged Nyoze-hime, but a fearsome plague swept the kingdom, infecting his daughter and many others. When even the best physicians were unable to cure Nyoze-hime, Gakkai's friends urged him to consult with Shaka, who was living nearby with his followers. Previously, Gakkai had shunned Shaka, refusing to give alms or listen to his holy message, but now, swallowing his pride, Gakkai approached Shaka and begged for a cure for his daughter. Shaka replied that in the West lived another Buddha, Amida, and if Gakkai prayed to Amida his daughter would surely be cured. By this stage Nyoze-hime was deathly ill, but when Gakkai prayed to Amida, Amida and his two attendant Bodhisattvas, Kannon and Seishi, appeared magically in the sky over Gakkai's gate and drove away the demons who were causing the plague. Nyoze-hime and the other sufferers were all revived as a result of this miracle.

When the Amida Triad was about to return to the Western Paradise, Gakkai was distraught and begged Shaka and Amida for a copy of the triad. The two Buddhas obliged, producing a magical copy by projecting brilliant light from their *urnas*, which transformed miraculously-obtained gold into an exact replica of the "real" Amida Triad. The result of this miracle was the creation of a "Living Buddha," which Gakkai cherished for the rest of his life. The exact relationship between the two triads, the "original" and the "copy," is mysterious, although clearly both were considered to be fully animate.

Gakkai died and was reincarnated as the famous King Song of the Korean kingdom of Paekche. Hearing that King Song had fallen into evil ways, the Amida Triad flew from India to Paekche, where it immediately was successful in reforming the king. Subsequently, the triad delivered an oracle, saying that it wished to go to Japan. This trip by the Amida Triad is made to coincide in the Zenkoji legends with the so-called "official" introduction of Buddhism to Japan, when King Song presented a Buddhist icon to Emperor Kinmei in 538 or 552. *Zenkoji engi* relates how the Amida Triad became the central icon in the controversy surrounding the adoption of Buddhism in Japan, graphically describing how the anti-Buddhist faction attempted, without success, to destroy the image. Ultimately they gave up, and threw the triad into Naniwa Canal.

King Song was reincarnated as a humble Japanese man from Shinano Province named Honda Yoshimitsu. Upon completing labor service in the capital, Yoshimitsu began to return to his home in Shinano when, walking past Naniwa Canal, he heard a voice calling: "Yoshimitsu, Yoshimitsu." Miraculously, the Amida Triad jumped out of the canal, settled on Yoshimitsu's back, and asked to be taken to Shinano. Yoshimitsu took the triad on the long journey to Shinano, where he installed the icon on a stone mortar, the purest place in his house. A variety of miracles occurred. Since Yayoi, his wife, did not believe her husband's story, the Buddha granted the couple a magical vision whereby they became aware of their previous incarnations. At one point, Yoshimitsu was concerned that it was inappropriate to keep the triad on a mortar within his humble dwelling, and so he built a chapel outside the house and enshrined the triad there. Surprisingly, every night the Amida Triad returned to its original place in the house, so after several attempts Yoshimitsu gave up and allowed the triad to rejoin the family in the house.

The central miracle of the Zenkoji legend occurred next. Yoshimitsu and Yayoi had a son, named Yoshisuke, who, very tragically, predeceased them. Yoshimitsu complained to the Amida Triad about this great misfortune, begging to have his son returned. Amida dispatched his attendant Kannon to Hell, where Yoshisuke was dwelling, and Kannon begged the ruler of Hell, King Enma, to release Yoshisuke. The king agreed, releasing Yoshisuke, who returned to his grieving family after completing an archetypal "otherworld journey."[6] It is, of course, Yoshisuke's death, otherworld journey, and revival which guarantee to those who believe the message of the Zenkoji Amida Triad the possibility of personal release from Hell and subsequent rebirth in the Western Paradise.

*The Seiryoji Shaka*[7]

Unlike the Zenkoji Amida Triad, there are no problems in describing the Seiryoji Shaka, for the actual image is available for inspection in its shrine at Seiryoji in Kyoto (see Figure 8).[8] In this icon, Shaka stands 160 cm tall, the average height for a male in pre-modern times. The sculpture is made in a joined-wood technique, and it has some polychromy and gold leaf (*kirikane*) surface decoration. Its specific identification is based on the two spiral coils of hair which make up the coiffure; this trait is a constant in Seiryoji-type Shaka images. There is a jewel at the front of the *ushnisha*, jewels inserted in each ear, and a silver *urna* on which a Buddha figure is incised. A cavity at the back contains a great number of deposits including relics, scriptures, jewels, and most importantly, representations of the internal organs, all made of silk. (The replications very seldom contain this range of deposits, or the jewels on the head.) The Shaka wears a heavy monastic robe, but unlike the drapery arrangement seen in the Zenkoji Amida, here the folds loop across the upper body, and are then forced between the legs, producing separate ovoid configurations over each leg. The history of Seiryoji and its icon is complex.[9] As we will see in a moment, the Shaka, which was made in China in 985, was brought to Japan about one year later, and was displayed in Kyoto early in 987. Chonen (938-1016), the monk responsible for this, wished to have a temple built for his wonderful icon on Mt. Atago, to the west of Kyoto, opposite Mt. Hiei, where the great Tendai center Enryakuji was located, but this goal went unrealized. Shortly after Chonen's death, his disciples obtained permission from the court to construct a Shaka Hall at Seikaji, a temple situated below Mt. Atago. Over the centuries, the cult of the Shaka superseded the previous beliefs, and the temple was transformed into Seiryoji, with the original Seikaji component becoming minor.

While there may be one extant replication of the Seiryoji Shaka made in Japan during the Heian period,[10] like the Zenkoji tradition, the vast majority of Seiryoji replications falls in the Kamakura period, especially after the mid-thirteenth century. Also analogous to the Zenkoji tradition, the copies of the Seiryoji Shaka are found throughout Japan. Here too, then, we see a flourishing cult centering on a miraculous image, a state of affairs requiring some explanation.

The Seiryoji Shaka legend begins with King Udayana of Vatsa, in India, who is said to have lived at the time of the historical Buddha.[11] Although it seems certain that King Udayana was a historical figure, there is no evidence to suggest that he had anything to do with Buddhism; in fact, this part of the story is certainly legendary embellishment. In any event, at one stage Shaka left this earth and ascended to one of the paradises to preach to his late mother, who was dwelling there. King Udayana bitterly lamented Shaka's absence and decided to have a representation made to remind him of his teacher's appearance. Craftsmen were magically sent to paradise, where they produced a portrait of Shaka carved from sandalwood. The image was brought back to earth, where it was worshiped by the king and his court. Undoubtedly, this story was created retrospectively to explain the production and worship of anthropomorphic Buddhist icons.

Early Chinese texts provide diverse accounts of how the Udayana Shaka left India, traveled through Central Asia, and arrived in China. The version adopted in Japan relates that the father of a famous translator, Kumarajiva, carried the image from India to the oasis city of Kucha, where various miracles associated with the icon were witnessed. The illustrated *Seiryoji engi* shows Kumarajiva's father carrying the icon during the day, while at night the icon carried the father.[12] Subsequently, Kumarajiva and the icon were taken to the Chinese capital, where the image was worshiped. Whatever the precise location of the Udayana Shaka (accounts vary), by the later Six Dynasties, Sui, and T'ang Dynasties the legend was well known.

Chonen, the Japanese priest referred to earlier, was associated with Nara's Todaiji, a key center of traditional Buddhism which, however, had fallen into hard times because of the overwhelming dominance of the newer Tendai School headquartered at Enryakuji on Mt. Hiei to the east of Kyoto.[13] Disturbed by the decline of the older schools of Nara Buddhism, Chonen adopted a standard strategy, and traveled to China in 983 in order to gain the knowledge and sacred objects necessary to reinvigorate his lineage. In particular, he wished to visit Mt. Wu-t'ai, the most sacred Buddhist site in East Asia. This goal was accomplished, and in addition to pilgrimages to other holy places, Chonen was able to study with learned theologians, mastering some of the newest ideas and practices, especially those connected with esoteric Buddhism. Chonen, warmly received by the Sung Emperor, was granted various titles and symbols of esteem as well as the extraordinarily generous gift of the newly printed version of the Buddhist scriptures, which he subsequently took back to Japan.

During his stay in China, Chonen realized the importance of the Udayana Shaka and decided to have a copy made. It is important to note that the Udayana image is a representation of Shaka, for the Tendai school with which Chonen was competing was increasingly favoring Amida and Amidist teachings. In 985, Chonen commissioned two Buddhist sculptors in T'ai-chou to carve a representation of the Udayana Shaka, and it is this icon, of course, which is the image now installed at Seiryoji in Kyoto. While the image was being carved, a drop of blood magically appeared on the surface of the image, a miraculous occurrence at which all present marveled.[14]

As related earlier, Chonen returned to Japan in 986, spent some months in Kyushu, and then entered Kyoto in triumphal procession in early 987. Although Chonen was greeted with tremendous enthusiasm by the court, nobles, and populace, his dream of erecting a great temple, to be called Dai Seiryoji (The Great Temple of Pure Coolness), on Mt. Atago was frustrated by the political maneuvers of his arch-rivals at Enryakuji, who were unwilling to tolerate the prospect of even a symbolic competitor at Mt. Atago. Only with Chonen's death was the Udayana Shaka properly enshrined at Seikaiji, in the Saga district of Kyoto, and even then it was given only a modest hall. To obtain even this much, Chonen's followers had to offer the enormous printed edition of the scriptures, which had been bestowed on

Chonen by the Chinese emperor, to Fujiwara Michinaga, the dominant figure in Japanese politics at the time.[15]

As was the case with the Zenkoji cult, that of Seiryoji experienced rapid growth during the Kamakura period. Particularly interesting, in the present context, is the Japanese belief that during the night, just after the sculpting of the copy was finished in China, the "copy" and the "original" Udayana images traded places, so that the icon now enshrined at Seiryoji is not a replication, but the *actual* image carved in the presence of the historic Buddha.[16]

## Replications as Primary Objects of Worship

Both of the icons just discussed are clearly imbued with wonderful miraculous powers of a type found in special religious imagery throughout the world. What is so remarkable about these two traditions, however, is the very large number of replications produced over the centuries. Here I am speaking not of devotional objects purchased by pious pilgrims, a topic that will be addressed presently, but rather of "exact" copies of the Main Icons of Zenkoji and Seiryoji which were then enshrined in other temples where each, in turn, ordinarily became the Main Icon of its own temple. This seems to be a relatively unusual phenomenon.[17]

Approximately two hundred pre-modern replications of the Zenkoji icon and about one hundred of the Seiryoji icon are extant, spread throughout most regions of Japan. The majority of important examples was made during the thirteenth and fourteenth centuries, although there are also examples which were produced in later centuries. As just noted, these replicated images are now, or were in the past, intended as the Main Icon of a temple. While a given temple could have some, often many, other icons, the usual situation was for the Zenkoji Amida Triad or the Seiryoji Shaka to serve as the central focus of worship. Needless to say, in neither case are we dealing with the generalized worship of Amida or Shaka, but rather with specific cult beliefs and practices associated with the lineage in question. Evidently, these cults were motivated by belief in the miraculous "original" icon in their respective home temples in Nagano and Kyoto.

The most difficult question is how the replications were conceptualized. Clearly, the copies were not entirely equivalent to the original, but, on the other hand, all had to participate in the power of the originals if they were to function effectively as the Main Icons of their own temples. It is my impression that there is some ambiguity in the conceptualization of the prime object/replication relationship, a vagueness that was perhaps purposely designed to direct attention away from the somewhat problematic status of the copies. When asked, local worshipers would not pose theologically sophisticated questions about the nature of their icon, nor would the priests volunteer opinions about this subject, assuming that it was even something about which they thought.

Our questions may be clarified to some extent by considering a specific example from each tradition. For this purpose, I have selected key monuments that both date to the middle of the thirteenth century, the Saidaiji Shaka of 1249 and the Tokyo National Museum Amida Triad of 1254.

## Saidaiji Shaka[18]

Although some replications of the Seiryoji Shaka were made during the first part of the Kamakura period, the flourishing period of production was inaugurated with the Saidaiji Shaka of 1249 (see Figure 9).[19] The Saidaiji Shaka, while following quite closely the forms of the Seiryoji Shaka (Figure 8), clearly shows a strong tendency toward a more Japanese style, whereby the exotic, rather harsh quality of the earlier work is softened. Such traits can be seen in the more gentle facial expression, the schematized drapery folds, and the more lavish treatment of the surface.

This icon is associated with the career of the great prelate Eison (1201-1290), who revived the Nara period temple Saidaiji during the middle decades of the thirteenth century.[20] Eison, like Chonen before him, was committed to traditional Buddhism, and thus it is not surprising that he was devoted to Shaka, and especially to the image which is supposed to be an exact copy of the Udayana Shaka, housed at Seiryoji. Consequently, in 1248 Eison asked one of his followers, Kennin, to gather funds and arrange for the making of a copy of the Seiryoji Shaka.[21]

The next year a party of priests and sculptors traveled from Saidaiji in Nara to Seiryoji to carry out the replication. Here we have clear documentary evidence that the copy was made in front of the original icon, thereby allowing the art historian to assess the degree to which the copy is related to the image copied. For about eighteen days the sculptors labored at their work, and then the new image was brought back to Saidaiji, where the surface decoration was completed. On the first year of Kencho (1249), fifth month, seventh day, the eye-opening consecration ceremony was performed, thereby animating the new icon. Just before this ceremony, on the evening of the fifth day of the fifth month, a great miracle occurred which, presumably, was a divine acknowledgment of the sacred power of the new icon. *Gakushoki*, Eison's autobiography, tells us that during that night relics "gushed forth" in the monks' quarters. Relics, of course, are closely related to the cult of the historic Buddha, Shaka, so the relationship between the appearance of these relics and the Udayana Buddha is obvious.

The image produced from Eison's commission is now the Main Icon of Saidaiji, although it should be mentioned that Saidaiji houses a great number of other images, of diverse iconography. Furthermore, the Saidaiji replication of the Seiryoji Shaka becomes something like a new "prime object," forming the basis for a number of other replications housed in temples connected with Eison's Shingon Ritsu School.

## Tokyo National Museum Amida Triad[22]

In discussing the Saidaiji Shaka, we were able to compare it with the prototype at Seiryoji and thus recognize the degree of development that had occurred in Japan. Obviously, for reasons stated earlier, this is not possible in the case of the Zenkoji tradition, so I have selected an important triad that is representative of the situation at mid-thirteenth century. This triad, now housed at the Tokyo National Museum, was made in 1254 for a temple in the Nasu region of Tochigi Prefecture (see Figure 10). The triad now lacks the mandorla and pedestals, but the three figures display most of the defining characteristics of mainstream replications, especially the hexagonal crowns of the flanking Bodhisattvas. A number of other Zenkoji icons are associated with the Nasu region, indicating that it was a major center of the cult after the middle of the thirteenth century.

Particularly interesting in the case of this icon is the long inscription incised on the back of the Amida. (Shorter, less informative inscriptions are found on the two flanking Bodhisattvas.) In addition to providing the location and date of the image, the inscription also tells us that it is a Zenkoji Nyorai (Zenkoji Buddha), made in the *ikko sanzon* or "One Mandorla Triad" format. The patron is identified as Sainin, a man with the priestly title of *Kanjin Shonin* (Alms-gathering priest),[23] who is twenty-seven years old. Most significantly, we are told that Sainin had the triad made as a result of a dream-oracle, thus suggesting it was made under miraculous circumstances. The earliest known replication, commissioned by Joson for Shinano Zenkoji in 1195, was also produced as a result of various mysterious oracles. In fact, oracles are an important component of the Zenkoji legend and cult, and so the reference to a dream-oracle in the inscription of the present image is especially important.[24]

Reference was made earlier to the miracle which occurred when the new Seiryoji-style icon was installed at Saidaiji. Presumably there are other miracle tales associated with Seiryoji lineage icons. With the Zenkoji tradition there are numerous legends describing the miracles associated with various icons. For example, one of the largest Shin (New) Zenkoji is Byodosan Zenkoji in Kawaguchi City, Saitama Prefecture. This temple has a legend associating its icon with the activities of Joson, the priest just mentioned, who is said to have made the first replication in 1195. According to the story, the icon which Joson had commissioned for Shinano Zenkoji was traveling with him a couple of years after it was made. When the icon, enshrined in a portable shrine (*oi*), reached Kawaguchi, it would not move. Joson interpreted this as a sacred oracle of the Zenkoji Buddha, and the new temple was built at this location.[25] The icon at another Shin Zenkoji in the distant island of Sado appeared under the following mysterious circumstances. An itinerant priest was preaching on Sado when, one evening, thunder rolled, the rain suddenly ceased, and the moon began to shine brightly. The priest went outside and discovered an Amida Triad under an old tree; this image turned out to be a divine copy of the Main Icon of Shinano Zenkoji--the Living Buddha--and so the Sado Shin Zenkoji was established at this site.[26] There are also less miraculous stories. A stone relief replication of the Zenkoji Amida Triad at Kankiin in Saitama, for example, is said to have the power to cure warts![27]

## Replications that did not serve as Main Icons

The preceding pages have considered replications of the Zenkoji and Seiryoji images which served as the Main Icons of their temples, as the central objects of worship. There are, however, numerous replications, ranging from small, crudely-executed prints or sculptures, to large-scale paintings which were purchased by the faithful to remind them of the main object of worship and to aid them in their own religious devotions. This practice, of course, is found in icon cults throughout the world, and during all periods.[28]

The most common form of replication in the Zenkoji tradition is the wood-block print, a format cheaply produced and easy to take home from the temple. Fortunately, a relatively early example, probably dating to the Kamakura period, is preserved at the Nara National Museum (Figure 11).[29] The double lines at the borders of this print indicate that it was made as an *ofuda* (talisman). This type of *ofuda* would have been used for devotion to the deity. Although badly damaged, especially at the left side, the basic features of the Zenkoji Amida Triad can be clearly distinguished, including the pedestal base element referred to earlier. In contrast to other pictorial representations, this print lacks the representation of Gakkai and his wife, usually placed in front of the base. Particularly interesting are the inscriptions along the left margin: at top, the temple name, Zenkoji; in the middle, the fact that this print is one of a run of 60,000 copies; and at the base, the name of the donor, a monk named Kengyo. The extremely large number apparently produced at one time clearly demonstrates the popularity of this type of print and its subject matter.

Somewhat later, dating to the Edo period, is a related print (Figure 12). Presumably this work was also made as an *ofuda*. Although lacking an inscription as seen in the Nara National Museum print, this example does include the figures of Gakkai and his wife, shown at the base paying homage to the triad.[30] Later still is a tiny, modestly executed print that must have been within the means of even the poorest worshiper (Figure 13).

There are also a variety of paintings representing the Amida Triad. These, of course, would be substantially more expensive to produce, and thus would only be available to those with considerable resources. An especially fine example, dating to the late Kamakura or early Muromachi (1333-1568) period, is at the Freer Gallery in Washington (Figure 14). This work also shows Gakkai and his wife worshiping the Amida Triad. Interestingly, the Freer painting and the two works to be cited next all show Amida with hands held in a mudra which is different from the standard form. This may perhaps indicate a separate lineage of pictorial representations of the icon. A similar work from the early Muromachi period, executed in color on silk (89 x 37.6 cm), is kept at Seiganji in Tochigi Prefecture (Figure 15). The colors are still fresh, and the *kirikane* decor on the robes of the three figures is extremely well preserved. An Edo example, in the collection of the Hoshi Bukkyo Bijutsukan in Fukushima Prefecture (Figure 16), follows the same format as the other two examples, although its schematized execution indicates a later date.

Generally speaking, the types of icons considered in this section are graphic, two-dimensional objects, rather than three-dimensional sculptures. One does, however, also find small-scale sculptures, such as a 5 cm tall piece dated Bunka eighth year (1811) (Figure 17). While the graphic icons are clearly *representations* of the deity, the sculptural versions seem to come closer to the animate quality of the actual icon than do the pictorial examples.[31]

Prints were also made depicting the Seiryoji Shaka. A very large print, measuring 130 x 55.5 cm, in a private collection, Portland, shows Shaka in a hieratic, frontal view (Figure 18).[32] Smaller prints occur as well.

As was the case with the Zenkoji tradition, more expensive, large-scale paintings of the Seiryoji Shaka were executed. There is a painting in Konrenji in Kyoto (Figure 19) done in colors on silk (113 x 53.2 cm) dated to the Kamakura period. This painting shows Shaka standing at a slight angle, gazing off to the side, rather than in the normal frontal position. The artist probably intended this pose to give the icon a somewhat more informal quality than is usual. Perhaps this representation reflects the influence of Amidist imagery that was increasingly important during the Kamakura period.[33] At the temple itself is a large (132.5 x 79.7 cm), richly-colored painting on silk, attributed to the famous Muromachi artist Kano Motonobu (Figure 20).[34] This painting, which shows the icon in its shrine, with curtains opened at either side, is interesting in that it is a *representation* of the icon at Seiryoji rather than an ideal depiction of the deity. Possibly the Motonobu painting relates to an earlier work that is now lost. Such paintings were sent to distant temples, where they could be used as re-presentations of the original icon in special ceremonies. Certainly the scale and expense of this type of work suggests that it was intended for temple rather than personal use.[35] A related, but much smaller, painting is in the collection of the Royal Ontario Museum (Figure 21). This work, 58.4 x 23.7 cm, is executed in ink, colors, and gold on paper, and dates from the Edo period. In contrast to the painting attributed to Kano Motonobu, the present work does not show Shaka in a shrine, behind curtains, but repre-sents him in a more iconic manner. This hieratic quality is enhanced by the inscriptions that flank the pedestal: at right "Saga godaizan" (Wu-t'ai-shan of Saga), and at left "Seiryoji."[36]

## Conclusion

This paper has considered icons at three different levels of significance. At the summit, of course, are the Amida Triad enshrined at Shinano Zenkoji and the Udayana Shaka at Seiryoji in Kyoto. The former is con-sidered the "original" icon, the Living Buddha created through the joint efforts of Shaka and Amida in ancient India. The latter is generally acknowledged to be a copy, commissioned by Chonen in 985, of an Udayana Buddha kept in China, although, as we saw earlier, one Japanese legend holds that the copy was left behind in China, with the "original" being brought back to Japan. The claims made for these two icons surpass those made for most other icons, thus explaining in part how they became central to important cults. Many other icons in Japan are of great prestige, but few, if any, resulted in the productions of replications in the way seen in the Zenkoji and Seiryoji traditions.[37]

At the intermediate level are the numerous replications that serve or served as the Main Icon of an independent temple. Here it is essential to keep in mind that these icons are not conceptualized as unique representations or direct embodiments of the deity but are, rather, replications of the "original" icons at Zenkoji or Seiryoji. There is an intimate relationship between original and copy, based not on stylistic lineage, but on the miraculous efficacy of the Shinano Zenkoji Amida Triad or the Seiryoji Shaka. In some mysterious manner, the replication participates in the power of the original, thereby enabling it to function as the Main Icon of its own temple.[38] As I suggested earlier, we do not have evidence of much analytic effort having been spent on trying to clarify the status of the replicated Main Icons. What, then, guaranteed their power and efficacy?

I assume that the principal consideration was with the accuracy of the copy. If the replication resembled the original to the appropriate degree, it would automatically embody something of that icon's spiritual force.[39] Of course, consecration ceremonies were performed, but they would be of no significance if the icon in question was not seen as an "exact" copy of the original icon. In the case of more remote temples, where knowledge of the Seiryoji Shaka was limited, perhaps a priest of high authority sanctioned the replication, thereby rendering it authentic.

Finally, in terms of our three levels, are the various replications that were made not as Main Icons, but as devotional objects to be taken home by pilgrims and other worshipers. I believe that it is significant that in both of these iconic traditions, the replications in question are usually graphic, two-dimensional representations rather than sculptures. Space is lacking to consider in detail the respective implications of sculptural versus graphic representation/manifestation of the deity, but suffice it to say that three-dimensional forms are almost universally considered to be more able to embody the divinity's living presence.[40] With only rare exceptions, the Main Icons of Japanese Buddhist temples are virtually all sculptures, not paintings. Consequently, I would like to suggest that the prints and paintings which we have examined should be seen as reminders of their prototypes rather than as direct embodiments of the power of the prototype. In this respect, these replications are of a distinctly lesser degree of importance than the icons at the higher levels.

What responses did the icons at our three levels evoke from the worshipers? Some distinctions must be made between Shinano Zenkoji and Seiryoji before this question can be addressed. Most important, perhaps, is Zenkoji's situation as a great pilgrimage center. Today, as in previous centuries, enormous numbers of pilgrims visit Zenkoji each year; many, perhaps the majority, of these pilgrims in earlier times were associated with a Shin Zenkoji (New Zenkoji) in their native regions, and thus their pilgrimages were an aspect of a hierarchical religious practice.[41] Normal devotions could be carried out at the home temple, but the believer would also hope to have at least one opportunity to worship the "Living Buddha" at Shinano Zenkoji. In contrast, Seiryoji is not primarily a pilgrimage site. Many worshipers attend its great ceremonies, but not usually as pilgrims coming from afar. Furthermore, it does not seem to be the case that the devotees at local temples enshrining a Seiryoji-type Shaka felt the need to visit the main temple in Kyoto in order to worship the "original" icon. In this sense, temples housing a Seiryoji-type Shaka seem more autonomous from a religious standpoint than Zenkoji-related temples.

Regardless of these differences, it is evident that in both cases the "original" icons housed at Shinano Zenkoji and Seiryoji were held in the greatest awe and respect. Both were truly miraculous icons. When we turn to the replications serving as Main Icons in their various temples, the situation is somewhat more complicated. Only the most uninformed visitor would not have known the relationship between the local replication and the Main Icon at Shinano Zenkoji or Seiryoji. This relationship was frankly acknowledged--in fact, it was the raison d'être for the temple enshrining the replication. And yet, these replicated icons do not seem to have been thought of as somehow inferior or ineffective; quite the opposite, for within their own temples and local communities, they were very much venerated. I have to stress here once again that the original/replication relationship is mysterious and somewhat ambiguous.

The replications purchased by pilgrims or worshipers had a decidedly more modest status. They, like the great variety of charms, texts, and iconic objects that are ubiquitous in Japanese temples and shrines, served the devotional needs of the individual believers.[42] Some were little more than souvenirs, others may have been ascribed powers close to those of the prime icons. But in all cases, their status as *representations* of the original icons would have been understood. This, as stated above, is why they are frequently in graphic form.

Crucial to the thesis of this paper is the categorization of the imagery into three levels of signification. I am fully aware that these are not airtight categories, and clearly there is some slippage from one category to the next. Nevertheless, as an analytic strategy I believe that this tripartite scheme is helpful in illuminating key phenomena in Japanese religious practice. Hopefully, enough has been said to convince the reader of the extraordinary status granted to the miraculous icons enshrined at Zenkoji in Nagano and Seiryoji in Kyoto. More problematic is the conceptualization of the second level, those images copied after the prototypes in Nagano and Kyoto which then functioned as Main Icons in their own temples. Stated in neutral terms, this relationship is one of "prime object" and "replication"–a secondary temple that wished to have an icon directly based on the holy icon in the main temple.

Art historians studying these prime object/replication sequences will note varying degrees of diversity, but the fact remains that the principal characteristic of both traditions considered in this paper is the extremely high degree of similarity among the extant monuments. In that respect, the replication process must be deemed "successful," since any knowledgeable observer will instantly recognize a given example of a Zenkoji Amida or Seiryoji Shaka sculpture as replication of its respective prime object. This is the reason for insisting the process of replication, as defined in this paper, is different from the production of more generally delineated iconographical or stylistic lineages, since in the latter individual examples are not placed in a direct spiritual relationship with the prototype. Of course, there are highly influential images produced by sculptors such as Jocho and Kaikei, but normally these works subsequently modeled after such images are thought of as embodying the qualities (dare we call it style?) Of the masters, and individual replications are not referred back directly in a spiritual or theological sense to a specific prime object that is thought to embody miraculous powers.

A wide variety of images have been considered in this paper, extending from two of the most awe-inspiring, spiritually powerful icons to some of the most humble images. The very breadth of the imagery surveyed enables us to grasp with particular clarity significant ideological and practical dimensions of the worship of miraculous icons. Especially important, in my view, is the very extensive process of replication seen in both the Zenkoji Amida Triad and the Seiryoji Shaka traditions. While certainly not a unique phenomenon, the sheer extent of replication observed in these two traditions, from highly crafted, expensive Main Icons to cheap prints, speaks eloquently of a range of patronage and a variety of function. It is my hope that the material surveyed here will be of use to students and scholars who are investigating the broader implications of the commission, production, and worship of miraculous icons in world religion and religious art.

## Notes

1. This paper developed from a talk, given at the 1987 annual meeting of the College Art Association in Boston, entitled: "The Seiryoji Shaka and Zenkoji Amida Traditions in Japanese Buddhist Sculpture." My thanks to John Rosenfield, the organizer of the panel, for his suggestions.

2. I have presented a full account of this tradition in *Zenkoji and Its Icon: A Study in Medieval Japanese Religious Art*, Princeton, New Jersey, Princeton University Press, 1994. (Hereafter abbreviated as *Zenkoji and Its Icon*.)

3. For an excellent account of the *hibutsu* phenomenon see Sherry Fowler, "Hibutsu: Secret Buddhist Images of Japan," *Journal of Asian Culture* 15 (1991-1992): 137-161.

4. The present Maedachi Honzon is a work of the Muromachi period. For an illustration see Ito Nobuo, et al., eds., *Zenkoji: kokoro to katachi* (*Zenkoji: Spirit and Form*), Tokyo: Daiichi hoki shuppan, 1991, pl. 1.

5. The extant evidence on the continent indicates that the prototype for the Zenkoji Amida Triad was probably an example of the three-figures-standing triad format which was especially popular in Three Kingdoms period Korea. I deal at length with possible sources in *Zenkoji and Its Icon*, pp. 54-62. See also my "The Buddhist Triad in Three Kingdoms Sculpture," *Korean Culture* 16.4 (1995): 18-35.

6. Carol Zaleski, *Otherworld Journeys: Accounts of Near-Death Experience in Medieval and Modern Times*, New York and Oxford: Oxford University Press, 1987.

7. I am preparing a study which will consider all aspects of the Udayana Shaka tradition, especially as seen in Japan, as the Seiryoji Shaka lineage.

8. See Gregory Henderson and Leon Hurvitz, "The Buddha of Seiryoji: New Finds and New Theory," *Artibus Asiae* 19.1 (1956): 5-55. For detailed description and illustration see Maruo Shozaburo, ed., *Nihon chokuku-shi kiso shiryo shusei: zozo meiki ban* (Fundamental Collection of Documentary Sources for the History of Japanese Sculpture), vol. 1, text vol., pp. 42-65, plate vol., pp. 43-75, Tokyo: Chuo koron bijutsu shuppan, 1966.

9. For a succinct history of Seiryoji see Sakaki Kozo, *Seiryoji*, Tokyo: Chuo koron bijutsu shuppan, 1965.

10. On the basis of documentary evidence, the image of Shaka at Mimurododera has been dated to the year 1098 by some scholars, although I doubt that this image was made prior to the Kamakura period. For excellent photographic coverage see Nara National Museum, ed., *Nihon bukkyo bijutsu no genryu* (Origins of Japanese Buddhist Art), Kyoto: Dohosha shuppan, 1984, vol. 1, pls. 93a-e.

11. For information on King Udayana see Nita Adaval, *The Story of King Udayana*, Chowkhamba Sanskrit Studies, LXXIV, Varanasi, 1970. For the Udayana-tradition Shaka see Martha L. Carter, *The Mystery of the Udayana Buddha*, Istituto Universitario Orientale, Supplemento n. 64 agli Annali-vol. 50 (1990), fasc. 3, Napoli, 1990.

12.The entire *Seiryoji engi* (referred to as the *Shakado engi*) is illustrated in Kyoto Kokuritsu Hakubutsukan, ed., *Tokubetsu tenrankai: Shaka shinko to Seiryoji* (Special exhibition: Belief in Shaka and Seiryoji), Kyoto, 1982, pp. 68-75. The scene discussed here is found on p. 72. For a color illustration of this scene see Setouchi Jakucho and Ugai Kojun, eds., *Seiryoji (Koji junrei: Kyoto 21)*, Kyoto: Tankosha, 1978, pl. 61.

13. In addition to the challenge presented by Enryakuji, the Kofukuji/Kasuga multiplex was becoming increasingly powerful at this period. See Allan G. Grapard, *The Protocol of the Gods: A Study of the Kasuga Cult in Japanese History*, Berkeley and Los Angeles: University of California Press, 1992, especially chapter two, "Kasuga Daimyojin: Protector or Ruler?" pp. 71-118.

14. Hurvitz, as cited in note 8 above, p. 48, provides a translation of the document which says that the blood drop appeared at the top of the Buddha's "head," on the basis of an emendation of a character he had difficulty reading (his footnote 22). It is clear, however, from the photograph of the text in *Nihon chokoku-shi kiso shiryo shusei*, p. 55, pl. 27, that the character in question is "back." This minor error should not be seen as detracting from the brilliance of Hurvitz's translation.

15. For Chonen see Tsukamoto Zenryu, "Seiryoji Shaka zo fuzo no Todaiji Chonen no shuin risseisho," in *Tsukamoto Zenryu chosakushu*, vol. 7, Tokyo: Daito shuppansho, 1975, pp. 167-204. (Originally published in *Bukkyo bunka kenkyu* 4 [1954]: 5-22.)

16. See the *Tokubetsu tenrankai: Shaka shinko to Seiryoji*, p. 75.

17. Much of my research in recent years has been devoted to the issue of replicated icons in Buddhist art and practice. A preliminary statement will be found in my unpublished paper, "The Power of Replication: The Seiryoji Shaka Tradition in Kamakura Sculpture," presented at the International Symposium on Kamakura Sculpture held at the British Museum in 1991. The term "Main Icon" is a translation of the Japanese *honzon*, and is capitalized in order to indicate the status of the given image as the most important icon of a temple.

18. I have dealt with this image and its lineage in detail in "The Saidaiji Lineage of the Seriyoji Shaka Tradition," *Archives of Asian Art* 49 (1996): 51-67.

19. Excellent illustrations and analysis can be found in *Nara rokudaiji taikan*, vol. 14, *Saidaiji*, Tokyo: Iwanami shoten, 1973, pls. 12-13, 50-53, and pp. 41-46, (Tanabe Saburosuke). This image was included in the recent exhibition of the Tokyo National Museum; see Tokyo Kokuritsu Hakubutsukan, ed., *Yamato koji no hotoke-tachi* (Buddhist Images of the Ancient Temples of the Yamato Region), Tokyo: NHK, 1993, number 18.

20. For a biography of Eison and his disciple Ninsho, see Wajima Yoshio, *Eison-Ninsho*, Tokyo: Yoshikawa kobunko, 1959. Essays devoted to his life and career can be found in Nakao Takashi and Imai Masaharu, eds., *Chogen, Eison, Ninsho*, Tokyo: Yoshikawa kobunka, 1983. The most up-to-date material is in *Bukkyo geijutsu* 199 (1991) "Tokushu: Eison to Saidai-ha bijutsu" (Special issue: Priest Eison and the Saidai-ji School of Buddhist Art). See especially the article by Hamada Takashi, "Eison no shinko to bijutsu" (The Faith and Art of Priest Eison), pp. 11-31. Two forthcoming papers by Paul Groner will clarify many of the important issues: "The Role of Images in Eison's Religious Activities" and "Tradition and Innovation: Eison, Kakujo, and the Re-establishment of Orders of Monks and Nuns during the Kamakura Period."

21. For the making of the Saidaiji Shaka see Tanabe Saburosuke as cited in note 19, above.

22. I have dealt with this image in detail in "Tokyo Kokuritsu Hakubutsukan hokan Zenkoji-shiki Amida sanzon zo ni tsuite" (A Zenkoji Triad in the Tokyo National Museum), *Museum* 441 (1987): 21-28.

23. For an excellent discussion of the nature of alms gathering, see Janet R. Goodwin, *Alms and Vagabonds: Buddhist Temples and Popular Patronage in Medieval Japan*, Honolulu: University of Hawaii Press, 1994.

24. See *Zenkoji and Its Icon* for the significance of oracles in the Zenkoji cult. For Joson's reception of oracles, ibid., p. 110.

25. Ito Hirofumi and Kasuya Masaaki, *Zenkoji--sono rekishi to nyorai no fushigi* (Zenkoji: Its History and the Strangeness of the Buddha), Matsumoto: Kyodo Shuppansha, 1987, pp. 236-238.

26. Ibid. pp. 272-273.

27. Ibid. p. 239.

28. For valuable material see David Freedberg, *The Power of Images: Studies in the History and Theory of Response*, Chicago and London: University of Chicago Press, 1989, pp. 99-160.

29. For Buddhist prints see Mosaku Ishida, ed., *Japanese Buddhist Prints*, New York: Abrams, 1964. (The print considered here is shown on pl. 44.) Also, Mary W. Baskett, *Footprints of the Buddha: Japanese Buddhist Prints from American and Japanese Collections*, Philadelphia: Philadelphia Museum of Art, 1980. In Japanese see Kikuchi Jun'ichi, *Bukkyo hanga* (Buddhist Prints), vol. 218 of *Nihon no bijutsu*, Tokyo: Shibundo, 1984; Kanagawa Kenritsu Kanazawa Bunko, ed., *Bukkyo hanga*, Yokohama, 1993.

30. These two people are clearly not Honda Yoshimitsu and his wife Yayoi, because they are represented as wearing exotic costumes which are theoretically those of ancient India.

31. A large amount of relevant material in the Zenkoji tradition will be found in Yoshihara Hiroto, "Waseda Daigaku Toshokan: Zenkoji shinko shiryo ko--fukaidai" (On the archival collection of the Zenkoji religion in the Library with its bibliographical annotations), *Waseda Daigaku Toshokan kiyo* 39 (1994): 97-124. I owe this source to Nakaya Hikari of the Waseda Library.

32. Two closely related prints in the collection of Kanazawa Bunko are illustrated in their *Bukkyo hanga*, catalogue entries nos. 14 and 57.

33. For examples of Amida images depicted at an angle see Kyoto National Museum, ed., *Jodo-kyo kaiga* (The Painting of Pure Land Buddhism), Kyoto: Kyoto Kokuritsu hakubutsukan, 1975, pls. 104, 105, 107, 108.

34. A color illustration of this painting can be found in Setouchi and Ugai, as in note 10, pl. 67. For Kano Motonobu see Yamaoka Taizo, *Kano Masanobu-Motonobu*, Tokyo: Shueisha, 1978. It is likely that this painting indicates to some extent the original color scheme of the Seiryoji Shaka, since the latter image still has slight traces of red pigment on the main robe. (The scene showing Kumarajiva's father carrying the icon is illustrated in Yamaoka, pl. 48, in a large-scale reproduction.)

35. There is another, later painting at Seiryoji by Kano Dorin, which is an exact copy of the Motonobu attribution, indicating that just as sculptural replications were made, so too were painted versions. See Shimizu Zenzo in Setouchi and Ugai, pp. 143-144.

36. As mentioned above, Chonen's principal goal in traveling to China was to visit Mt. Wu-t'ai (Wu-t'ai-shan), and he wished his temple planned for Mt. Atago to be called Godaizan Seiryoji.

37. The matter of stylistic or iconographical lineage versus what I define as a replication lineage is complicated. Virtually all icons belong to a specific iconographical lineage, but normally such lineages are not as clearly and precisely defined as is the case with the Zenkoji or Seiryoji icons. In the case of stylistic lineages the relationship among examples is even less clearly articulated. For a discussion of the concept of replication as used by contemporary scholars, see Whitney Davis, *Replications: Archaeology, Art History, Psychoanalysis*, University Park, Pennsylvania, The Pennsylvania State University Press, 1996, especially pp. 1-31.

38. A great deal of fascinating material on the status of Hindu sculptural icons can be found in Richard H. Davis, *Lives of Indian Images*, Princeton, New Jersey, Princeton University Press, 1997. Especially important is Chapter 1, "Living Images" (pp. 15-50), where Davis discusses in detail the animate status normally ascribed to Indian icons. The fact that Japanese believers refer to only certain specific icons as "living" (*shojin*) suggests that not all icons in Japan were explicitly granted this status. Consequently, those images having this characteristic, especially the Zenkoji Amida Triad and to a lesser extent the Seiryoji Shaka, are conceived of as more miraculous than other icons. This status, of course, is the primary motivating factor for the production of replications.

39. The issue of resemblance has been discussed in detail in Christian thought concerning icons. For a good summary of some of the arguments see Mosche Barasch, *Icon: Studies in the History of an Idea*, New York: New York University Press, 1992, especially pp. 63-91. A recent work covers much of the same ground, but with greater attention to the art historical issues: Paul Corby Finney, *The Invisible God: The Earliest Christians on Art*, New York and Oxford: Oxford University Press, 1994. Also important is Hans Belting, *Likeness and Presence: A History of the Image before the Era of Art*, Chicago and London: University of Chicago Press, 1994.

40. In the early Christian world sculptural icons were so strongly associated with pagan deities that often their status did not even enter into the debate about icons; they were completely out of the question, and the debate centered on whether or not it was acceptable to represent Christ, Mary, and the saints in two-dimensional form. For example, the sixth-century cleric Julian of Atramytion opposed sculptural icons but was willing to accept paintings. See Ernst Kitzinger, "The Cult of Images in the Age Before Iconoclasm," *Dumbarton Oaks Papers* 8 (1954): 131-132, n. 211. The issue is also discussed by Edwyn Bevan, *Holy Images: An Inquiry into Idolatry and Image-Worship in Ancient Paganism and in Christianity*, New York: AMS Press, 1940, pp. 51-56.

41. For pilgrimage to Zenkoji see *Zenkoji and Its Icon*, pp. 190-191. There is a very extensive network of temples throughout Japan housing Zenkoji Amida triads, which are usually called Shin Zenkoji, ibid, pp. 86-99.

42. For a probing analysis of the medieval Japanese Buddhism see James H. Foard, "In Search of a Lost Reformation: A Reconsideration of Kamakura Buddhism," *Japanese Journal of Religious Studies* 7:4 (1980): 261-291. More specialized, but also highly relevant, is William M. Bodiford, *Soto Zen in Medieval Japan*, Honolulu: University of Hawaii Press, 1993. Bodiford's work, like that of Foard, aims to show what sort of practices and beliefs were *really* current, in distinction to abstract, theologically sophisticated conceptions which never had much impact on the laity (and little enough on the clergy).

# Bibliography

Adaval, Nita. 1970. *The Story of King Udayana*. Chowkhamba Sanskrit Studies, LXXIV. Varanasi.

*Adbhutasagara*. 1977. Ed. Smt. Pramila Misra. Orissan Oriental Text Series (Sanskrit) 6. Bhubaneswar: Directorate of Tourism and Cultural Affairs (Cultural Wing).

Anavaratavinayakar Pillai, S. 1936. Nulacciriyar. In Sivagrayogin, *Civaneriprakasam*. Madras: Madras University Tamil Series.

*Annadakalpatantra*. Bengali year 1383. Ed. Bengali script, Calcutta: Nabvabharata Publishers.

Anonymous 1981. *Mutt and Temples*. Dharmapuram: Gnanasambandam Press.

*A.R.E. Annual Report on (South) Indian Epigraphy*. Serial for the years 1887-1944/45. Madras: Archaeological Survey of India.

Appadurai, Arjun. 1978. Kings, Sects and Temples in South India, 1350-1700 A.D. In *South Indian Temples, An Analytical Reconsideration*. Ed. Burton Stein. New Delhi: Vikas Publishing House. Pp. 47-74.

Apte, Vaman Shivram. 1893. *The Student's English-Sanskrit Dictionary*. Bombay: Mrs. Radhabai Atmaram Sagoon.

Aquinas, Thomas. 1945. *Basic Writings*. Trans. Anton C. Pegis. New York: Random House.

Aravamuthan, T. G. 1931. *Portrait Sculpture in South India*. London: Indian Society.

Arunachalam, M. 1972. *Guru Jnana Sambandhar: The Philosopher Inspired by Madurai*. Dharmapuram: Dharmapuram Adhinam.

Augustine, Aurelius. 1950. *The City of God*. Trans. Marcus Dods. New York: The Modern Library.

Balbir, Nalini. 1982. *Danastakakatha, Receuil Jaina de Huit Histories sur le Don*. Paris: Publications de l'Institut Civilisation Indienne, vol. 48.

Barasch, Moshe. 1992. *Icon: Studies in the History of an Idea*. New York: New York University Press.

Barrett, T. H. 1990. Exploratory Observations on Some Weeping Pilgrims. In *The Buddhist Forum. Vol. I: Seminar Papers 1987-1988*. Ed. Tadeusz Skorupski. London: School of Oriental and African Studies, University of London.

Barua, B. M. 1931-34. Reprint 1979. *Barhut*. 3 Vols. Calcutta: India Research Institute Publications.

Baskett, Mary W. 1980. *Footprints of the Buddha: Japanese Buddhist Prints from American and Japanese Collections*. Philadelphia: Philadelphia Museum of Art.

Bays, Gwendolyn, trans. 1983. *The Voice of the Buddha: The Beauty of Compassion* [*Lalitavistara Sutra*]. Berkeley: Dharma Publishing.

Beal, Samuel, trans. 1884. *Si-yu-ki. Buddhist Records of the Western World. Translated from the Chinese of Hiuen Tsiang (A.D. 629)*. London: Kegan Paul, Trench, Trübner.

Bechert, Heinz, ed. 1991. *The Dating of the Historical Buddha (Die Datierung des historischen Buddha*, Part 1. Göttingen: Vandenhoeck & Ruprecht.

Belting, Hans. 1994. *Likeness and Presence: A History of the Image before the Era of Art*. Chicago and London: University of Chicago Press.

Benisti, Mireille. 1986. Observations concernant le *stupa* no. 2 de Sanci. *Bulletin d'Études Indiennes* 4: 165-170.

Bevan, Edwyn. 1940. *Holy Images: An Inquiry into Idolatry and Image-Worship in Ancient Paganism and in Christianity*. New York: AMS Press.

Bodiford, William M. 1993. *Soto Zen in Medieval Japan*. Honolulu: University of Hawaii Press.

Bosch, F. D. K. 1932. La procession du feu sacré. *Bulletin de l'École Française d'Extreme-Orient* 32.

*Brhannaradiya Purana*. 1975. Ed. Pandit Hrishikeshashastri. Varanasi: Chaukhamba Press.

*Brhatkathakosa of Harinena*. 1943. Ed. by A. N. Upadhye. Singhi Jain Series, vol. 17. Bombay: Bharatiya Vidya Bhavan.

Briggs, Lawrence Palmer. 1951. *The Ancient Khmer Empire Transactions of the American Philosophical Society*, n.s. 41, part 1. Philadelphia: The American Philosophical Society.

Brown, Robert L. 1997a. The Emaciated Gandharan Buddha Images: Asceticism, Health, and the Body. In *Living a Life in Accord with Dhamma: Papers in Honor of Professor Jean Boisselier*. Ed. Natasha Eilenber, M.C. Subhadradis Diskul, and Robert L. Brown. Bangkok: Fine Arts University.

————. 1997b. The Jataka Stories in Ancient Indian and Southeast Asian Architecture. In *Sacred Biography in the Buddhist Traditions of South and Southeast Asia*. Ed. Juliane Schober. Honolulu: University of Hawaii Press.

Bruce, Helen. 1960. *Nine Temples of Bangkok*. Bangkok: Chalermnit Press.

Brunner, Hélène. 1990. Atmarthapuja Versus Pararthapuja. In *Panels of the VIIth World Sanskrit Conference. Vol. 1. The Sanskrit Tradition and Tantrism*. Ed. Teun Goudriaan. Leiden: E. J. Brill, 5-23.

————. 1962. Les categories sociales vediques dans le Sivaisme du sud. *Journal asiatique* 252: 451-72.

Brunner-Lachaux, Hélène. 1963. Introduction. In *Somasambhupaddhati. Première Partie*. Pondichéry: Institut français d'Indologie.

Bühler, Georg. 1936. *The Life of Hemachandra*. Eng. trans. Dr. Manilal Patel. Singhi Jain Series, no.11. Santiniketan: Singhi Jaina Pitha.

*Bukkyo geijutsu* 1991. Tokushu: Eison to Saidai-ha bijutsu (Special issue: *Priest Eison and the Saidai-ji School of Buddhist Art*).

Caillat, Colette. 1975. *Atonements in the Ancient Ritual of the Jaina Monks*. L.D. Institute Series, no. 49. Ahmedabad: L.D. Institute.

Carter, Martha L. 1985. Hsuan-Tsang and the Colossal Buddhas at Bamiyan. In *Studies in Buddhist Art of South Asia*. Ed. A. K. Narain. New Delhi: Kanak Publications.

Carter, Martha L. 1990. *The Mystery of the Udayana Buddha*. Napoli: Istituto Universitario Orientale.

*Caurasi Vaisnavan ki Varta*. 1977. Mathura: Govardhana Granthamala Karyalaya.

Celvakkanapati, Ira. 1984. Tarumatina Kuruparamparai Varalaru. In *Anaitulak Caiva Cittanta Mutal Kuruttarankan Vila Malar*. Tarumapuram: Tarumai Atinam, 108-75.

Chandra, Moti. 1949. *Jain Miniature Paintings from Western India*. Ahmedabad: Sarabhai Manilal Nawab.

Clausen, Christopher. 1975. Victorian Buddhism and the Origins of Comparative Religion. *Religion* 5, no. 1 (Spring 1975): 1-15.

Conze, Edward. 1973. *Buddhist Thought in India*. Ann Arbor: The University of Michigan Press.

Cort, John. 1990. The Jain Sacred Cosmos: Selections from a Medieval Pilgrimage Text. In *The Clever Adulteress: A Treasury of Jain Literature*. Edited by Phyllis Granoff. Oakville, Ontario: Mosaic Press. Pp. 245-90.

Cunningham, Alexander. 1871. *The Ancient Geography of India. I, The Buddhist Period*. London: Trübner.

Cuppiramaniyan, Me. Co. 1928. *Tiruvavatuturai Atinam Kuruparamparai Vilakkam*. Citamparam.

*Dainihon bukkyo zensho*. 1931. Ed. Takakusu Junjiro et al. 150 vols. Tokyo: Dainihon kukkyo zensho kankokai. Reprint. Ed. Suzuki gakujutsu zaidan. 100 vols. Tokyo: Kodansha, 1970-73.

*Dainihon zokuzokyo*. 1903-12. Ed. Nakano Tatsue. 150 vols. Kyoto: Zokyo shoin, Reprint. Taibei: Xinwenfeng, 1968-1970.

Davis, Richard H. 1991. *Ritual in an Oscillating Universe: Worshiping Siva in Medieval India*. Princeton: Princeton University Press.

_____ . 1994. Trophies of War: The Case of the Calukya Intruder. In *Perceptions of South Asia's Visual Past*. Eds. Catherine B. Asher and Thomas R. Metcalf. New Delhi: American Institute of Indian Studies. Pp. 161-77.

_____ . 1997. *Lives of Indian Images*. Princeton: Princeton University Press.

Davis, Whitney. 1996. *Replications: Archaeology, Art History, Psychoanalysis*. University Park, Pennsylvania: The Pennsylvania University Press.

Dehejia, Vidya. 1991. Aniconism and the Multivalence of Emblems. *Ars Orientalis* 21: 45-66.

Desai, Vishakha and Denise Patry Leidy. 1989. *Faces of Asia: Portraits from the Permanent Collection*. Boston: Museum of Fine Arts.

Desikacharya, N. 1949. *The Origin and Growth of the Sri Brahmatantra Prakala Mutt*.

Dirks, Nicholas B. 1987. *The Hollow Crown: Ethnohistory of an Indian Kingdom*. Cambridge: Cambridge University Press.

Diskul, Professor M. C. Subhadradis. n.d. *History of the Temple of the Emerald Buddha*. Bangkok: Bureau of the Royal Household.

*Divyavadana*. 1959. Ed. P. L. Vaidya. Buddhist Sanskrit Text Series, vol. 20. Darbhanga: Mithila Institute of Post-Graduate Studies and Research in Sanskrit Learning.

Dundas, Paul. Forthcoming. Becoming Gautama: Mantra and History in Jainism. Paper delivered at the Jain Conference, Amherst, Mass. June 1993.

Ekalalingamahatmya. 1976. Ed. Dr. Premlata Sarma. Delhi: Motilal Banarsidass.

Falk, Nancy. 1977. To Gaze on the Sacred Traces. History of Religions 16(4): 281-93.

Faure, Bernard. 1991. The Rhetoric of Immediacy: A Cultural Critique of Chan/Zen Buddhism. Princeton: Princeton University Press.

Feer, M. Leon, ed. 1884. The Samyutta-nikaya of the Sutta-pitaka, Part I. Sagatha-vagga. Pali Text Society Text Series, vol. 8. London: Pali Text Society.

Finney, Paul Corby. 1994. The Invisible God: The Earliest Christians on Art. New York and Oxford: Oxford University Press.

Fleet, J. F. 1877. Sanskrit and Old Canarese Inscriptions. The Indian Antiquary 16: 30.

Foard, James H. 1980. In Search of a Lost Reformation: A Reconsideration of Kamakura Buddhism. Japanese Journal of Religious Studies 7.4: 261-291.

Fowler, Sherry. 1991-92. Hibutsu: Secret Buddhist Images of Japan. Journal of Asian Culture 15: 137-161.

Freedberg, David. 1989. The Power of Images: Studies in the History and Theory of Response. Chicago and London: University of Chicago Press.

Fuller, Christopher J. 1984. Servants of the Goddess: The Priests of a South Indian Temple. Cambridge: Cambridge University Press.

_____. 1992. The Camphor Flame: Popular Hinduism and Society in India. Princeton: Princeton University Press.

Ganapati Iyer, P.R. 1918. The Law Relating to Hindu and Mahommedan Endowments. Madras: Modern Printing Works.

Ghosh, Manmohan, tran. 1967. The Natyasastra (A Treatise on Ancient Indian Dramaturgy and Histrionics). 2nd ed. Calcutta: Manisha Granthalaya.

Gibbs, Nancy. 1995. The Message of Miracles. Time, 10 April, 64-73.

Glasenapp, Helmuth von. 1966. Buddhism--a Non-Theistic Religion. Trans. by Irmgard Schloegl. New York: George Braziller.

Gombrich, E. H. 1969. Art and Illusion: A Study in the Psychology of Pictorial Representation. Princeton: Princeton University Press.

Goodwin, Janet R. 1994. Alms and Vagabonds: Buddhist Temples and Popular Patronage in Medieval Japan. Honolulu: University of Hawaii Press.

Goswami, Hemcandra. 1924. Asamiya Sahitya Chaneki or Typical Selections from Assamese Literature, Vol. II: Vaisnava Period. Calcutta: University of Calcutta.

Granoff, Phyllis. 1988. The Jain Biographies of Haribhadra: An Inquiry into the Origin of the Legends. The Journal of Indian Philosophy 16: 109-125.

_____. 1989a. The Biographies of Arya Khapatacarya: A Preliminary Investigation into the Transmission and Adaptation of Biographical Legends. In P. Granoff and K. Shinohara, eds. Monks and Magicians: Religious Biography in Asia. Oakville, Ontario: Mosaic Press. Pp. 67-99.

_____. 1989b. The Biographies of Siddhasena: A Study of the Texture of Allusion and the Weaving of a Group Image: Part I. The Journal of Indian Philosophy 17: 329-384 .

_____. 1989c. Religious Biographies and Clan Histories Among the Svetambara Jains of North India. East and West 39.1-4: 195-217.

_____. 1990a. The Biographies of Siddhasena, Part II. The Journal of Indian Philosophy 18: 261-304.

Granoff, Phyllis. 1990b. *The Clever Adulteress: A Treasury of Jain Literature.* Oakville, Ontario: Mosaic Press.

_____. 1990c. Manicuda's Sacrifice: Narrative Context as a Guide to Interpretation. In V. N. Jha, ed., *Kalyanamitra: Festschrift for Hajime Nakamura.* Delhi: Indian Books Centre. Pp. 225-39.

_____. 1991a. The Politics of Religious Biography: The Biography of Balibhadra the Usurper. *Bulletin d'Études Indiennes* 9: 75-91.

_____. 1991b. Tales of Broken Limbs and Bleeding Wounds: A Study of Some Hindu Responses to Muslim Iconoclasm. *East and West* 41: 189-205.

_____. 1992a. Jinaprabhasuri and Jinadattasuri: Two Studies from the Svetambara Jain Tradition. In Phyllis Granoff and Koichi Shinohara, eds., *Speaking of Monks: Religious Biography in India and China.* Oakville, Ontario: Mosaic Press. Pp. 1-97.

_____. 1992b. The Violence of Non-Violence: A Study of Some Jain Responses to Non-Jain Religious Practices. *Journal of the International Association of Buddhist Studies* 15.1: 1-42.

_____. 1992c. When Jina Bleeds: Threats to the Faith and the Rescue of the Faithful in Medieval Jain Stories. Paper presented at the annual meeting of the Association of Asian Studies. Washington D.C.

_____. 1992d. Worship as Commemoration: Pilgrimage, Death and Dying in Medieval Jainism. *Bulletin d'Etudes Sanskrite et Indiennes* 10: 181-202.

_____. 1993. Halayudha's Prism: The Experience of Religion in Medieval Hymns and Stories. In Vishakha Desai and Darielle Mason, eds., *Gods, Guardians and Lovers: Temple Sculptures from North India A.D. 700-1200.* New York: The Asia Society Galleries. Pp. 66-94.

_____. 1994a. Being in the Minority: Medieval Jain Reactions to Other Religious Groups. In N. N. Bhattacharya, ed., *Jainism and Prakrit in Ancient and Medieval India: Essays for Jagdish Chandra Jain.* New Delhi: Manohar. Pp. 241-266.

_____. 1994b. Ritual and Biography: The Case of Bappahattisuri. In Phyllis Granoff and Koichi Shinohara, eds., *Other Selves: Biography and Autobiography in Cross Cultural Perspectives.* Oakville, Ontario: Mosaic Press. Pp. 150-207.

_____. 1995. Jain Pilgrimage: In Memory and Celebration of the Jinas. In Pratapaditya Pal, ed., *The Peaceful Liberators: Art from India.* Thames and Hudson. Pp. 63-77.

_____. Forthcoming a. The Ambiguity of Miracles: Buddhist Understandings of Supernatural Power. *East and West.*

_____. Forthcoming b. Heaven on Earth: Temples and Temple Cities of Medieval India. Festschrift for Frits Staal.

_____. Forthcoming c. Patrons, Overlords and Artisans: Some Comments on the Intricacies of Religious Donations in Medieval Jainism. In V. N. Misra, ed., *Sir William Jones Bicentennary of Death Commemoration Volume.*

Granoff, Phyllis, and Koichi Shinohara. 1992. *Speaking of Monks : Religious Biography in India and China.* Oakville, Ontario: Mosaic Press.

Grapard, Allan G. 1992. *The Protocol of the Gods: A Study of the Kasuga Cult in Japanese History.* Berkeley and Los Angeles: University of California Press.

Griswold, Alexander B. 1953. The Buddhas of Sukhodaya. *Archives of the Chinese Art Society of America* 7: 5-41.

_____. 1960. The Architecture and Sculpture of Siam. In *The Arts of Thailand: A Handbook of the Architecture, Sculpture and Painting of Thailand (Siam), and a Catalogue of the Exhibition in the United States in 1960-61-62.* Ed. Theodore Bowie. Bloomington: Indiana University.

_____. 1961. *King Mongkut of Siam.* New York: The Asia Society.

_____. 1974. *What is a Buddha Image?* 2nd ed. Bangkok: The Fine Arts Department.

Griswold, Alexander B. and Prasert na Nagara. 1971. The Inscription of King Rama Gamhen of Sukhodaya (1292 A.D.): Epigraphic and Historical Studies No. 9. *Journal of the Siam Society* 59, part 2:179-228.

_____. 1972. King Lodaiya of Sukhodaya and his Contemporaries: Epigraphical and Historical Studies, No. 10. *Journal of the Siam Society* 60, part 1:21-152.

_____. 1973. The Epigraphy of Mahadharmaraja I of Sukhodaya: Epigraphic and Historical Studies No. 11 Part I. *Journal of the Siam Society* 61, part 1:71-179.

Groner, Paul. Forthcoming a. The Role of Images in Eison's Religious Activities.

_____. Forthcoming b. Tradition and Innovation: Eison, Kakujo, and the Re-establishment of Orders of Monks and Nuns during the Kamakura Period.

Gupta, Sanjukta. 1979. Modes of Worship and Meditation. In Sanjukta Gupta, Dirk Jan Hoens and Teun Goudriaan, eds., *Hindu Tantrism.* Leiden and Köln: E. J. Brill.

Hackin, J. 1914. Sur les illustration Tibétaines d'une légende du Divyavadana. *Annales du Musee Guimet,* 40.

Hamada Takashi. 1991. Eison no shinko to bijutsu (The Faith and Art of Priest Eison). *Bukkyo geijutsu* 199: 11-31.

Harle, J. C. 1986. *The Art and Architecture of the Indian Subcontinent.* Harmondsworth: Penguin Books.

Härtel, Herbert. 1991. Archaeological Research on Ancient Buddhist Sites. In *The Dating of the Historical Buddha.* Ed. Heinz Bechert. Göttingen: Vandenhoeck & Ruprecht.

Harvey, Peter. 1983. The Nature of the Tathagata. In *Buddhist Studies: Ancient and Modern.* Eds. Philip Denwood and Alexander Piatigorsky. London: Curzon Press.

Hemmingsford, F. 1901. *Gazetteer of Tanjore District.* Madras: Superintendent of Government Press.

Henderson, Gregory, and Leon Hurvitz. 1956. The Buddha of Seiryoji: New Finds and New Theory. *Artibus Asiae* 19.1: 5-55.

*Hobogirin: Repertoire du canon bouddhique sino-japonais.* Adrien-Maisonneuve, 1978.

Horner, I. B., tran. 1952. *The Book of the Discipline (Vinaya-Pitaka), Vol. V (Cullavagga).* Sacred Books of the Buddhists, Vol. 20. London: Luzac & Company.

Hume, David. 1748. *Philosophical Essays Concerning Human Understanding.* London: Printed for A. Miller.

_____. 1980. *Enquiries Concerning the Human Understanding and Concerning the Principles of Morals.* Ed. L. A. Selby-Bigge. Westport, Conn.: Greenwood Press.

Huntington, Susan L. 1991. Early Buddhist Art and the Theory of Aniconism. *Art Journal* 49, 4: 401-408.

_____. 1992. Aniconism and the Multivalence of Emblems: Another Look. *Ars Orientalis* 22: 111-156.

Ikeda Rosan. 1982. *Kokusei hyakuroku no kenkyu.* Tokyo: Daoto shuppansha.

Inden, Ronald. 1978. Ritual, Authority and Cyclic Time in Hindu Kingship. In *Kingship and Authority in South Asia.* Ed. J. F. Richards. Madison: University of Wisconsin Publications Series. Pp. 28-74.

_____. 1981. Hierarchies of Kings in Early Medieval India. *Contributions to Indian Sociology* 15.1: 99-127.

I.L.R. 1887. Giyana Sambandha Pandara Sanadhi vs. Kanadasami Tambiran. *Indian Law Review* 10 Madras, 375-508.

_____. 1897. Dharmapuram Pandara Sannadhi vs. Virapandiyan Pillai. *Indian Law Review* 22: 302-4.

Inglis, Stephen. 1988. Making and Breaking: Craft Communities in South Asia. In Michael Meister, ed., *Making Things in South Asia: The Role of Artist and Craftsman.* Philadelphia: Department of South Asia Regional Studies.

Iracu, Ce. 1983. *Tancai Marattiyar Ceppetukal - 50.* Tancavur: Tamilp Palakalaik Kalakam.

Iramalinkat Tampiran. 1982. *Kuru Vilapatu.* Tarumapuram: Tarumai Atinam.

Ito Hirofumi and Kasuya Masaaki. 1987. *Zenkoji--sono rekishi to nyorai no fushigi* (*Zenkoji: Its History and the Strangeness of the Buddha*). Matsumoto: Kyodo Shuppansha.

Ito Nobuo, et al., eds. 1991. *Zenkoji: kokoro to katachi* (*Zenkoji: Spirit and Form*). Tokyo: Daiichi hoki shuppan.

Jan Yun-hua. 1965. Buddhist Self-immolation in Medieval China. *History of Religions* 4: 243-268.

*Jatakamala.* 1959. Ed. P.L. Vaidya. Buddhist Sanskrit Texts, vol.21. Darbhanga: Mithila Institute of Post-Graduate Studies and Research in Sanskrit Learning.

*Jatakas.* 1990. Ed. V Fausboll. Oxford: Pali Text Society.

Jayawickrama, N. S., trans. 1968. *The Sheaf of Garlands of the Epochs of the Conqueror* [*Jinakalamalipakarnam*]. London: Luzac & Company for the Pali Text Society.

Ji Xianlin, et al. 1985. *Tatang xiyouji xiaozhu.* Beijing: Zhonghua shuji.

*Jui tangshu.* 1975. Compiled by Liu Xu, et al. Zhonghua shuju edition. 16 vols. Beijing.

Kaimal, Padma. 1988. *Some Portraits at Pallava and Early Cola Temples: Kings, Patrons and Individual Identity.* Dissertation, University of California at Berkeley.

Kalupahana, David J. and Indrani. 1982. *The Way of Siddhartha: A Life of the Buddha.* Boulder & London: Shambhala.

Kalyanacuntara Tecikar, K. 1970. Tarumaiyatina Kuruparamparai Varalaru. In *Velur Kumpapiseka Malar.* Vaittisvarankoil. Pp. 373-81.

Kamata Shigeo. *Chugoku bukkyoshi.* Tokyo: Tokyodo.

Kanagawa Kenritsu Kanazawa Bunko, ed. 1993. *Bukkyo hanga.* Yokohama.

*Kanhadade Prabandha.* 1991. Trans. V.S. Bhatnagar. New Delhi: Aditya Prakashan.

Kennedy, Richard. 1976. The King in Early South India as Chieftain and Emperor. *The Indian Historical Review* 3.1: 1-15.

Keyes, Charles F. 1982. Death of Two Buddhist Saints in Thailand. In *Charisma and Sacred Biography*. Ed. Michael A. Williams. Journal of the American Academy of Religious Studies 48, nos. 3 and 4.

Kikuchi Jun'ichi. 1984. *Bukkyo hanga* (Buddhist Prints), vol. 218 of *Nihon no bijutsu*. Tokyo: Shibundo.

Kitzinger, Ernst. 1954. The Cult of Images in the Age Before Iconoclasm. *Dumbarton Oaks Papers* 8: 131-132.

Koppedrayer, K. I. 1990. The Sacred Presence of the Guru: The Velala Lineages of Tiruvavatuturai, Dharmapuram, and Tiruppanantal. Dissertation, McMaster University.

_____. 1991. The *Varnasramacandrika* and the *Sudra's* Right to Preceptorhood: The Social Background of a Philosophical Debate in Late Medieval South India. *Journal of Indian Philosophy* 19: 297-314.

_____. 1993. Remembering Tirumalikaittevar: The Relationship between an Early Saiva Mystic and a South Indian Matam. *East and West* 43.

Kulke, Hermann. 1978. Royal Temple Policy and the Structure of Medieval Hindu Kingdoms. In *The Cult of Jagannatha and the Regional Tradition of Orissa*, ed. Anncharlott Eschmann. Delhi: Manohar.

_____. 1992. Ksatra and Ksetra: The Cult of Jagannatha of Puri and the 'Royal Letters' of the Rajas of Khurda. In *The Sacred Centre as the Focus of Political Interest*, ed. Hans Bakker. Groningen: Egbert Forsten. Pp. 131-143.

Kyoto National Museum, ed. 1975. *Jodo-kyo kaiga* (The Painting of Pure Land Buddhism). Kyoto: Kyoto kokuritsu hakubutsukan.

_____. 1982. *Tokubetsu tenrankai: Shaka shinko to Seiryoji* (Special exhibition: Belief in Shaka and Seiryoji). Kyoto: Kyoto kokuritsu hakubutsukan.

Lalou, M. 1930. *Iconographie des Etoffes Peintes dans le Manjusrimulakalpa*. Paris.

Leoshko, Janice. 1993/94. Scenes of the Buddha's Life in Pala-Period Art. *Silk Road Art and Archaeology* 3:251-276.

Lingat, Robert. 1934. Le culte du Bouddha d'Emeraude. *Journal of the Siam Society* 27, pt. 1: 9-38.

_____. 1989. *Royautes Bouddhiques, Asoka, la Fonction Royale a Ceylan*. Paris: Éditions de l'École des Haute Études en Sciences Sociales.

*Los Angeles Times*. March 25, 1993: B, 2:1.

_____. July 13, 1994:E, 4:2.

McCallum, Donald F. 1987. Tokyo Kokuritsu Hakubutsukan hokan Zenkoji-shiki Amida sanzon zo ni tsuite (A Zenkoji Triad in the Tokyo National Museum). *Museum* 441: 21-28.

_____. 1991. The Power of Replication: The Seiryoji Shaka Tradition in Kamakura Sculpture. International Symposium on Kamakura Sculpture, British Museum.

_____. 1994. *Zenkoji and Its Icon: A Study in Medieval Japanese Religious Art*. Princeton: Princeton University Press.

_____. 1995. The Buddhist Triad in Three Kingdoms Sculpture. *Korean Culture* 16.4: 18-35.

_____. 1996. The Saidaiji Lineage of the Seriyoji Shaka Tradition. *Archives of Asian Art* 49: 51-67.

McKinnon, E. Edwards. 1985. Early Polities in Southern Sumatra: Some Preliminary Observations Based on Archaeological Evidence. *Indonesia* 40 (October): 1-36.

*Mahavagga*. 1956. Ed. Bhikkhu Jagadisakassapo. Nalanda Devanagari Pali Granthamala. Nalanda: Nava Nalanda Mahavihara.

Makita, Tairyo. 1976. *Gikyo kenkyu*. Kyoto: Kyoto daigaku jimbun kagaku kenkyusho

*Malli-Jnata, Das achte Kaptel des Nayadhammakahao im sechsten Anga des Svetambara Jainakanons*. 1983. Ed. and tran. Gustav Roth. Wiesbaden: Franz Steiner Verlag.

*Manjusrimulakalpa*. 1964. Ed. P. L. Vaidya. Buddhist Sanskrit Texts Series, vol. 18. Darbhanga: Mithila Institute of Post-Graduate Studies and Research in Sanskrit Learning.

*Manorathapurani*. 1976. Ed. Nand Kishore Prasad. Nalanda Devanagari Pali Granthamala, vol. 1. Nalanda: Nava Nalanda Mahavihara.

Maruo Shozaburo, ed. 1966. *Nihon chokoku-shi kiso shiryo shusei: zozo meiki ban* (Fundamental Collection of Documentary Sources for the History of Japanese Sculpture). Tokyo: Chuo koron bijutsu shuppan.

Matsunaga, Y. 1985. On the date of the Manjusrimulakalpa. In *Tantric and Taoist Studies in Honour of R.A. Stein, vol. III, Mélanges Chinois et Bouddhiques*, XXII. Bruxelles.

*Milinda Panha*. 1963. Tr. T. W. Rhys Davids. Vol. 2. New York: Dover Publications.

Minatcicuntarampillai, Ta. Ca. 1962. *Aracavanattu Aranilaiyam*. Tiruvavatuturai: Turaicai Atinam.

Mitra, Debala. 1971. *Buddhist Monuments*. Calcutta: Sahitya Samsad.

Mitra, Rajendralala. 1883. *The Yoga Aphorisms of Patanjali with the Commentary of Bhoja Raja*. Bibliotheca Indica. Calcutta: Baptist Mission Press.

Mosaku Ishida, ed. 1964. *Japanese Buddhist Prints*. New York: Abrams.

Mukherjee, Subodhchandra. 1926. *The Natyasastra of Bharata, Chapter Six: Rasadhyayah, with the Abhinavabharati*. Paris: University of Paris.

*Mulasarvastivadavinayavastu*. 1967. Ed. S. Bagchi. Buddhist Sanskrit Texts, no. 16. Darbhanga: Mithila Institute of Post-Graduate Studies and Research in Sanskrit Learning.

*Mulasuddhiprakarana with commentary of Devacandrasuri*. 1971. Ed. Amritlal Mohanlal Bhojak. Prakrit Text Society Series, vol. 15. Ahmedabad.

Mullin, Robert Bruce. 1996. *Miracles and the Modern Religious Imagination*. New Haven: Yale University Press.

Murugan, S. V. 1983. *The Tamil Nadu Hindu Religious and Charitable Endowments Act, 1959 (Tamil Nadu Act 22 of 1959) (as amended up to September 1983)*. Part I. Coimbatore: Coimbatore Book Agency.

Nagahiro Toshio. 1980. *Tonko Bakkokutsu*. Tokyo: Heibonsha

Nahar, Puran Chand. 1929. *Jain Inscriptions, vol. III. Jaisalmer*. Calcutta: Viswavinode Press.

Nakamura, Hajime. 1977. *Gotama Buddha*. Los Angeles-Tokyo: Buddhist Books International.

Nakao Takashi and Imai Masaharu, eds. 1983. *Chogen, Eison, Ninsho*. Tokyo: Yoshikawa kobunka.

Nallaswami Pillai, J.M. 1949. *Siva Jnana Bodham*. Dharmapuram: Dharmapuram Adhinam.

Nanamoli, Bhikkhu. 1972. *The Life of the Buddha*. Kandy: Buddhist Publication Society.

Nananata. 1961. Nularaycci. In *Turaicaippuranam*. Tiruvavatuturai: Tiruvavatuturai Atinam. Pp. 24-5.

Nara National Museum, ed. 1984. *Nihon bukkyo bijutsu no genryu* (Origins of Japanese Buddhist Art). Kyoto: Dohosha shuppan.

*Nara rokudaiji taikan, vol. 14. Saidaiji*. 1973. Tokyo: Iwanami shoten.

*Navasahasankacarita* of Padmagupta. 1963. Ed. Jitendrachandra Bharatiya. Vidyabhawan Sanskrit Granthamala, no. 66. Varanasi: Chowkhamba Vidyabhavan.

Neufeldt, Ronald W. 1980. Western Perceptions of Asia: The Romantic Vision of Max Müller. In *Traditions in Contact and Change: Selected Proceedings of the XIVth Congress of the International Association for the History of Religions*. Eds. Peter Slater and Ronald Wiebe. Waterloo, Ontario: Wilfrid Laurier University Press.

*Nisitha Sutra*. 1982. Ed. Upadhyay Amarchandjl Maharaj and Muni Shri Kanhaiya Laljl Maharaj. Agama Sahitya Ratnamala Series, no. 5. Delhi: Bharatiya Vidya Prakashan.

Oldenberg, Hermann, ed. 1880. *The Vinaya Pitakam, Vol. II: The Cullavagga*. London: Williams and Norgate.

Olivelle, Patrick. 1991. From Feast to Fast: Food and the Indian Ascetic. In Julia Leslie, ed. *Rules and Remedies in Classical Indian Law*. Leiden: E. J. Brill.

Omura Seigai. 1915. *Shina bijutsushi, Choso-hen*. Tokyo.

Ono Genmyo. 1932-36. *Bussha kaisetsu daijiten*. 12 vols. Tokyo: Daito shuppansha.

Osamu, Takata. 1967. *The Origin of the Buddha Image (Butsuzo no Kigen)*. Tokyo: Iwanami Shoten.

*Paumacariya* of Vimalasuri. 1968. Ed. Dr. H. Jabobi, rev. Muni Shri Punyavijayaji. Prakrit Text Society Series, vol. 12. Ahmedabad: Prakrit Text Society.

*Prabandhacintamani* of Merutunga. 1933. Ed. Jina Vijaya Muni. Singhi Jain Series, vol. 1. Santiniketan: Singhi Jaina Pitha.

_____. 1901. Trans. C. H. Tawney. Calcutta: Asiatic Society.

*Prabandhakosa of Rajasekharasuri*. 1935. Ed. Jina Vijaya Muni. Singhi Jain Series, vol. 6. Santiniketan: Singhi Jaina Pitha.

Prasada, Rama, trans. 1924. *Patanjali's Yoga Sutras with the Commentary of Vyasa and the Gloss of Vachaspati Misra*. Sacred Books of the Hindus, Vol. 4. Allahabad: Sudhindranath Vasu.

Pudukkottai. 1929. *Inscriptions (Texts) of the Pudukkottai State arranged according to Dynasties*. Pudukkottai: State Press.

*Puratanaprabandhasamgraha*. 1936. Ed. Jina Vijaya Muni. Singhi Jain Series, vol. 2. Santiniketan: Singhi Jaina Pitha.

Rajanubhab, Prince Damrong. 1973. *Monuments of the Buddha in Siam*. Trans. by Sulak Sivaraksa and A. B. Griswold with footnotes by Prince Subhadradis Diskul and A. B. Griswold. Bangkok: The Siam Society.

*Rajatarangini* of Jinaraja. 1967. Ed. Vishva Bandhu. Hosiharpur: Vishveshvaranand Institute.

Ramanujan, A. K. 1973. *Speaking of Siva*. Harmondsworth, England: Penguin Books.

Regmi, D. R. 1966. *Medieval Nepal: A History of the Three Kingdoms, 1520-1768 A.D.*, Part II. Calcutta: Firma K.L. Mukhopadhyay.

Reynolds, Frank. 1978. The Holy Emerald Jewel: Some Aspects of Buddhist Symbolism and Political Legitimation in Thailand. In *Religion and Legitimation of Power in Thailand, Laos, and Burma*, ed. Bardwell L. Smith. Chambersburg, Pa.: Anima.

Rhys Davids, Mrs., trans. 1918. *The Book of Kindred Sayings (Samyutta-nikaya) or Grouped Suttas, Part I. Kindred Sayings with Verses (Sagatha-vagga)*. Pali Text Society Translation Series, No. 7. London: Pali Text Society.

Rhys Davids, T. W., trans. 1899. *Dialogues of the Buddha*. Sacred Books of the Buddhists, vol. 2. London: Pali Text Society.

Rhys Davids, T. W., and J. Estlin Carpenter, eds. 1890. *The Digha Nikaya*. Pali Text Society Text series, vol. 22, vol. 1. London: Pali Text Society.

Sakaki Kozo. 1965. *Seiryoji*. Tokyo: Chuo koron bijutsu shuppan.

Sarasvati, Dayananda. 1879. The Autobiography of Dayanund Saraswati Swami. *The Theosophist* 1:9-13, 66-68.

_____. 1939. *The Light of Truth*. Trans. Ganga Prasad Upadhyaya. Allahabad: Kala Press.

Sasaki, Genjun H., ed. 1992. *Sarasangaha*. Oxford: Pali Text Society.

*Satrunjayakalpa with commentary of Subhasilagani*. n.d. Ed. Labhasagaragani. Agamoddharakagranthamala, vol. 41.

*Satsiddhantasamgraha*. 1942. Ed. Harisankara Shastri. Bombay:Nirnaya Sagara Press.

Schopen, Gregory. 1987. Burial 'Ad Sanctos' and the Physical Presence of the Buddha in Early Indian Buddhism: A Study in the Archaeology of Religions. *Religion* 17: 193-225.

_____. 1990. The Buddha as Owner of Property and Permanent Resident in Medieval Indian Monasteries. *The Journal of Indian Philosophy* 18.

_____. 1991. Archeology and Protestant Presuppositions in the Study of Indian Buddhism. *History of Religions* 31 (1):1-23.

Sen, Madhu. 1975. *A Cultural Study of the Nisitha Curn*. Parsvanatha Vidyashram Series, vol. 21. Varanasi: P.V. Research Institute.

Setouchi Jakucho and Ugai Kojun, eds. 1978. *Seiryoji (Koji junrai: Kyoto 21)*. Kyoto: Tankosha.

Settar, S. 1989. *Inviting Death: Indian Attitudes Toward Ritual Death*. Leiden: E. J. Brill.

Shankar, Uma. 1984. Brahmin, King and Bhakta in a Temple in Tamil Nadu. *Contributions to Indian Sociology*, n.s., 18.2: 169-189.

Shinohara, Koichi. 1988. Two Sources of Chinese Buddhist Biographies: Stupa Inscriptions and Miracle Stories. In *Monks and Magicians: Religious Biographies in Asia*. Edited by Phyllis Granoff and Koichi Shinohara. Oakville, Ontario: Mosaic Press. Pp. 119-228.

_____. 1990. Daoxuan's Collection of Miracle Stories about 'Supernatural Monks' (Shenseng gantong lu): An Analysis of its Sources. *Chung-Hwa Buddhist Journal* 3: 319-380.

_____. 1991a. *Ji shenzhou sanbao gantonglu*: Some Exploratory Notes. In *Kalyana Mitta: Professor Hajime Nakamura Felicitation Volume*. Edited by V. N. Jha. Delhi: Indian Book Center. Pp. 203-224.

Shinohara, Koichi. 1991b. The Maitreya Image in Shicheng and Guanding's Biography of Zhiyi. In *From Benares to Beijing: Essays in Buddhism and Chinese Religions in Honour of Prof. Jan Yün-hua*. Edited by Gregory Schopen and Koichi Shinohara. Oakville, Ontario: Mosaic Press. Pp. 203-228.

_____. 1991c. A Source Analysis of the *Ruijing lu* ("Records of Miraculous Scriptures"). *The Journal of the International Association of Buddhist Studies* 14, 1: 73-154.

_____. 1992. Guanding's Biography of Zhiyi: the Fourth Patriarch of the Tiantai tradition. In *Speaking of Monks: Religious Biography in Asia*. Edited by Phyllis Granoff and Koichi Shinohara. Oakville:, Ontario: Mosaic Press. Pp. 98-224.

_____. 1993. Dynastic Politics and Miraculous Images: The Example of Zhuli (544-623) of the Changlesi temple in Yangzhou. Paper presented at the annual meeting of the Association of Asian Studies, Los Angeles, California.

Sivadatta, Pandit, ed. 1894. *Natyasastra of Bharatamuni*. Kavyamala 42. Bombay: Nirnaya Sagara Press.

Sivagrayogin. 1932. *Saivasamnyasapaddhati*. Ed. Sriramasastri and Narayanasastri. Kumbhakonan: Kasi Matha of Tiruppanantal.

Smith, Bardwell. 1978. *Religion and Legitimation of Power in Sri Lanka* Chambersburg, Pa.: Anima Books.

*Somasambhupaddhati. 1977. Troisième Partie. Rituels occasionnels dans la tradition sivaïte de l'Inde du Sud selon Somasambhu. II. diksa, abhiseka, vratoddhara, antyesti, sraddha*. Text, Traduction et Notes, Hélène Brunner-Lachaux. Pondichéry: Institut français d'Indologie.

Soper, Alexander Coburn. 1959. *Literary Evidence for Early Buddhist Art in China. Artibus Asiae*, Supplementum XIX. Ascona, Switzerland: Artibus Asiae Publishers.

*Sripancapratikramanasutra*. 1925. Sri Jaina Atmananda Granthamala, vol.55. Bhavnagar: Atmananda Sabha.

Strong, John S. 1983. *The Legend of King Asoka: A Study and Translation of the Asokavadana*. Princeton: Princeton University Press.

*Sui shu*. 1973. Wei Zheng, et al. Zhonghua shuju edition. 6 vols. Beijing.

*Suvarnaprabhasottamasutra*. 1967. Ed. S. Bagchi. Buddhist Sanskrit Texts, no. 8. Darbhanga: Mithila Institute of Post-Graduate Studies and Research in Sanskrit Learning.

Suwa Gijn. 1988. *Chugoku chusei bukkyoshi kenkyu*. Tokyo: Daito shuppansha.

Swinburne, Richard. 1970. *The Concept of Miracle*. London: Macmillan.

*Taisho shinshu daizokyo*. 1922-33. Takakusu Junjiro, et al., eds. 100 vols. Tokyo: Daizo shuppankai.

Takada Osamu. 1967. *Butzuzo no kigen*. Tokyo: Iwanami shoten.

*Tarumai Kanakapiseka Vilamalar*. 1961. Tarumapuram: Tarumai Atinam.

*Le Temple d'Angkor Vat*. 1932. Reprint 1995. Mémoires Archéologiques Publiés par l'École Francçaise d'Extreme-Orient. Tome II. Paris: Les Éditions G. Van Oest.

Textor, Robert Bayard. 1966. An Inventory of Non-Buddhist Supernatural Objects in a Central Thai Village. Dissertation, Cornell University.

Tiruvambalavanadesikar. 1930. *Varnasramacandrika*. Ed. Narayanasastri. Kumbhakonan and Mayuram: Kasi Matha of Tiruppanantal.

Tokyo National Museum, ed. 1993. *Yamato koji no hotoke-tachi* (Buddhist Images of the Ancient Temples of the Yamato Region). Tokyo: NHK.

Tsukamoto Zenryu. 1975a. Zui no Konan seifuku to Bukkyo. *Tsukamoto Zenryu chosakushu* 3: 145-190. Tokyo: Daito shuppansha. Originally published in *Bukkyo Bunka Kenkyu*, vol. 3 (November, 1953)

_____. 1975b. Seiryoji Shaka zo fuzo no Todaiji Chonen no shuin risseisho. In *Tsukamoto Zenryu chosakushu*, vol. 7. Tokyo: Daito shuppansho. Pp. 167-204. (Originally published in *Bukkyo bunka kenkyu* 4 [1954]: 5-22.)

*Vidhimamrgaprapa.* 1941. Ed. Sri Jinavijaya. Jinadattasuri Pracinapustakoddhara Fund, vol.44. Surat: Jinadaddasuri Pracinapustakoddhara Fund.

Vijayamurti, Pandit M.A. Sastracarya. 1952. *Jaina Sila Lekha Samgraha*, vol. 2. Manikcandra Digambara Jainagranthamala, no.45. Bombay: Manikcandra Digambara Jaina Granthamalasamiti.

*Vinaya Pitaka.* 1969. Ed. Hermann Oldenberg. Pali Text Society. London: Luzac and Company.

*Visnudharmottarapurana.* 1985. Ed. Carudevasastrin. Delhi: Nag Publishers.

*Vividhatirthakalpa* of Jinaprabhasuri. 1934. Ed. Jina Vijaya Muni. Singhi Jain Series, vol. 10. Santiniketan: Singhi Jaina Pitha.

Wajima Yoshio. 1959. *Eison-Ninsho.* Tokyo: Yoshikawa kobunko.

Wang, Yi-t'ung. 1984. *A Record of Buddhist Monasteries in Lo-yang.* Princeton: Princeton University Press.

Weinstein, Stanley. 1973. Imperial Patronage in the Formation of T'ang Buddhism. In *Perspectives On The Tang.* Edited by Arthur E. Wright and Denis Twitchett. New Haven: Yale University Press. Pp. 265-306.

Werner, Karel. 1988. Indian Concepts of Human Personality in Relation to the Doctrine of the Soul. *Journal of the Royal Asiatic Society* no. 1.

Wriggins, Sally. 1987. A Buddhist Pilgrimage along the Silk Route. *Archaeology* 40, no. 5 (September/October): 35-41.

*Xin tangshu.* 1975. Compiled by Ouyang Xiu, et al. Zhonghua shuju edition. 20 vols. Beijing.

Yamaoka Taizo. 1978. *Kano Masanobu-Motonobu.* Tokyo: Shueisha.

Yocum, Glenn. 1990. A Field Study of the Thiruvavaduthurai Adheenam. In *Monastic Life in the Christian and Hindu Traditions: A Comparative Study,* Austin B. Creel and Vasuda Narayanan, eds. Lewiston NY: Edwin Mellen Press.

*Yogasastra of Hemacandra.* 1981. Ed. Muni Jambuvijaya. Bombay: Jaina Sahitya Vikas Mandal.

Yoshihara Hiroto. 1994. Waseda Daigaku Toshokan: Zenkoji shinko shiryo ko-- fukaidai (On the archival collection of the Zenkoji religion in the Library with its bibliographical annotations). *Waseda Daigaku Toshokan kiyo* 39: 97-124.

Zaleski, Carol. 1987. *Otherworld Journeys: Accounts of Near-Death Experience in Medieval and Modern Times.* New York and Oxford: Oxford University Press.

*Zhoushu.* 1974. Compiled by Lingu Defen. Zhonghua shuju edition. 3 vols. Beijing. (First edition, 1971).

Zvelebil, K.V. 1975. *Tamil Literature.* Leiden/Köln: E. J. Brill.